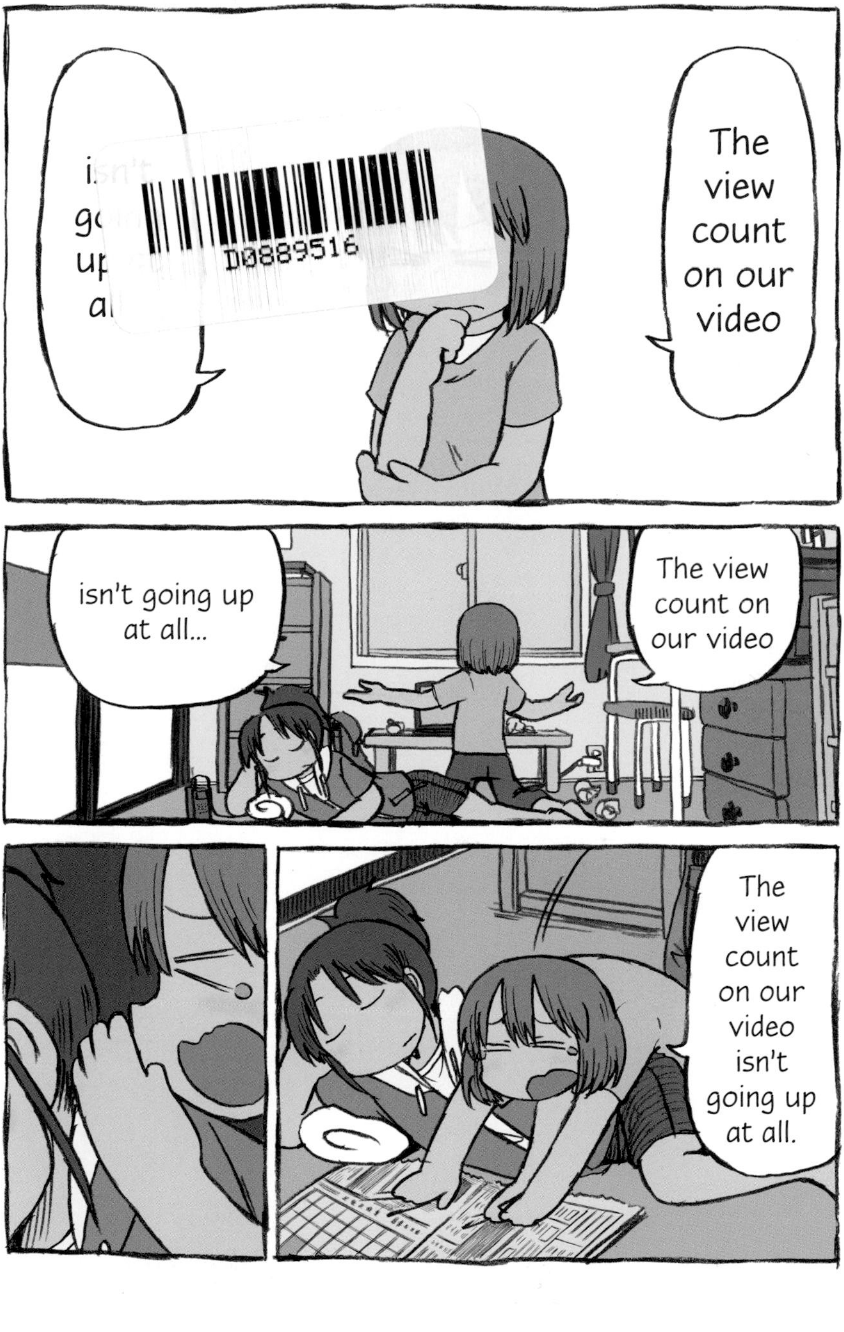
The view count on our video
The view count on our video
isn't going up at all...
The view count on our video isn't going up at all.

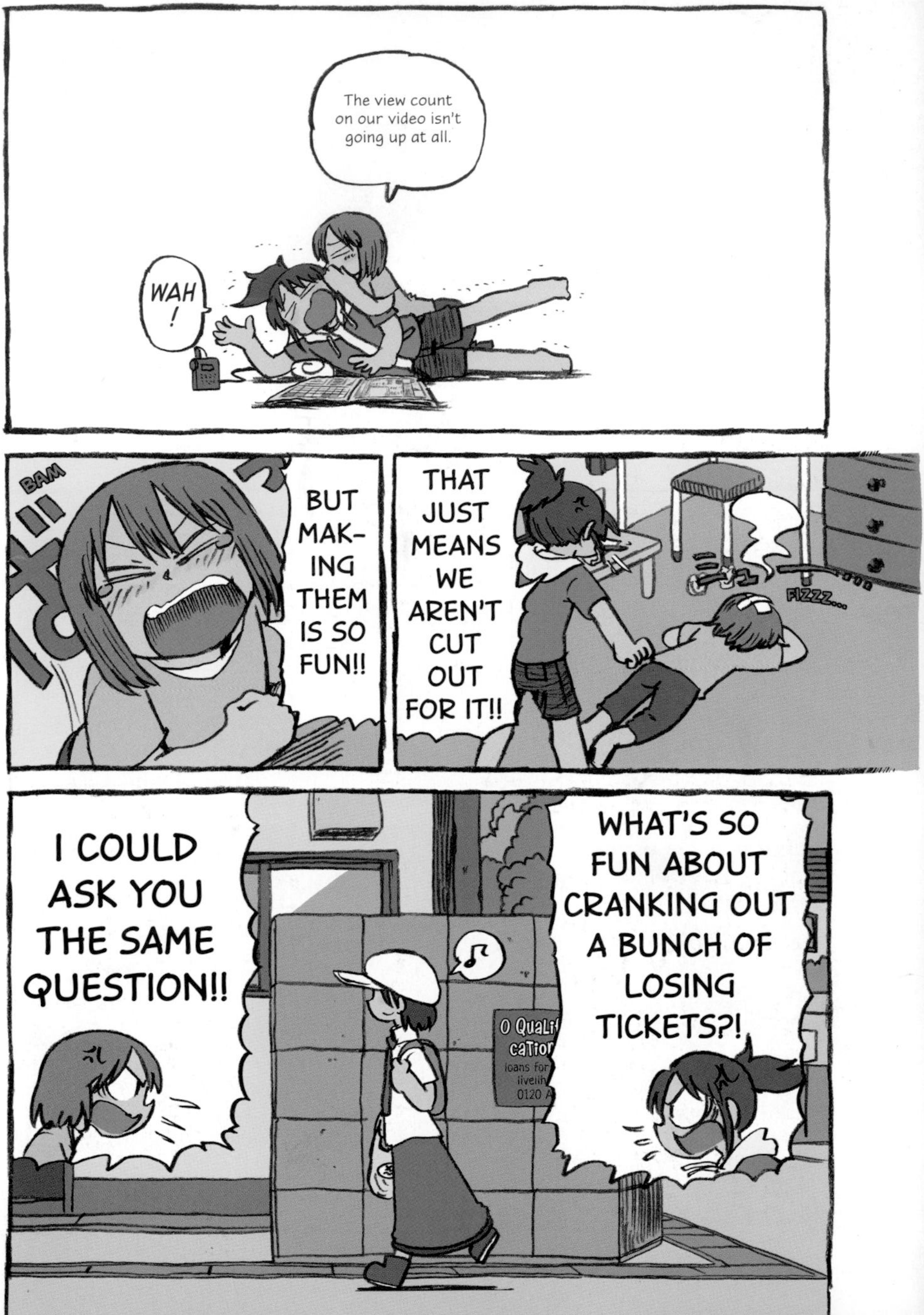

The view count on our video isn't going up at all.
WAH!
THAT JUST MEANS WE AREN'T CUT OUT FOR IT!!
FIZZZ...
BUT MAKING THEM IS SO FUN!!
BAM
WHAT'S SO FUN ABOUT CRANKING OUT A BUNCH OF LOSING TICKETS?!
I COULD ASK YOU THE SAME QUESTION!!

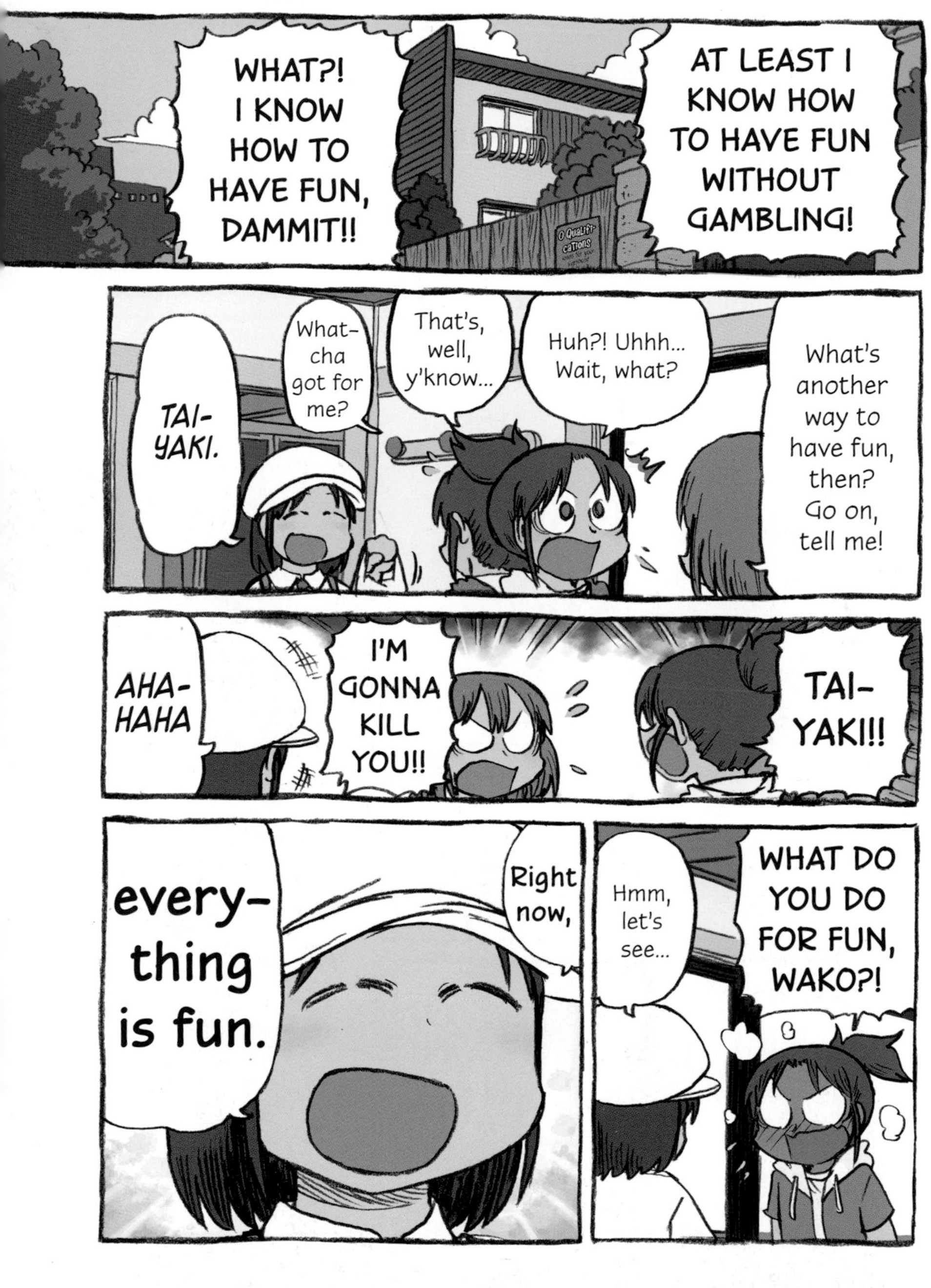
AT LEAST I KNOW HOW TO HAVE FUN WITHOUT GAMBLING!
WHAT?! I KNOW HOW TO HAVE FUN, DAMMIT!!
What's another way to have fun, then? Go on, tell me!
Huh?! Uhhh... Wait, what?
That's, well, y'know...
What-cha got for me?
TAI-YAKI.
TAI-YAKI!!!
I'M GONNA KILL YOU!!
AHA-HAHA
WHAT DO YOU DO FOR FUN, WAKO?!
Hmm, let's see...
Right now,
every-thing is fun.

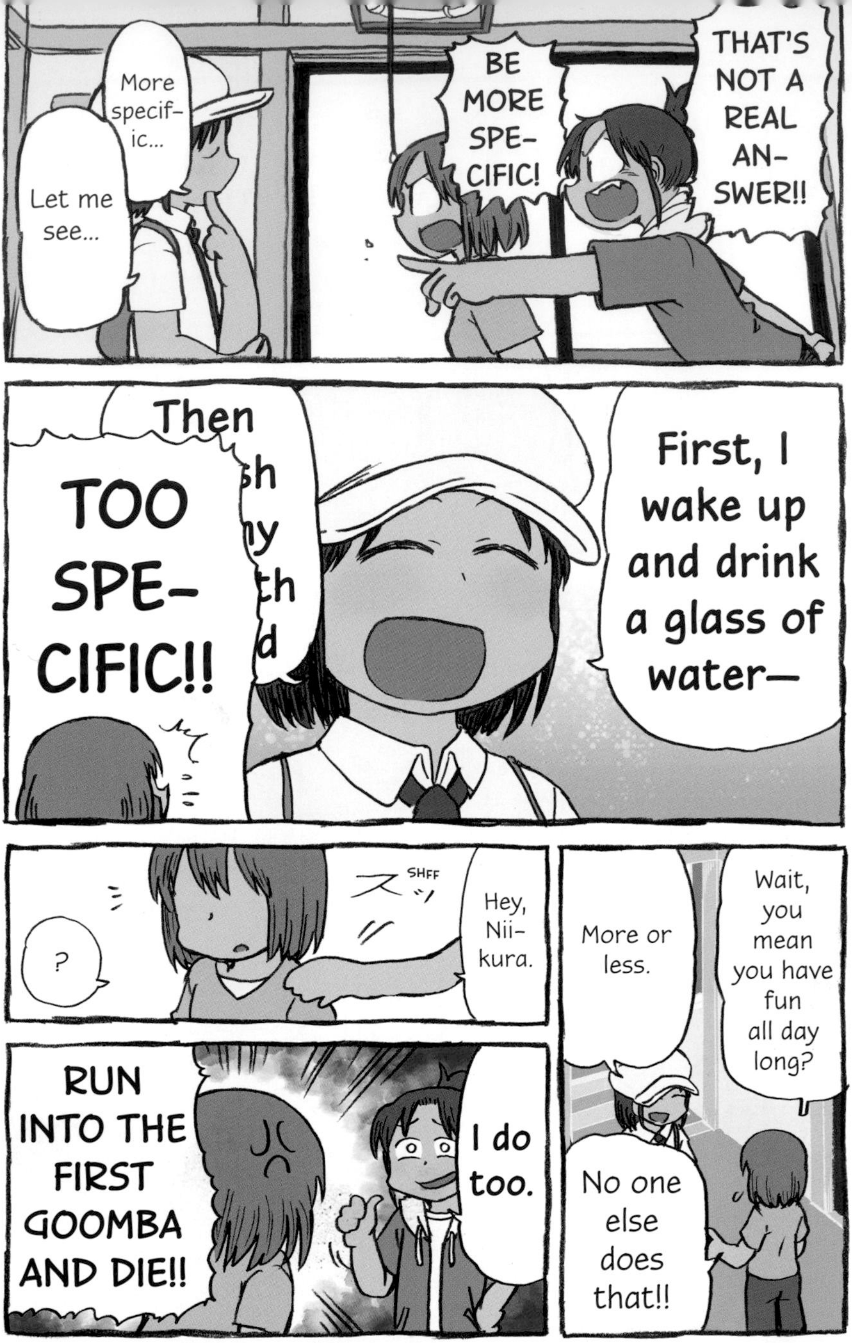
THAT'S NOT A REAL ANSWER!!
BE MORE SPECIFIC!
More specific...
Let me see...
First, I wake up and drink a glass of water—
Then
TOO SPECIFIC!!
Wait, you mean you have fun all day long?
More or less.
No one else does that!!
SHFF
Hey, Niikura.
?
I do too.
RUN INTO THE FIRST GOOMBA AND DIE!!

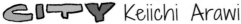

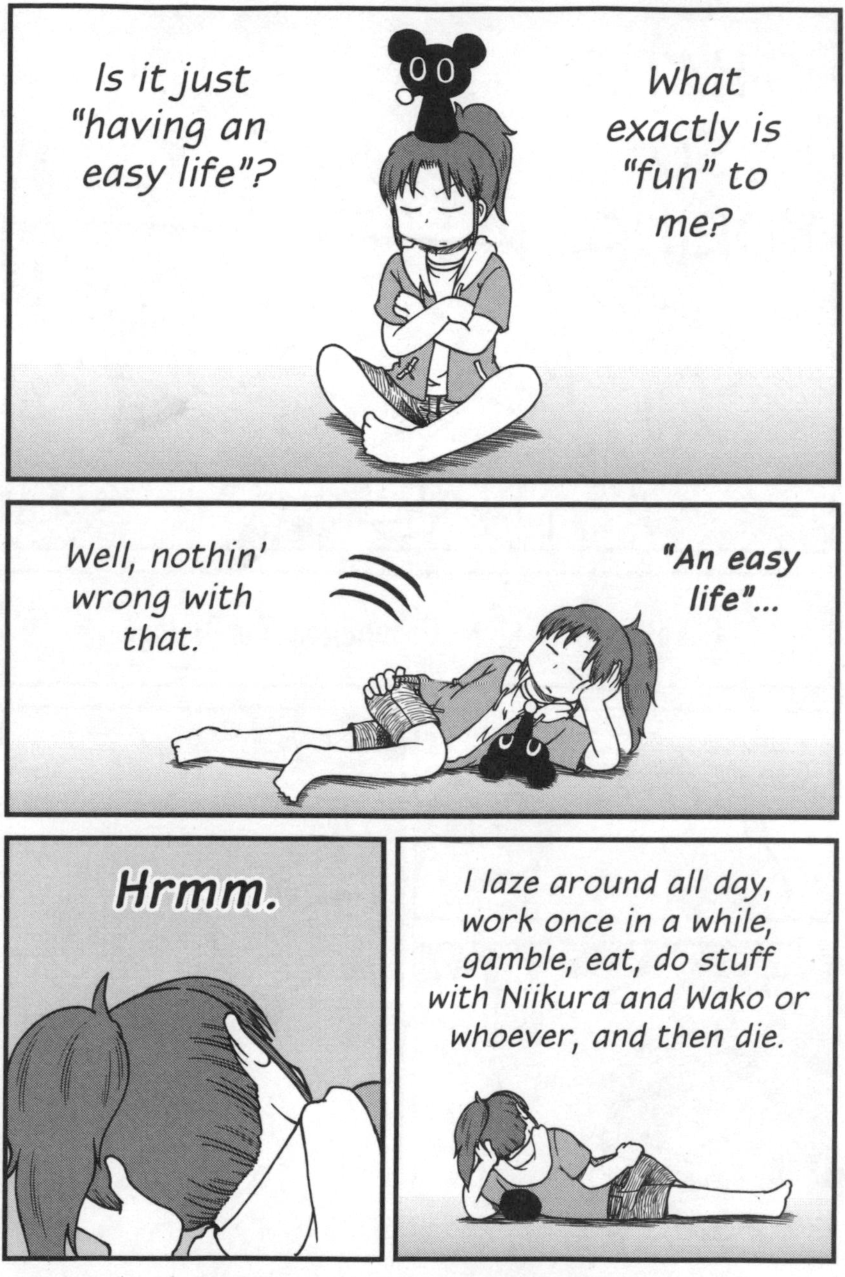
What exactly is "fun" to me?
Is it just "having an easy life"?
"An easy life"...
Well, nothin' wrong with that.
I laze around all day, work once in a while, gamble, eat, do stuff with Niikura and Wako or whoever, and then die.
Hrmm.

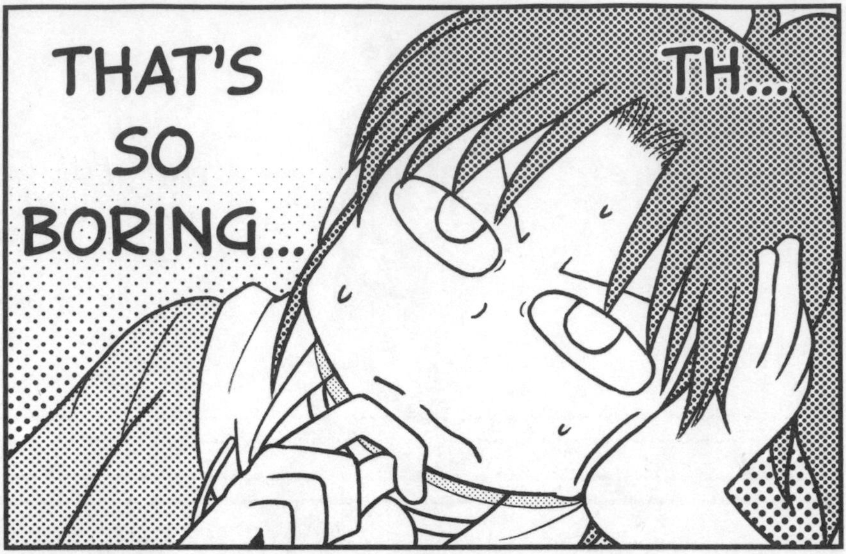
TH...
THAT'S SO BORING...

Chapter 153 Unsolicited Zen Dialogue

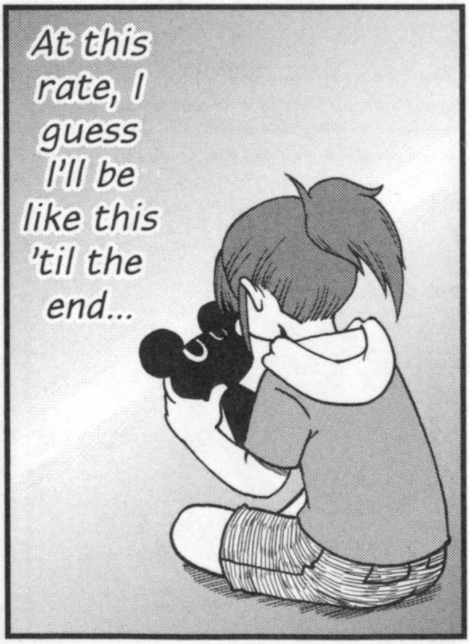
At this rate, I guess I'll be like this 'til the end...

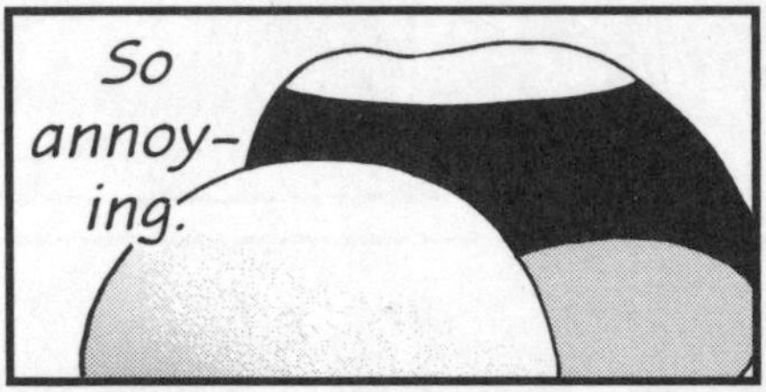
So annoy-ing.

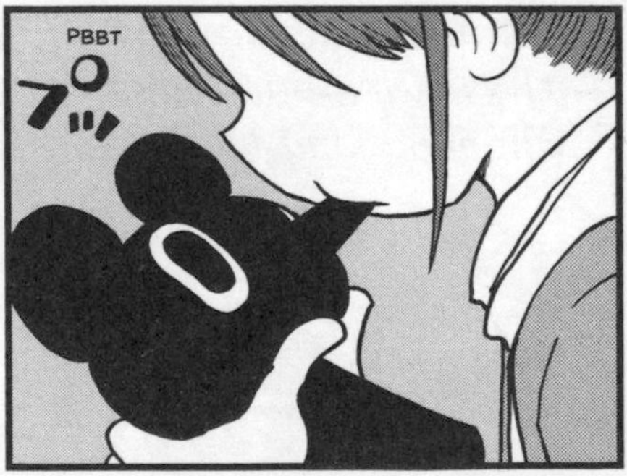
PBBT

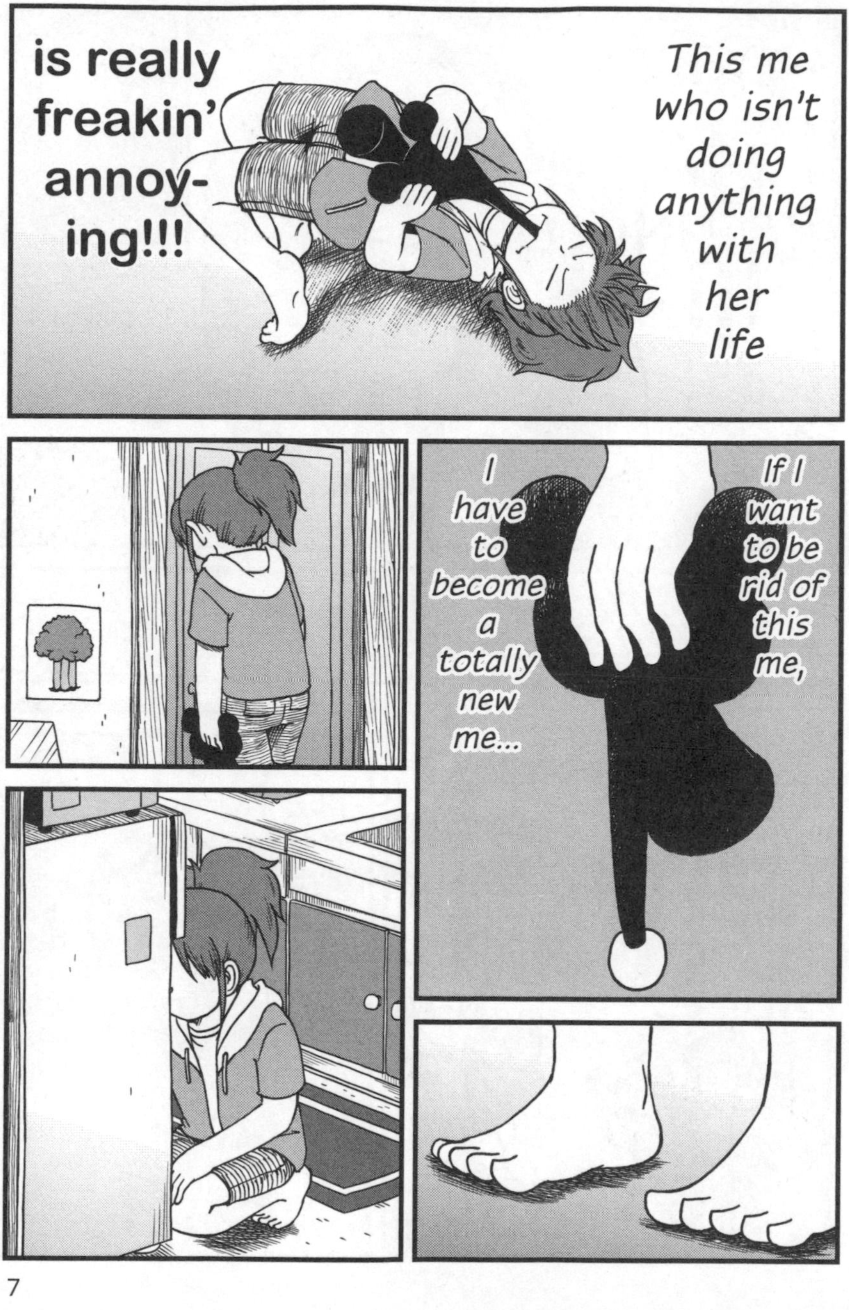
This me who isn't doing anything with her life
is really freakin' annoy-ing!!!
If I want to be rid of this me,
I have to become a totally new me...

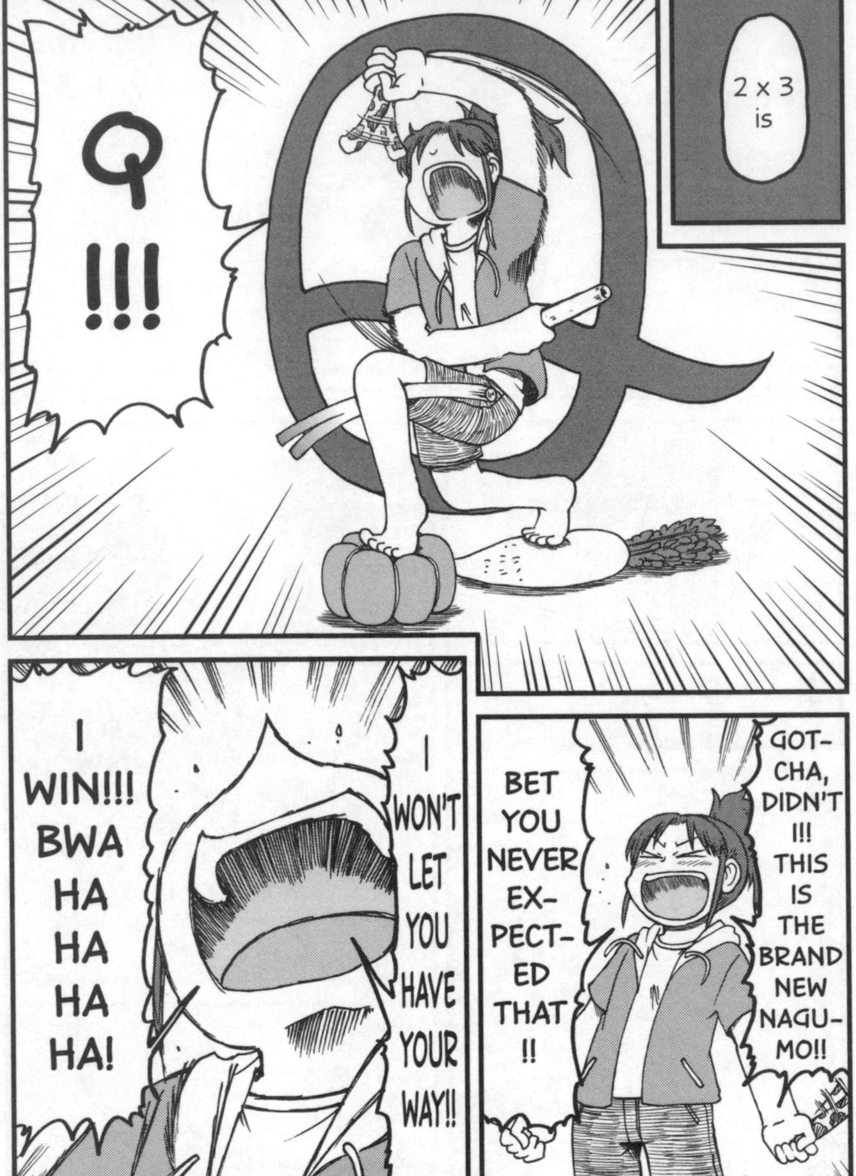
2 x 3 is
Q !!!
GOT-CHA, DIDN'T I!!! THIS IS THE BRAND NEW NAGU-MO!!
BET YOU NEVER EX-PECT-ED THAT !!
I WON'T LET YOU HAVE YOUR WAY!!
I WIN!!!! BWA HA HA HA HA HA!

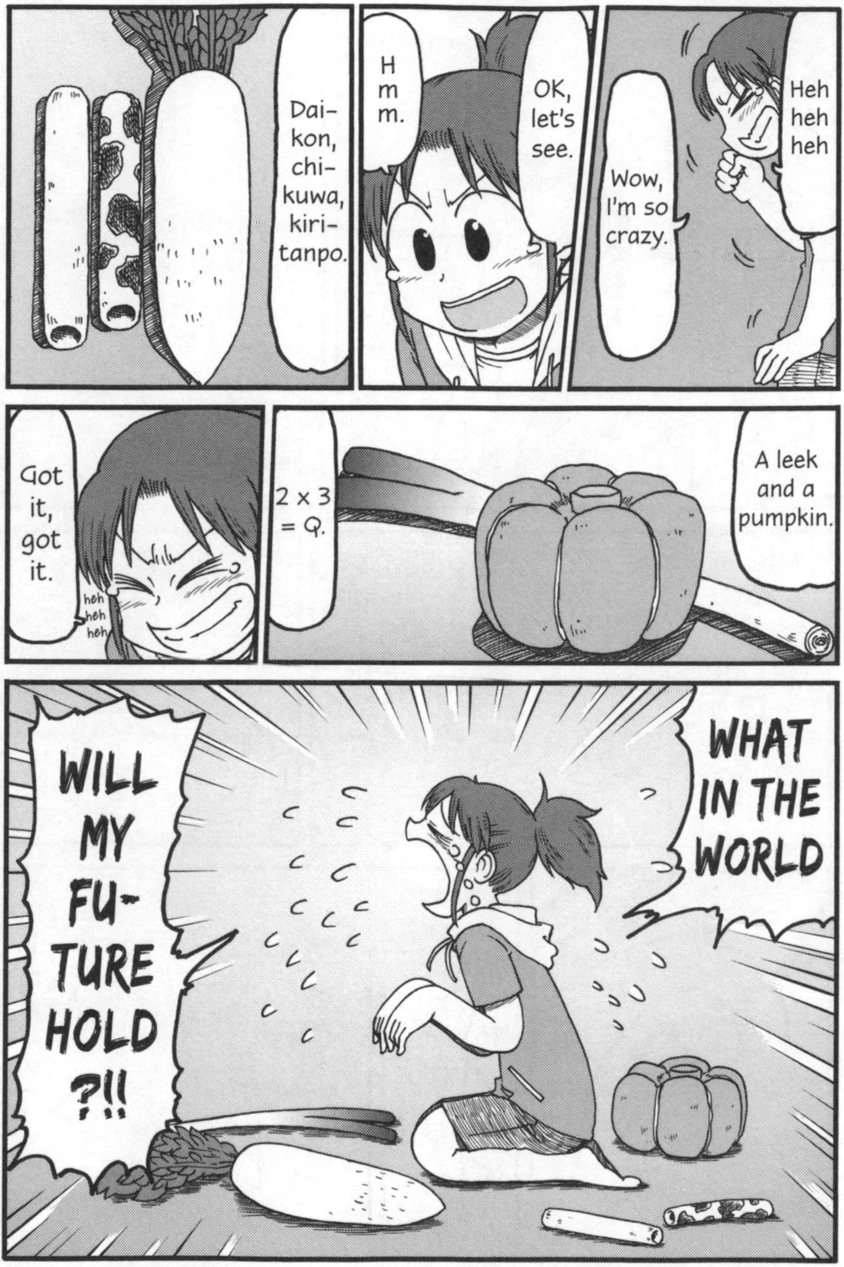

Heh heh heh
Wow, I'm so crazy.
OK, let's see.
Hmm.
Dai-kon, chi-kuwa, kiri-tanpo.
A leek and a pumpkin.
2 x 3 = Q.
Got it, got it.
heh heh heh
WHAT IN THE WORLD
WILL MY FU-TURE HOLD ?!!

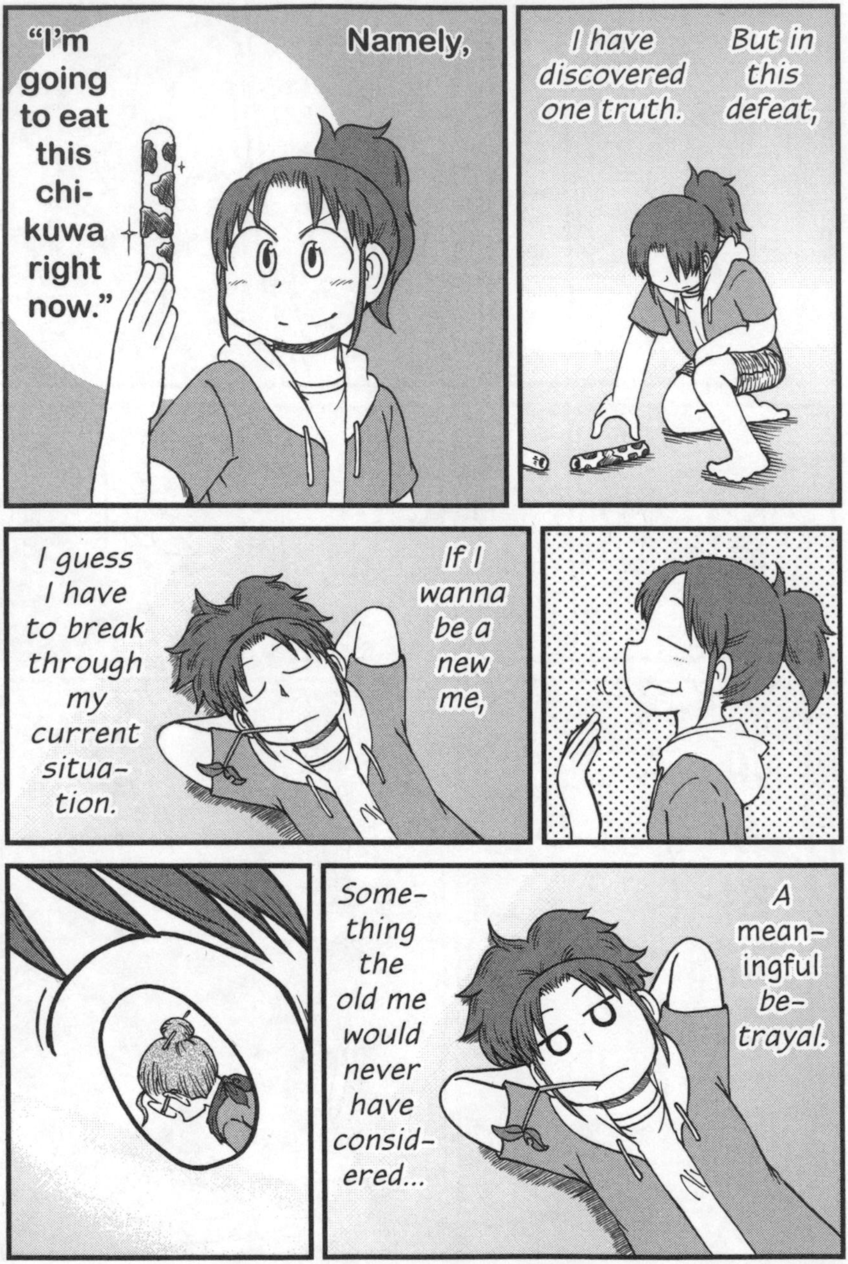
But in this defeat,
I have discovered one truth.
Namely,
“I'm going to eat this chikuwa right now.”
If I wanna be a new me,
I guess I have to break through my current situation.
A meaningful betrayal.
Something the old me would never have considered...

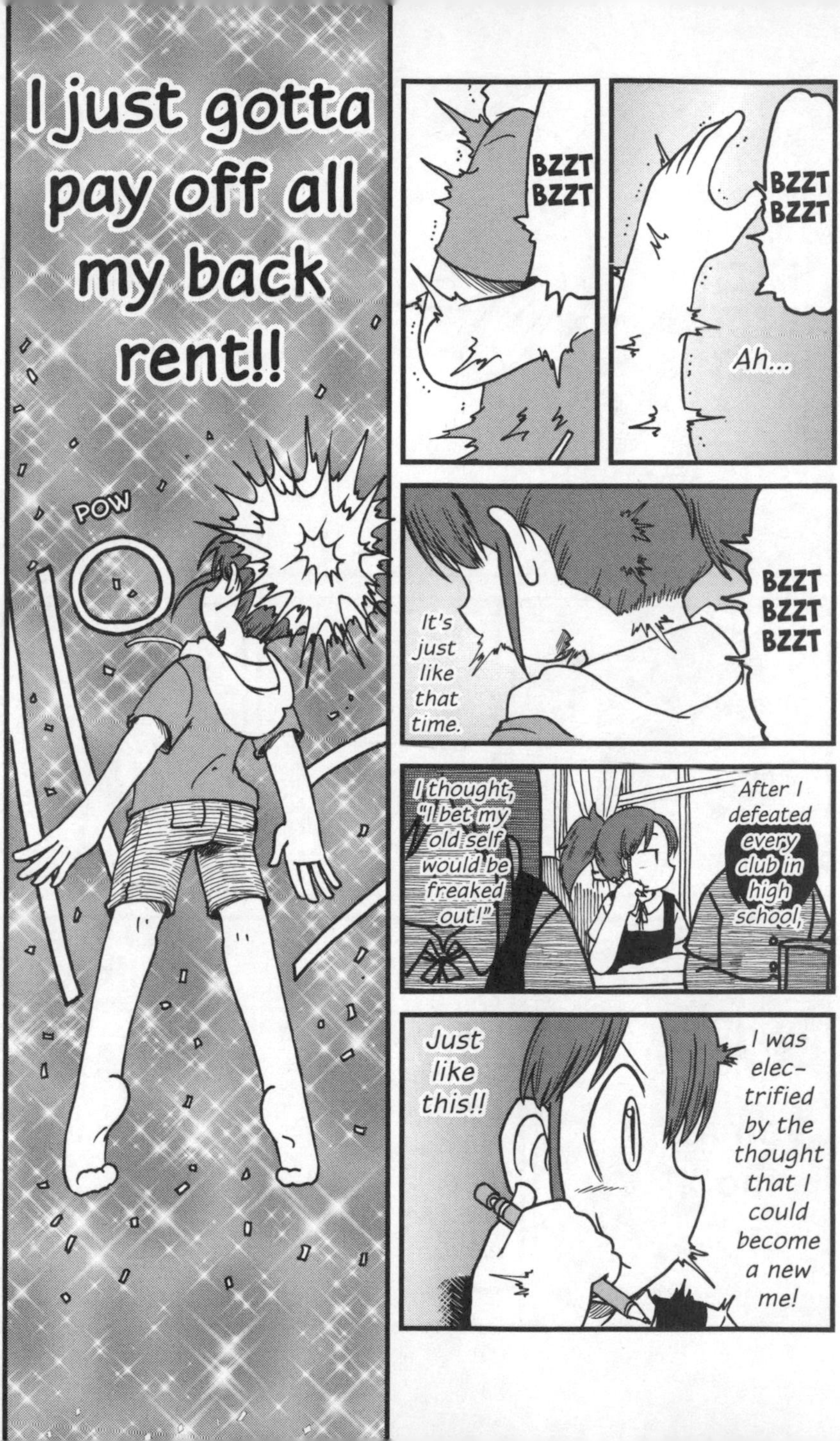
BZZT BZZT
Ah...
BZZT BZZT
BZZT BZZT BZZT
It's just like that time.
After I defeated every club in high school,
I thought, "I bet my old self would be freaked out!"
I was elec-trified by the thought that I could become a new me!
Just like this!!
I just gotta pay off all my back rent!!
POW

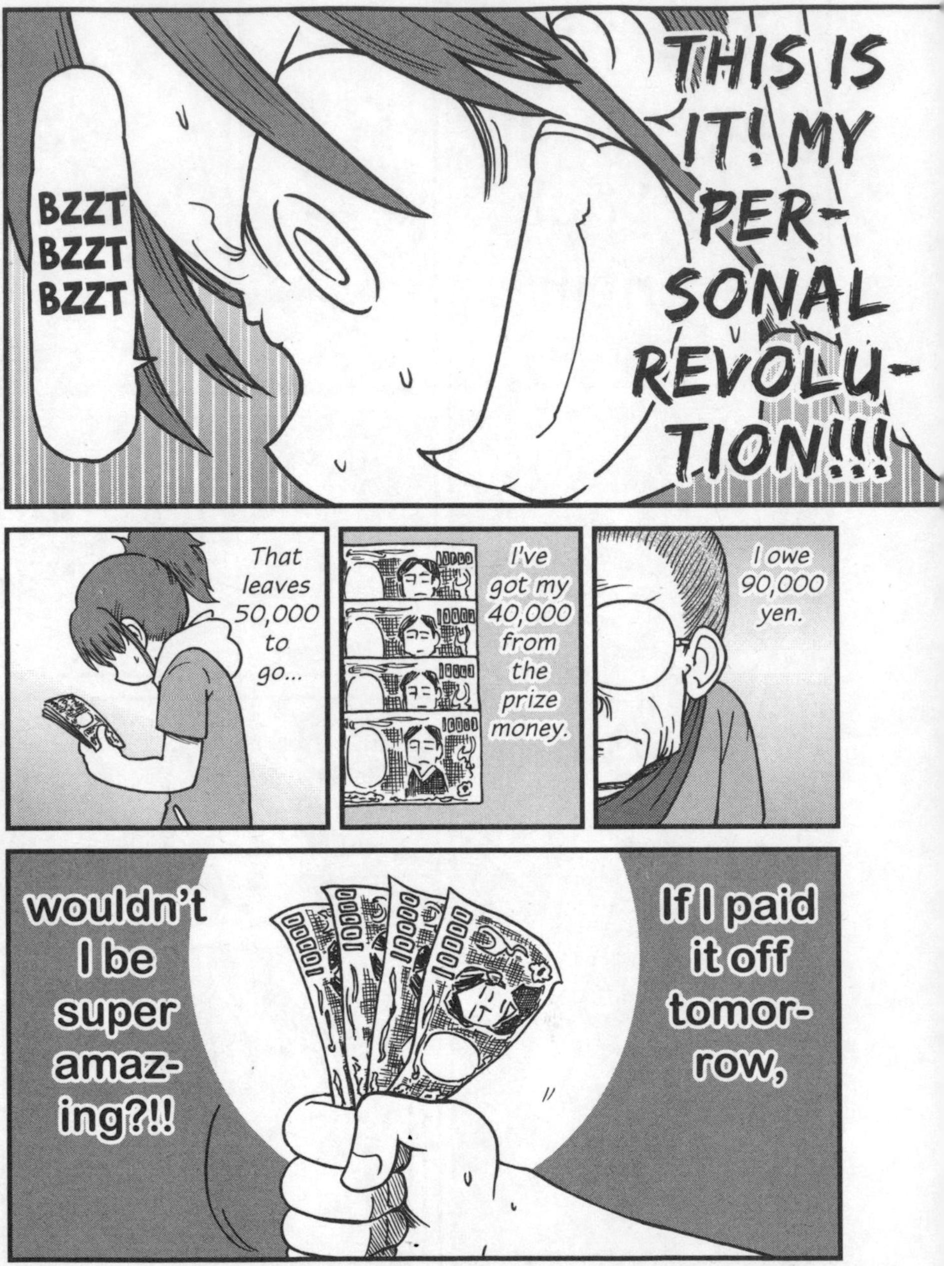
THIS IS IT! MY PERSONAL REVOLUTION!!!
BZZT BZZT BZZT
I owe 90,000 yen.
I've got my 40,000 from the prize money.
That leaves 50,000 to go...
If I paid it off tomorrow,
wouldn't I be super amazing?!!

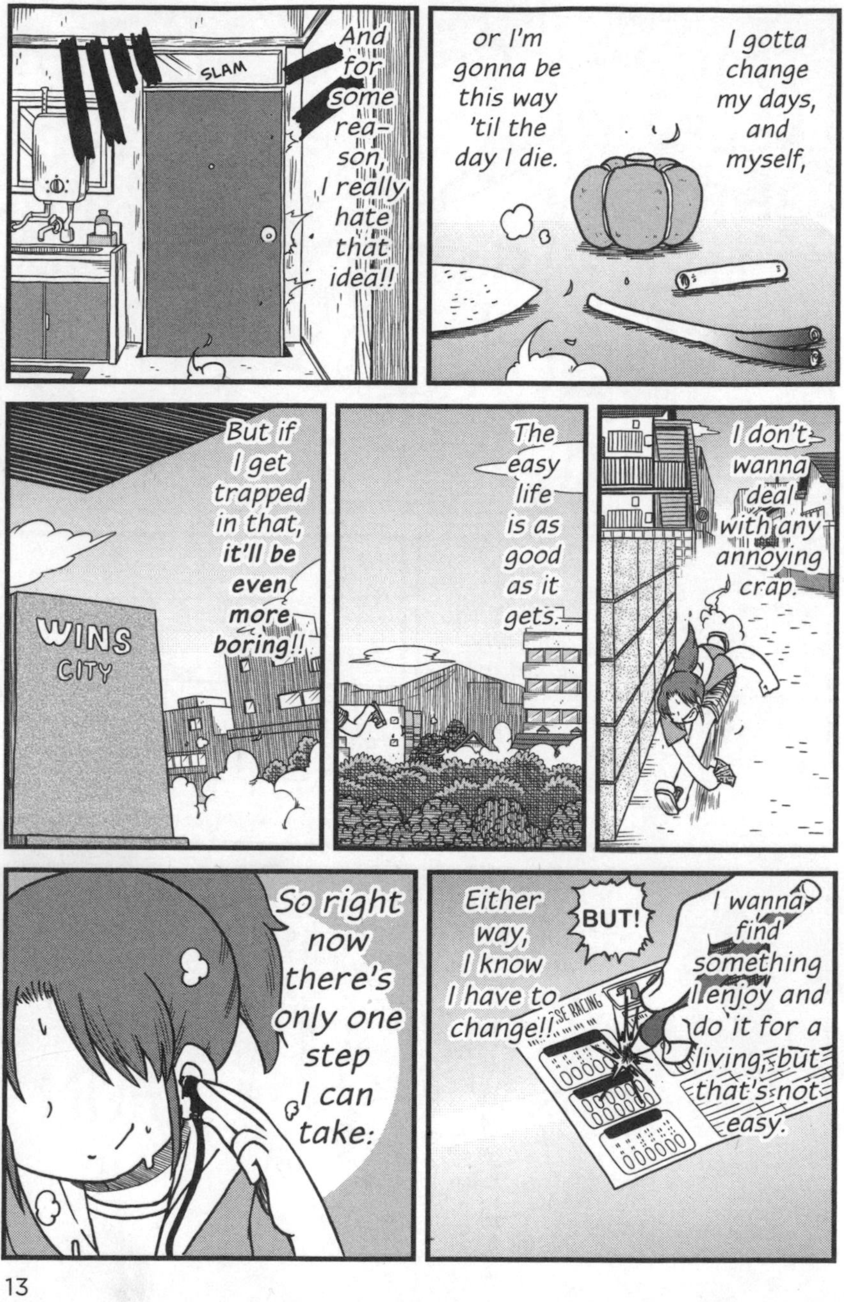
I gotta change my days, and myself,
or I'm gonna be this way 'til the day I die.
And for some rea-son, I really hate that idea!!
SLAM
I don't wanna deal with any annoying crap.
The easy life is as good as it gets.
But if I get trapped in that, **it'll be even more boring!!**
WINS
CITY
I wanna find something I enjoy and do it for a living, but that's not easy.
BUT!
Either way, I know I have to change!!
So right now there's only one step I can take:

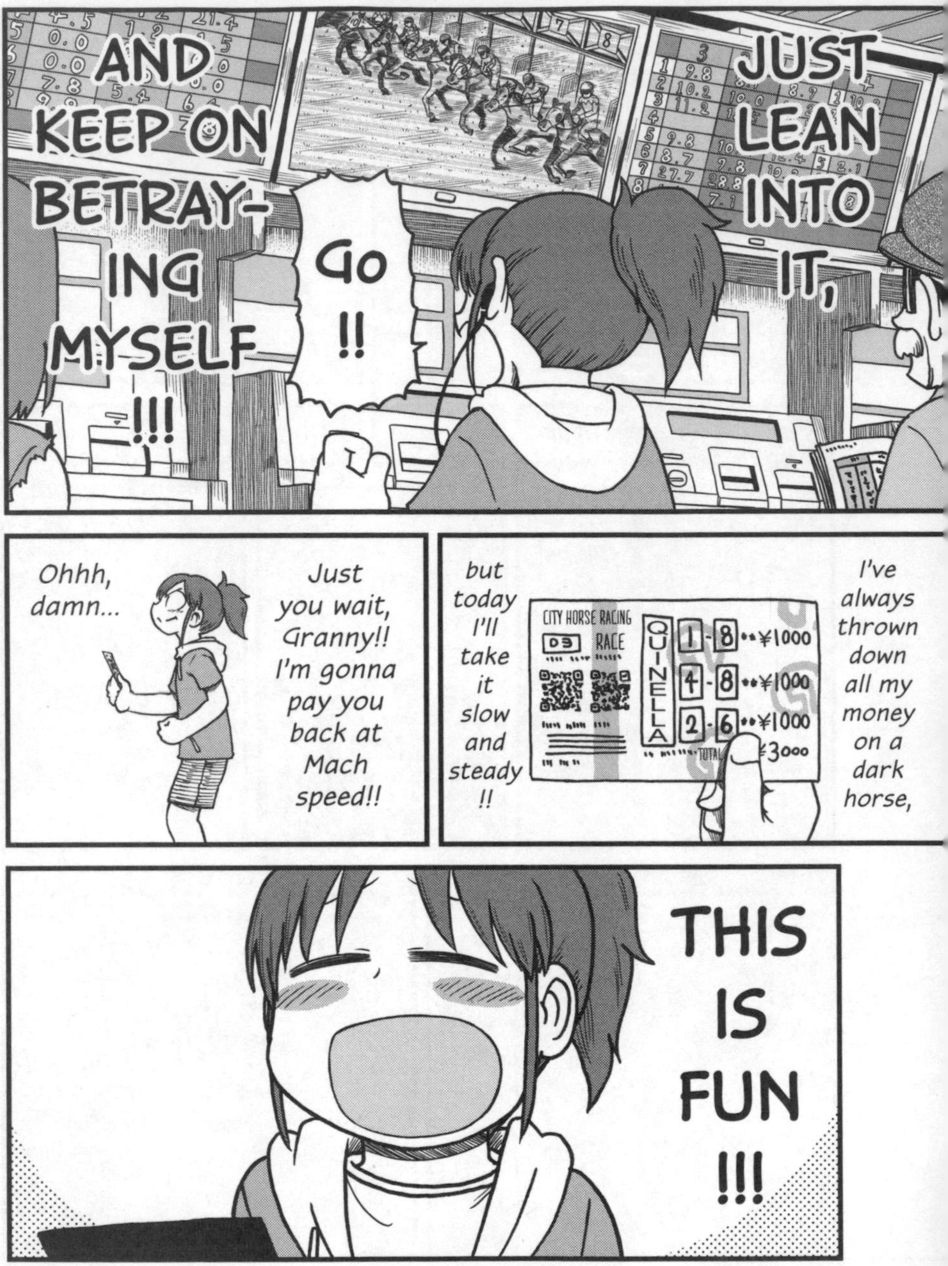
JUST LEAN INTO IT,
GO!!
AND KEEP ON BETRAYING MYSELF!!!
I've always thrown down all my money on a dark horse,
CITY HORSE RACING
D3 RACE
QUINELLA
1-8 ¥1000
4-8 ¥1000
2-6 ¥1000
TOTAL ¥3000
but today I'll take it slow and steady!!
Just you wait, Granny!! I'm gonna pay you back at Mach speed!!
Ohhh, damn...
THIS IS FUN!!!

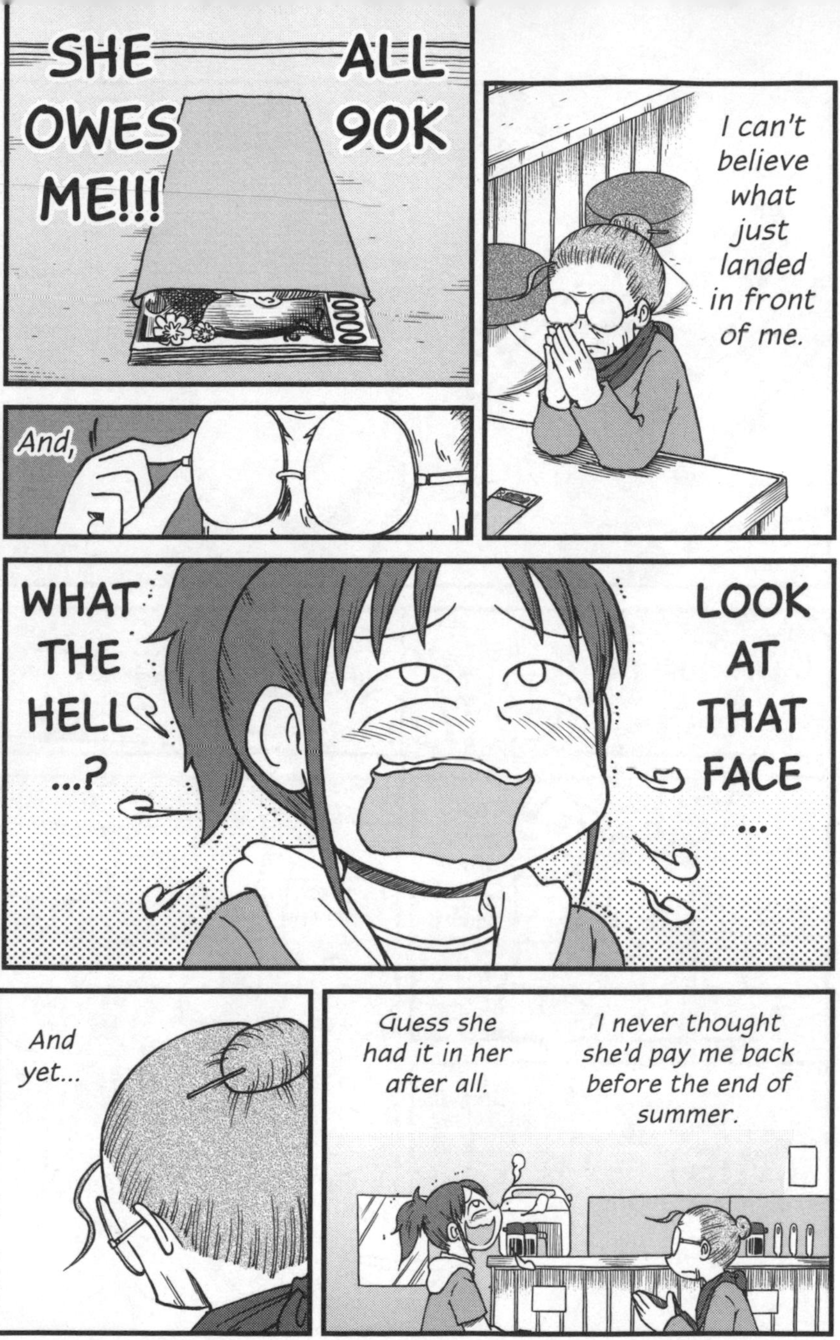
I can't believe what just landed in front of me.
ALL 90K
SHE OWES ME!!!
And,
LOOK AT THAT FACE ...
WHAT THE HELL ...?
I never thought she'd pay me back before the end of summer.
Guess she had it in her after all.
And yet...

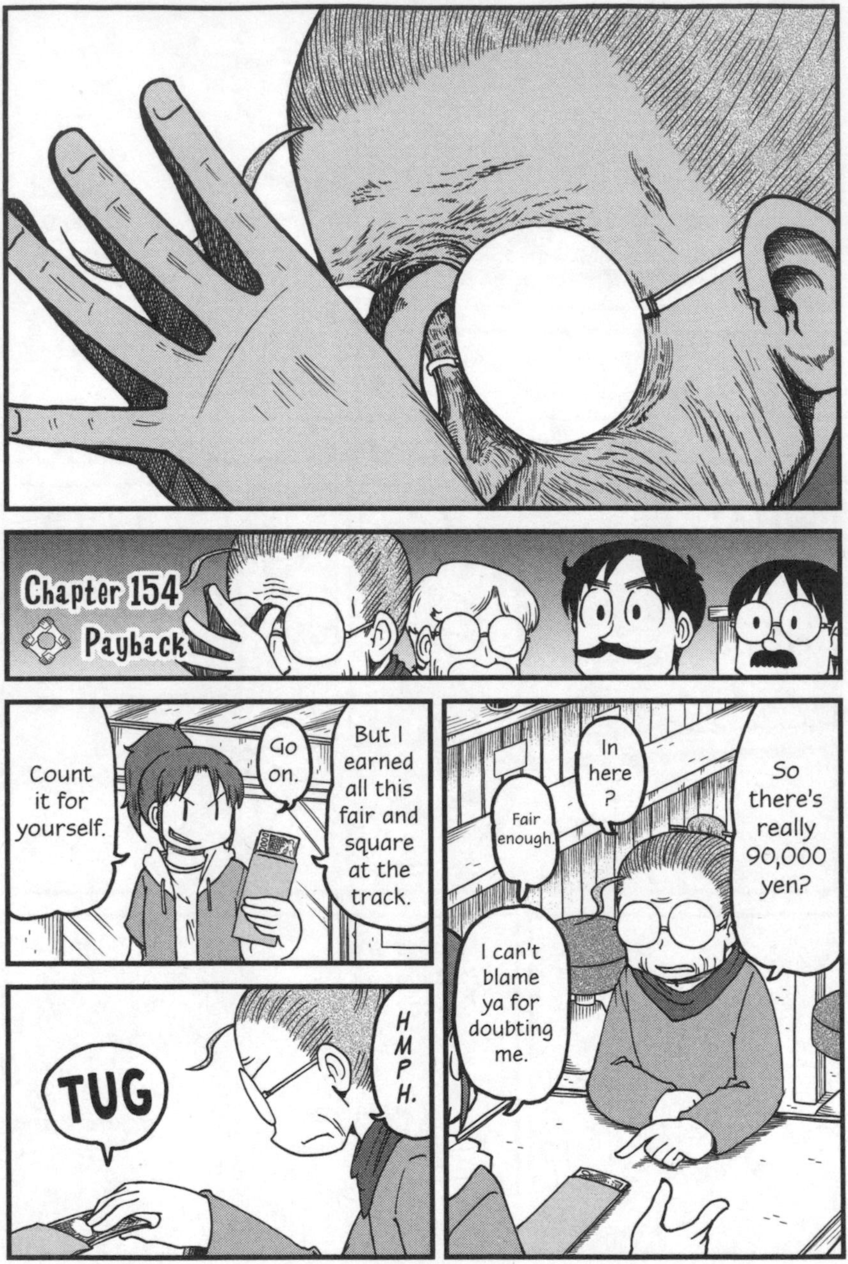

Chapter 154
Payback
So there's really 90,000 yen?
In here?
Fair enough.
I can't blame ya for doubting me.
But I earned all this fair and square at the track.
Go on.
Count it for yourself.
HMPH.
TUG

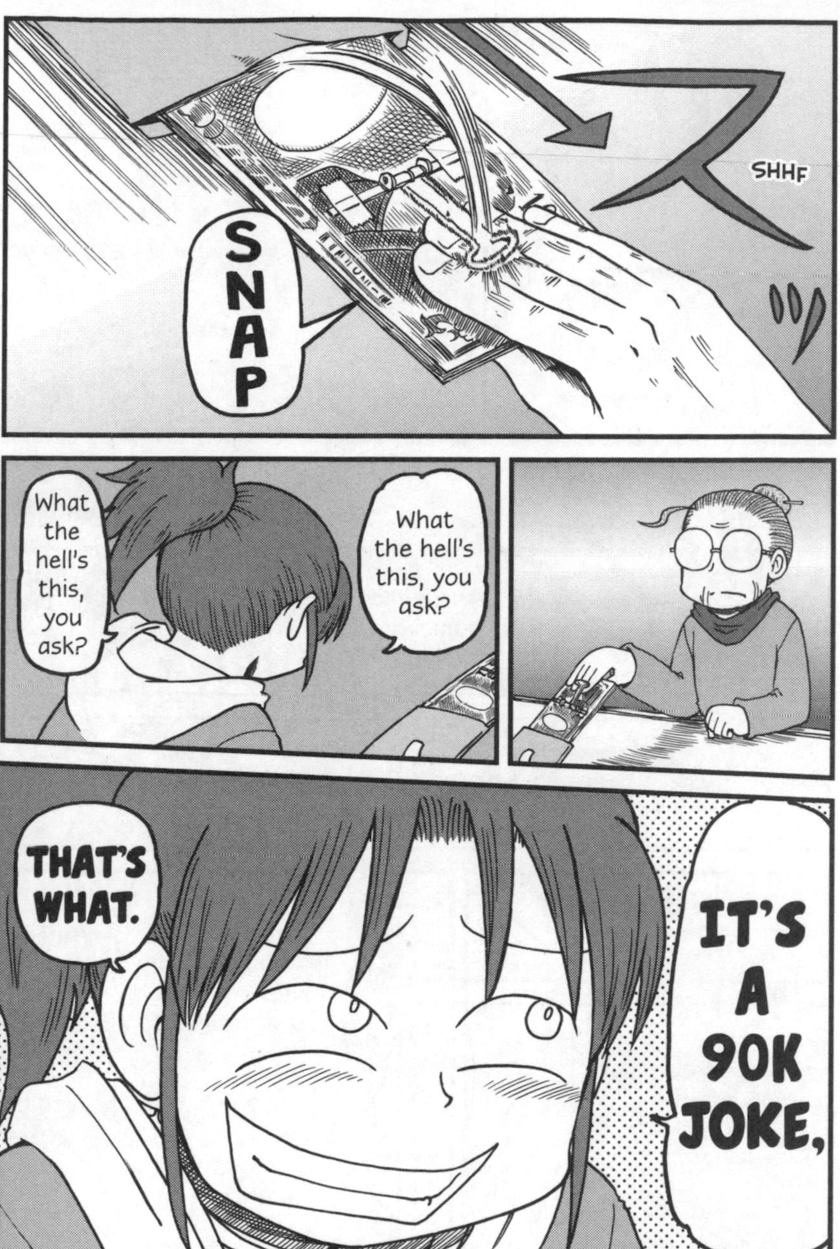
SHHF
SNAP
What the hell's this, you ask?
What the hell's this, you ask?
IT'S A 90K JOKE,
THAT'S WHAT.

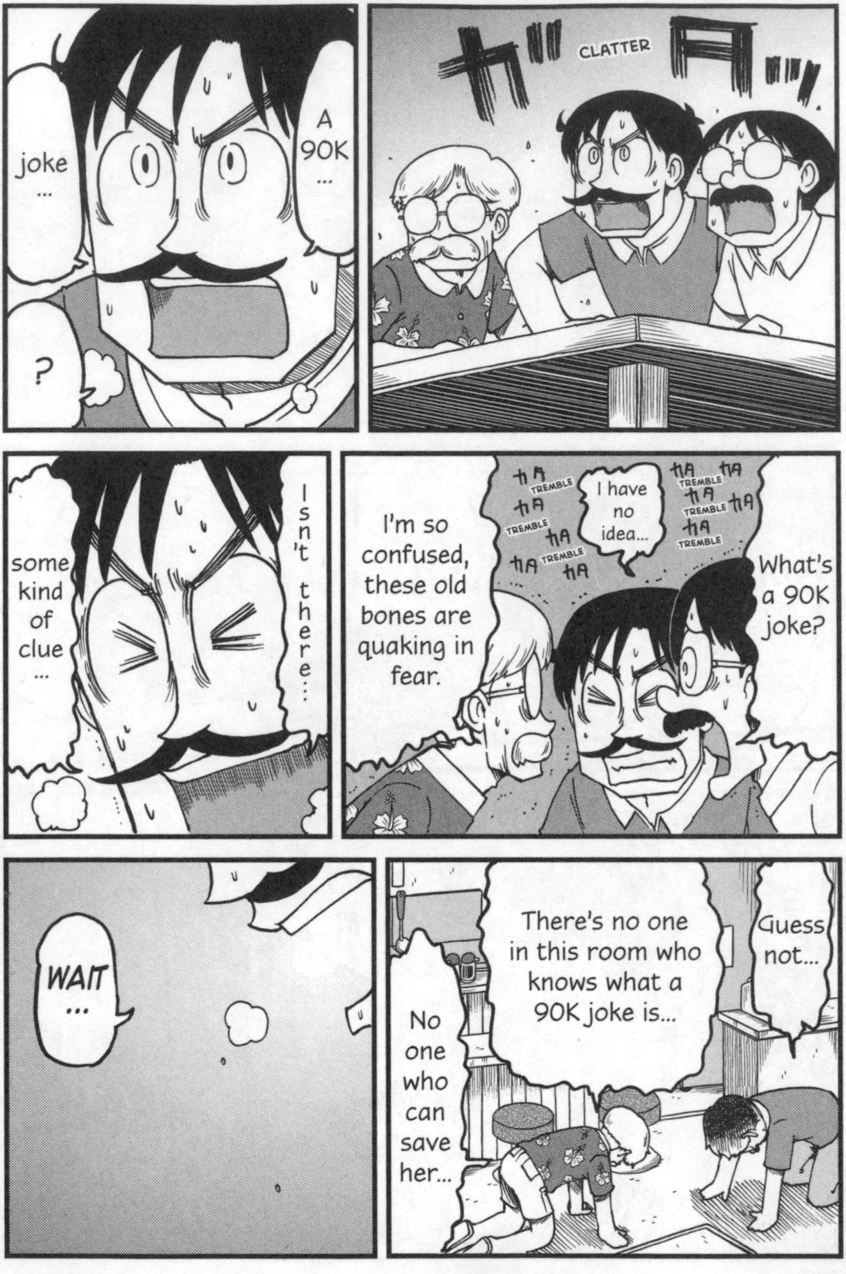
CLATTER
A 90K ...
joke ...
?
TREMBLE
What's a 90K joke?
I have no idea...
TREMBLE
I'm so confused, these old bones are quaking in fear.
Isn't there...
some kind of clue ...
Guess not...
There's no one in this room who knows what a 90K joke is...
No one who can save her...
WAIT ...

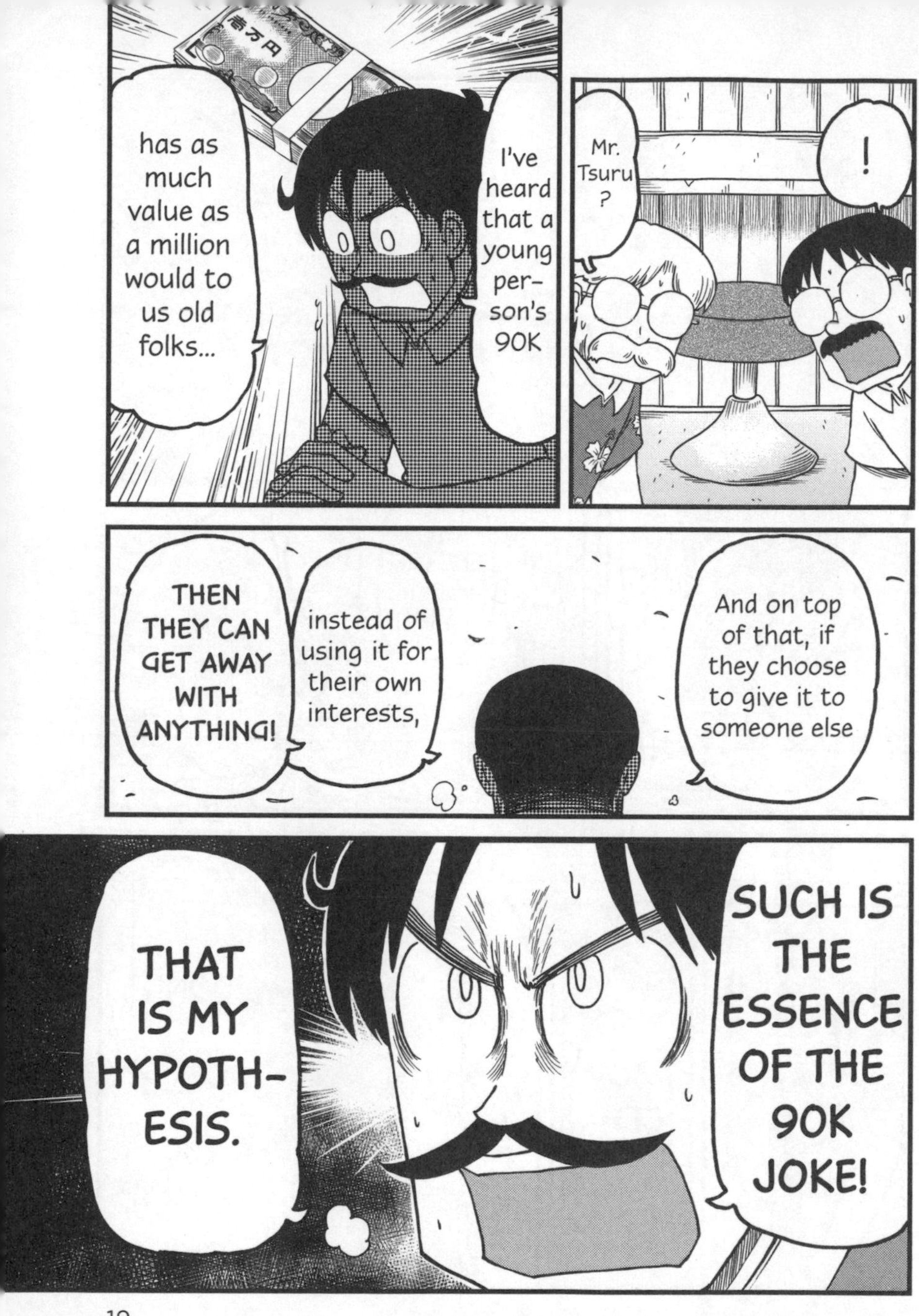
!
Mr. Tsuru?
I've heard that a young person's 90K
has as much value as a million would to us old folks...
And on top of that, if they choose to give it to someone else
instead of using it for their own interests,
THEN THEY CAN GET AWAY WITH ANYTHING!
SUCH IS THE ESSENCE OF THE 90K JOKE!
THAT IS MY HYPOTHESIS.

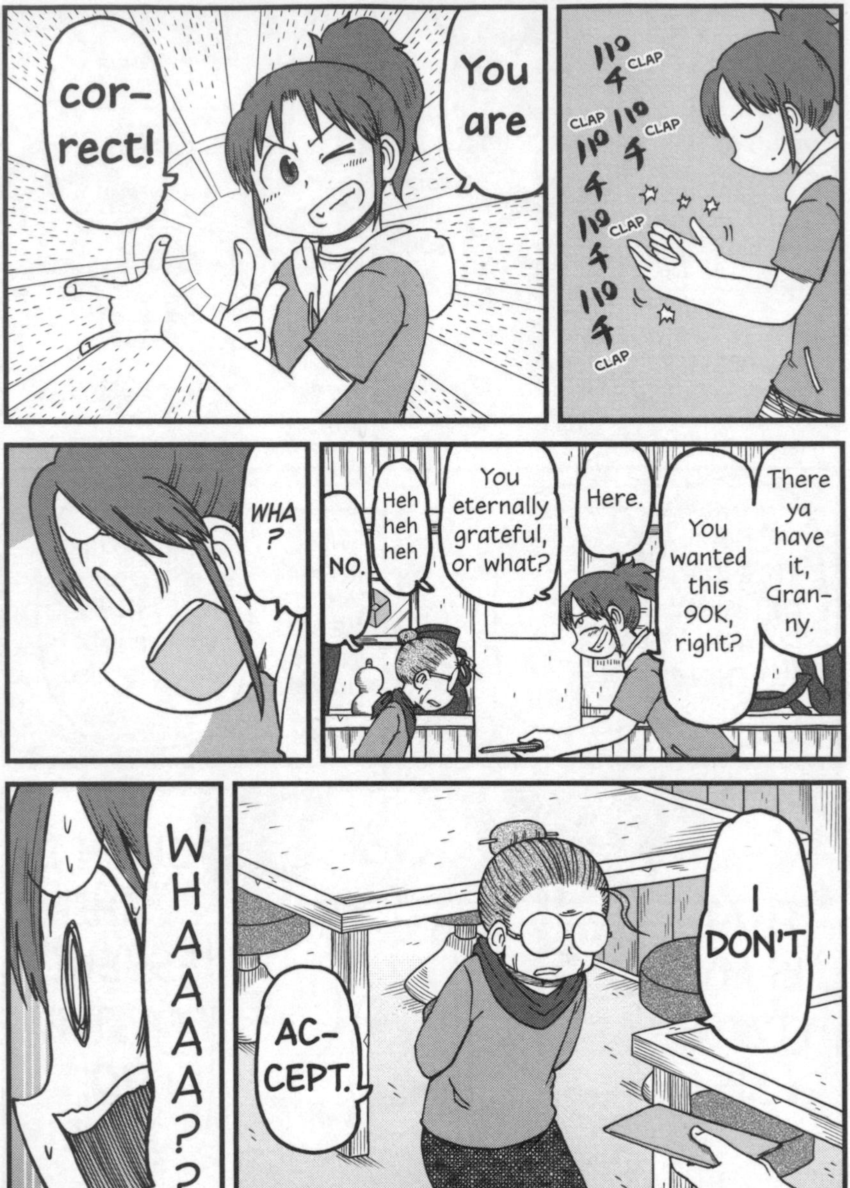
パチ CLAP
パチ CLAP
パチ CLAP
パチ CLAP
パチ CLAP
You are
cor-rect!
There ya have it, Gran-ny.
You wanted this 90K, right?
Here.
You eternally grateful, or what?
Heh heh heh
NO.
WHA?
I DON'T
AC-CEPT.
WHAAAA??

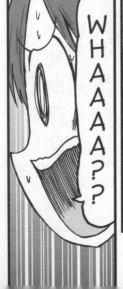

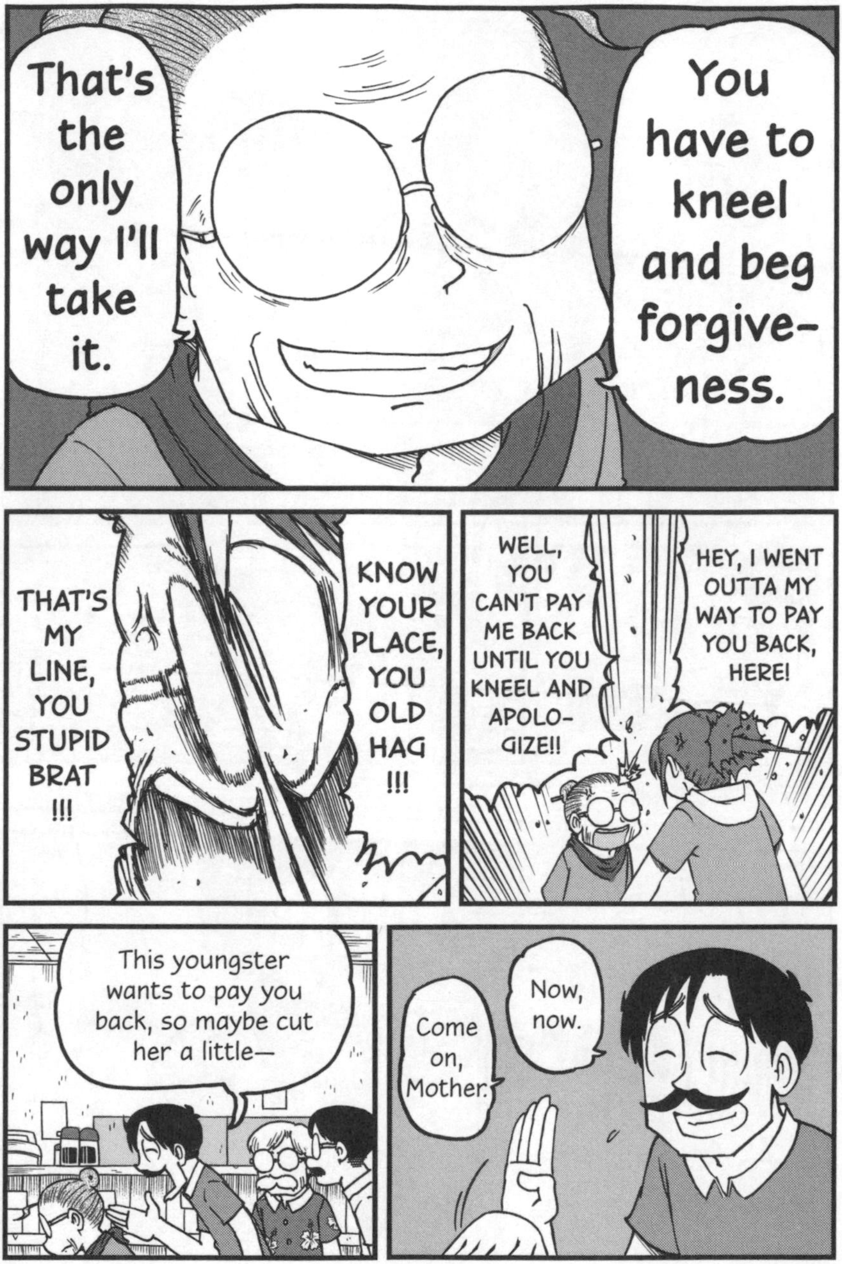
You have to kneel and beg forgive-ness.
That's the only way I'll take it.
HEY, I WENT OUTTA MY WAY TO PAY YOU BACK, HERE!
WELL, YOU CAN'T PAY ME BACK UNTIL YOU KNEEL AND APOLO-GIZE!!
KNOW YOUR PLACE, YOU OLD HAG!!!
THAT'S MY LINE, YOU STUPID BRAT!!!
Now, now.
Come on, Mother.
This youngster wants to pay you back, so maybe cut her a little—

I'LL AVENGE YOU!!!

DASH

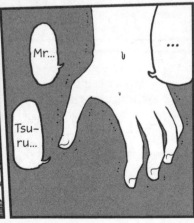

Mr...

Tsu-ru...

...

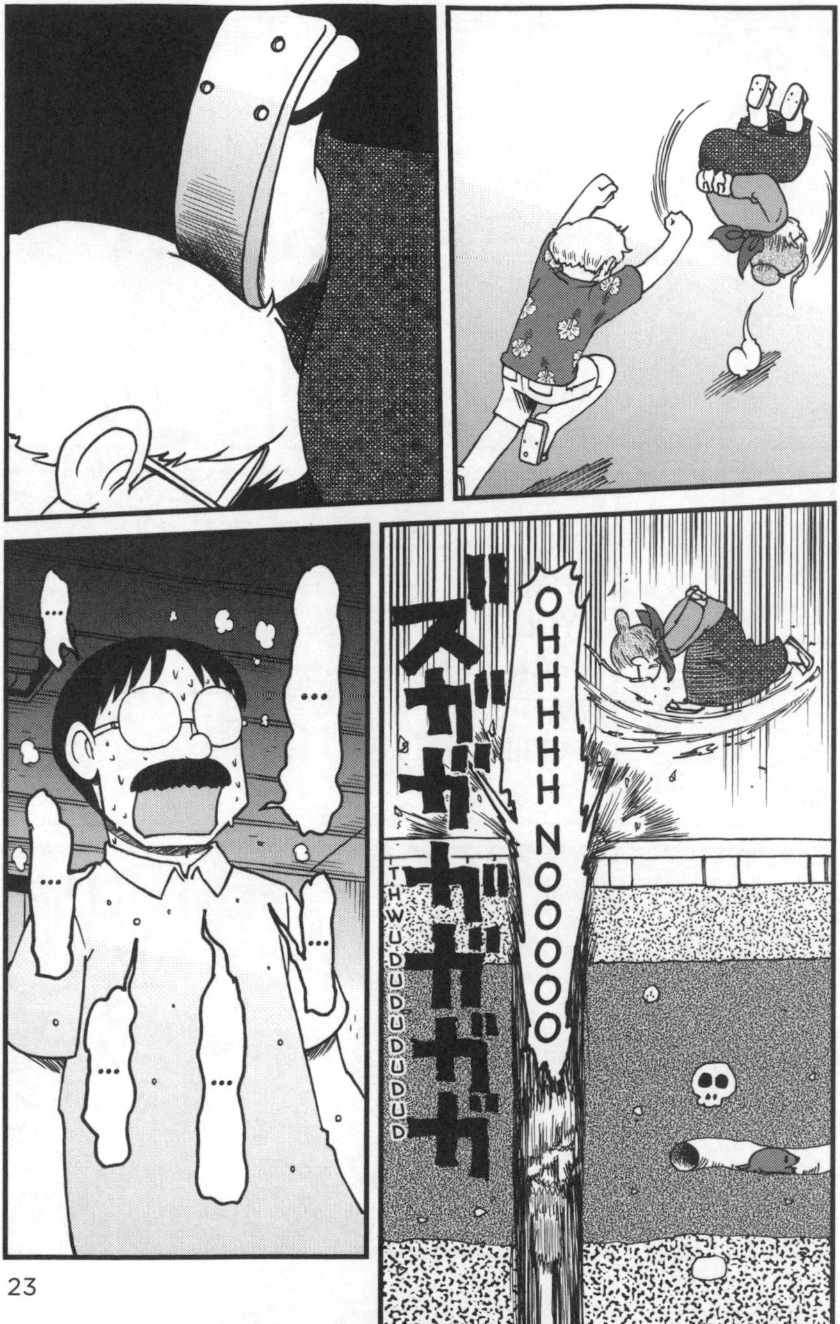
OHHHHH NOOOOO
ズガガガガガ
THWUDUDUDUDUD
...
...
...
...
...
...
...

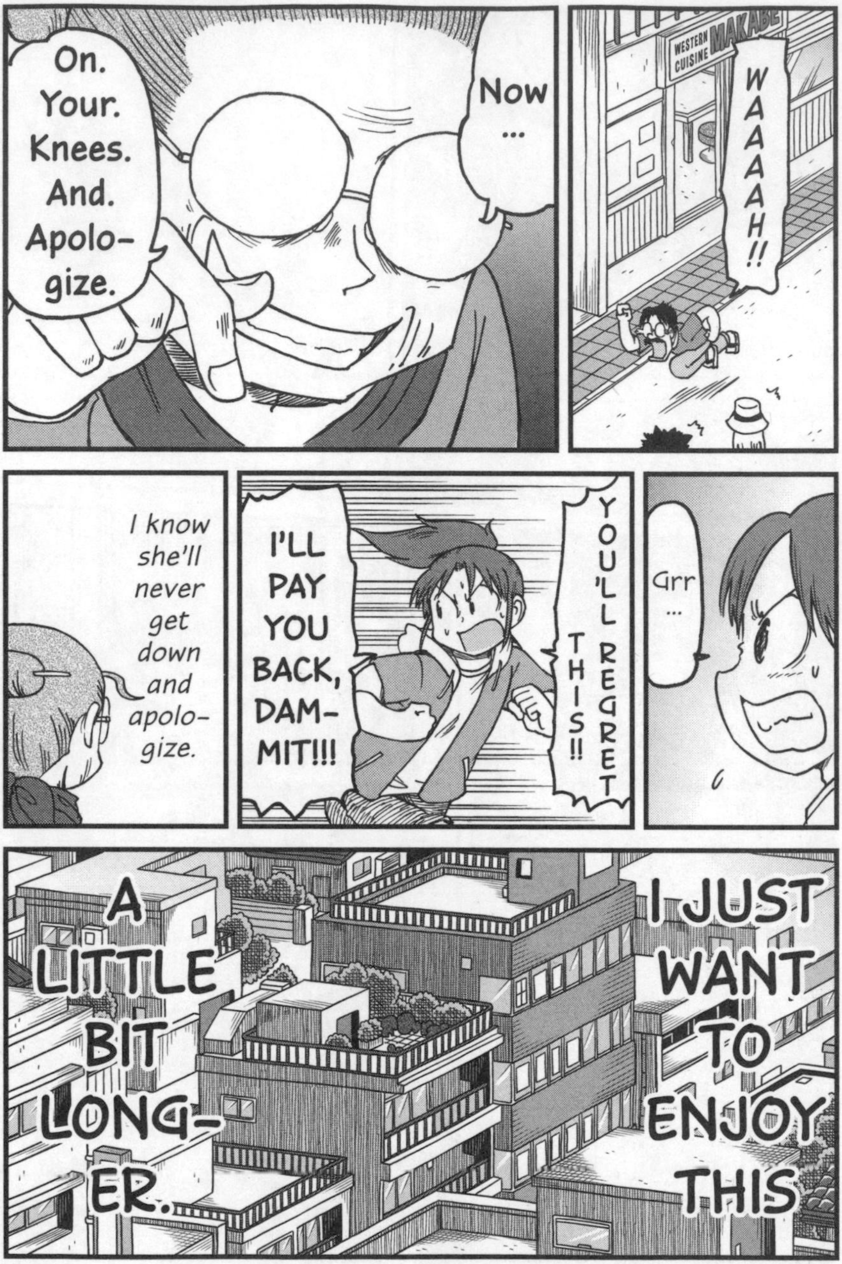
WESTERN CUISINE MAKABE
WAAAAAH!!
Now ...
On. Your. Knees. And. Apolo-gize.
Grr ...
YOU'LL REGRET THIS!!
I'LL PAY YOU BACK, DAM-MIT!!!
I know she'll never get down and apolo-gize.
I JUST WANT TO ENJOY THIS
A LITTLE BIT LONG-ER.

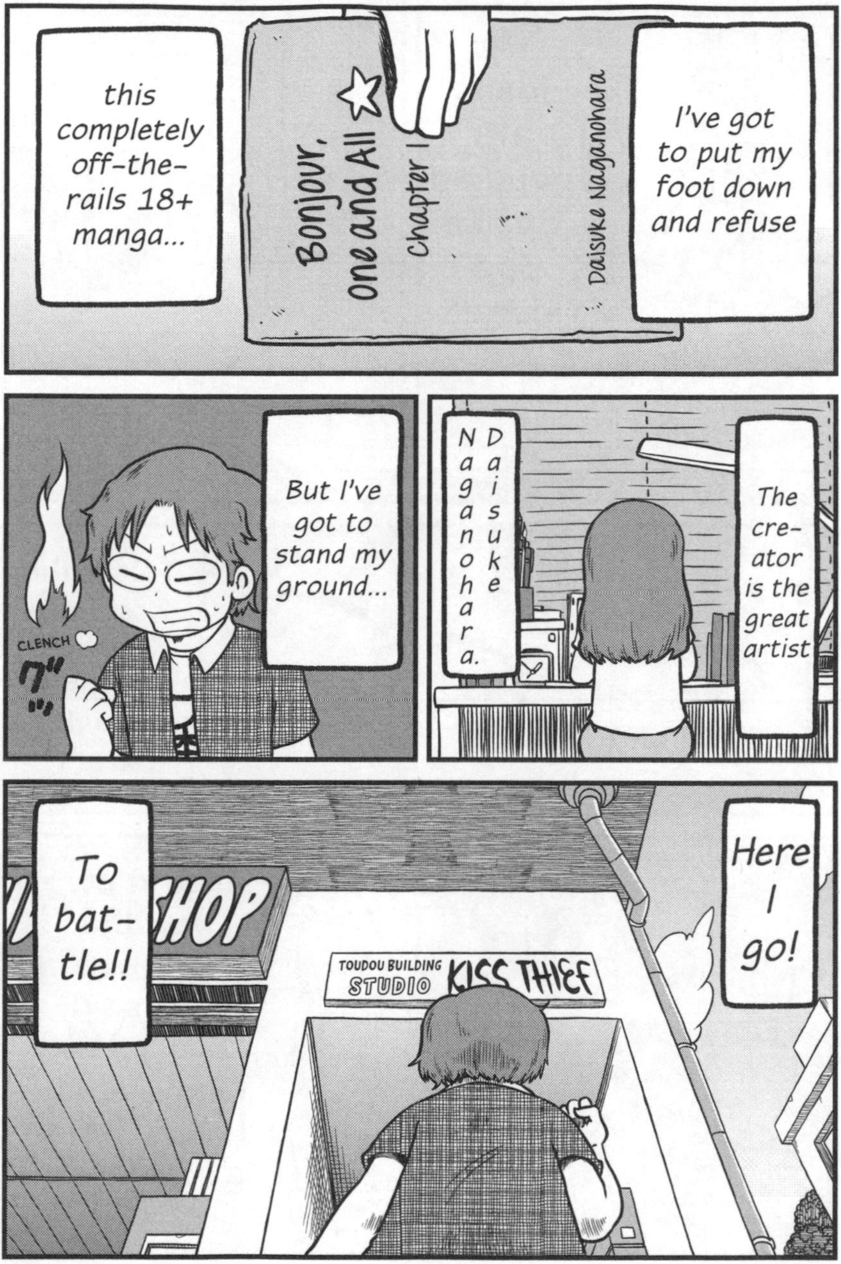
I've got to put my foot down and refuse
Bonjour, one and All
Chapter 1
Daisuke Naganohara
this completely off-the-rails 18+ manga...
The creator is the great artist
Daisuke Naganohara.
But I've got to stand my ground...
CLENCH
Here I go!
TOUDOU BUILDING STUDIO KISS THIEF
SHOP
To battle!!

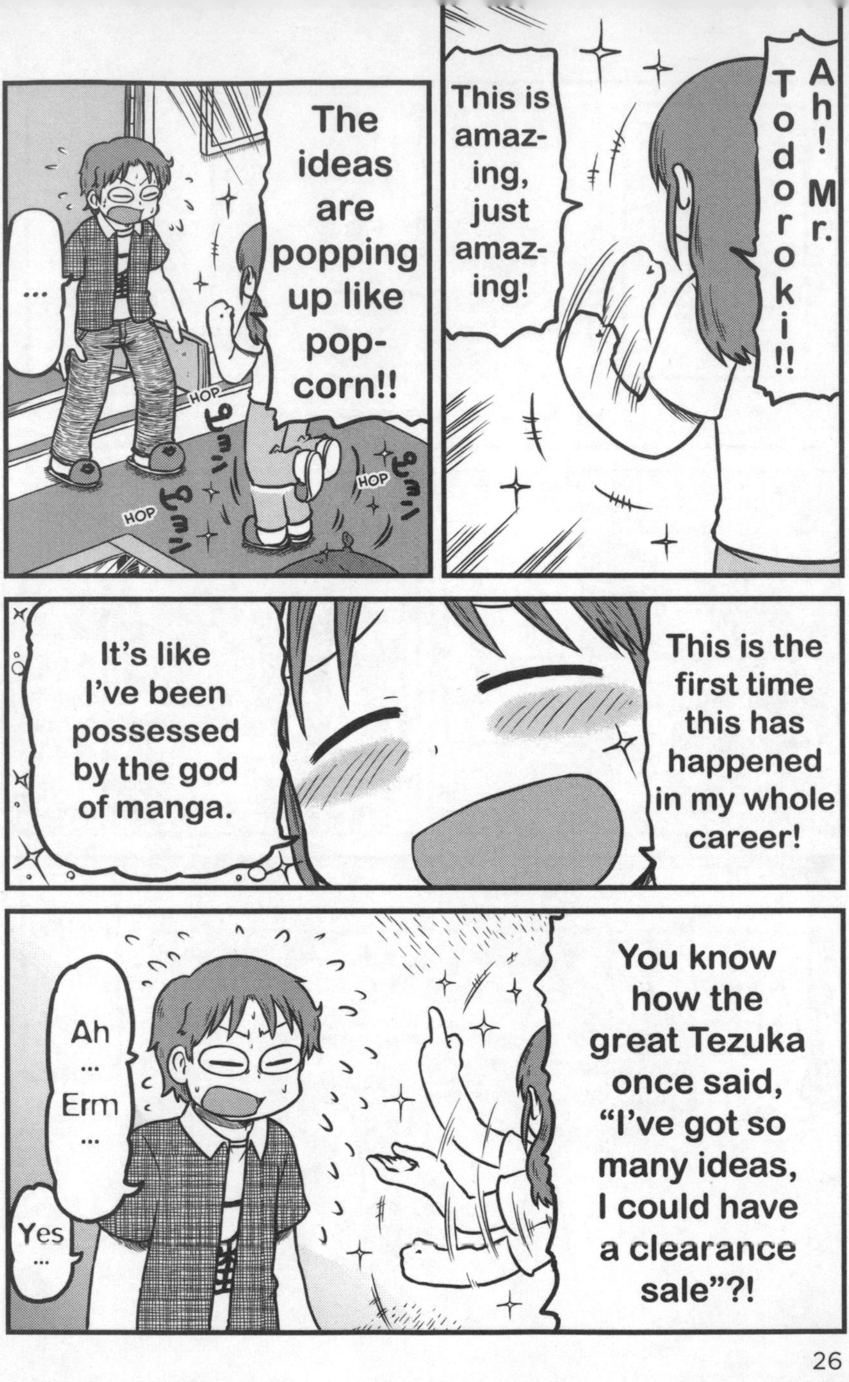
Ah! Mr. Todoroki!!
This is amazing, just amazing!
The ideas are popping up like popcorn!!
...
HOP
HOP
HOP
This is the first time this has happened in my whole career!
It's like I've been possessed by the god of manga.
You know how the great Tezuka once said, "I've got so many ideas, I could have a clearance sale"?!
Ah... Erm...
Yes...

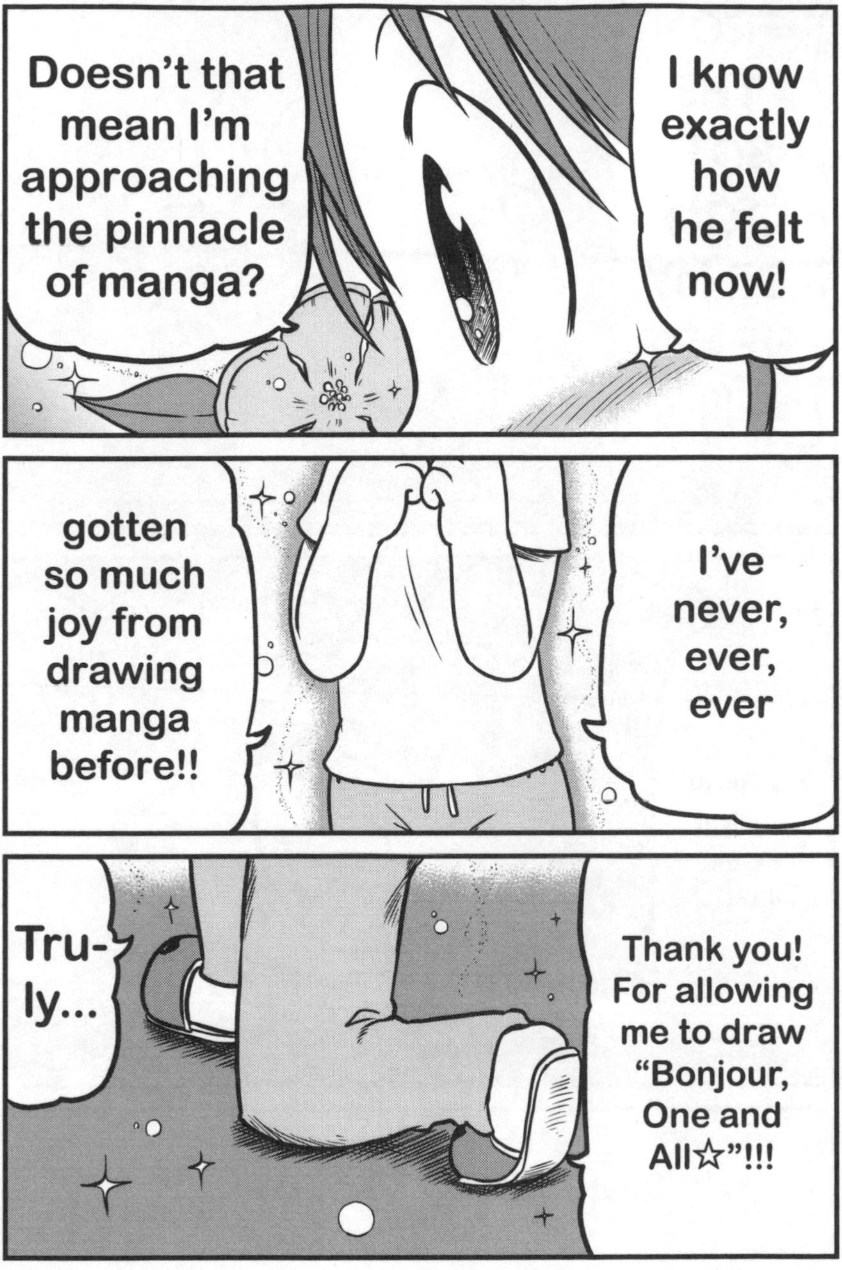
I know exactly how he felt now!
Doesn't that mean I'm approaching the pinnacle of manga?
I've never, ever, ever
gotten so much joy from drawing manga before!!
Thank you! For allowing me to draw "Bonjour, One and All☆"!!!
Tru-ly...

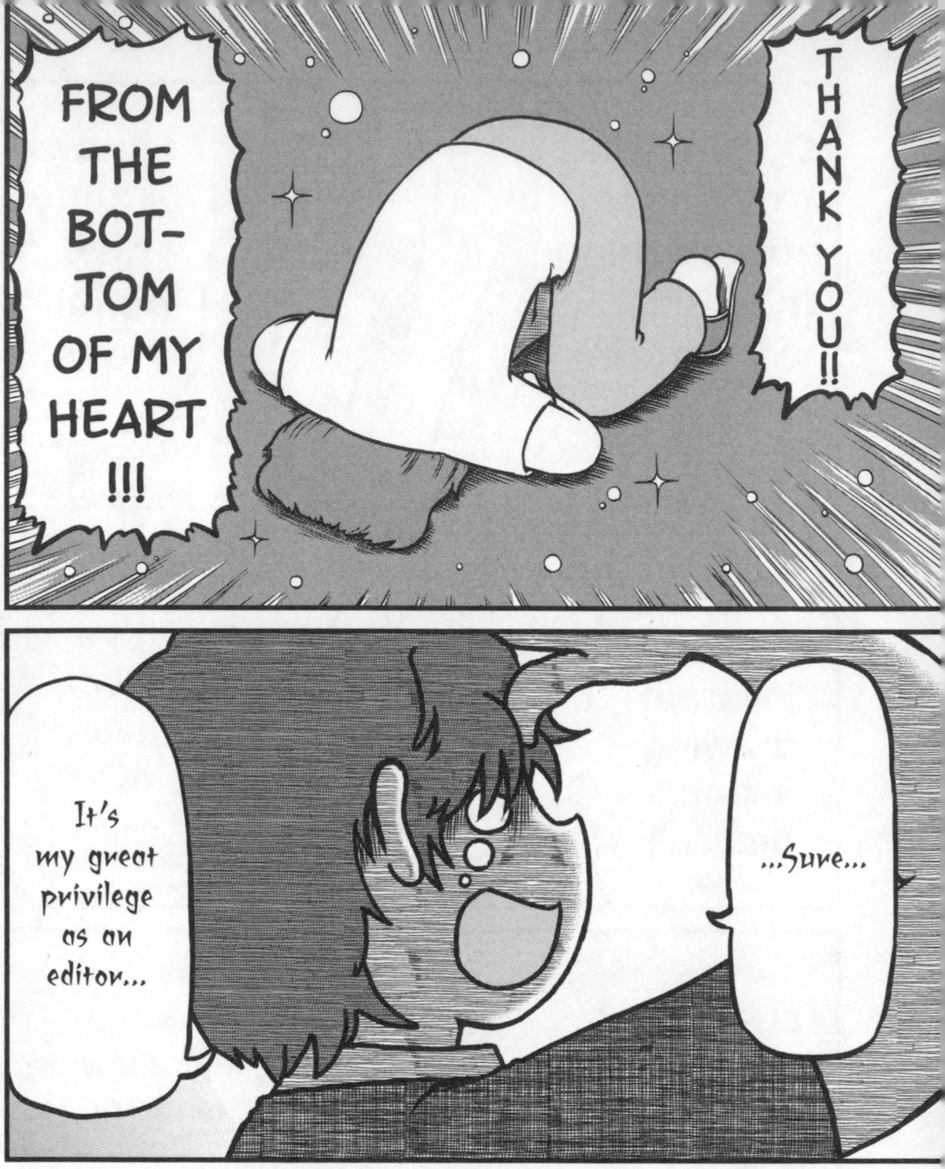
THANK YOU!!
FROM THE BOT-TOM OF MY HEART!!!
...Sure...
It's my great privilege as an editor...

Chapter 155 Back-and-Forth

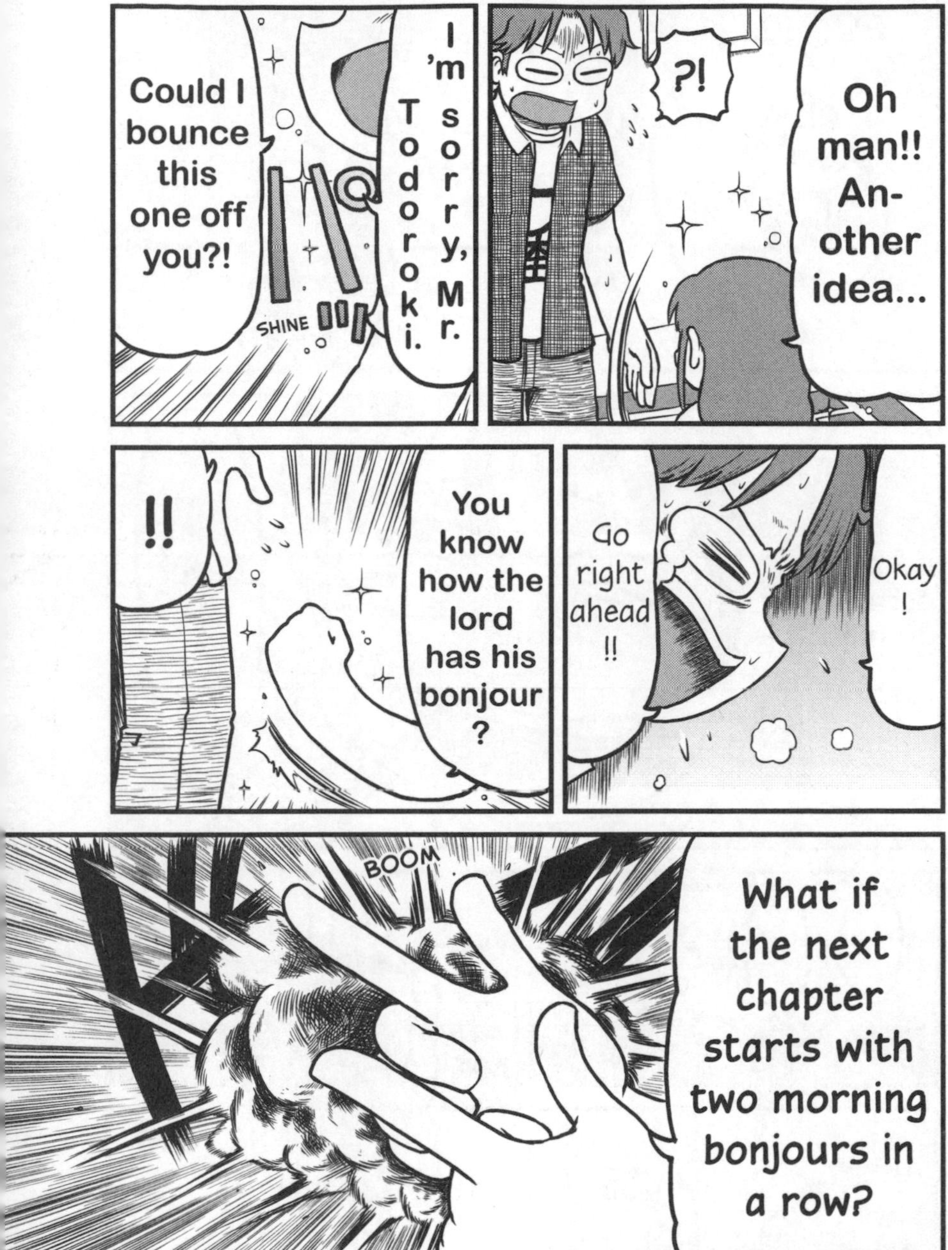
Oh man!! An-other idea...
?!
I'm sorry, Mr. Todoroki.
Could I bounce this one off you?!
SHINE
Okay!
Go right ahead!!
You know how the lord has his bonjour?
!!
What if the next chapter starts with two morning bonjours in a row?
BOOM

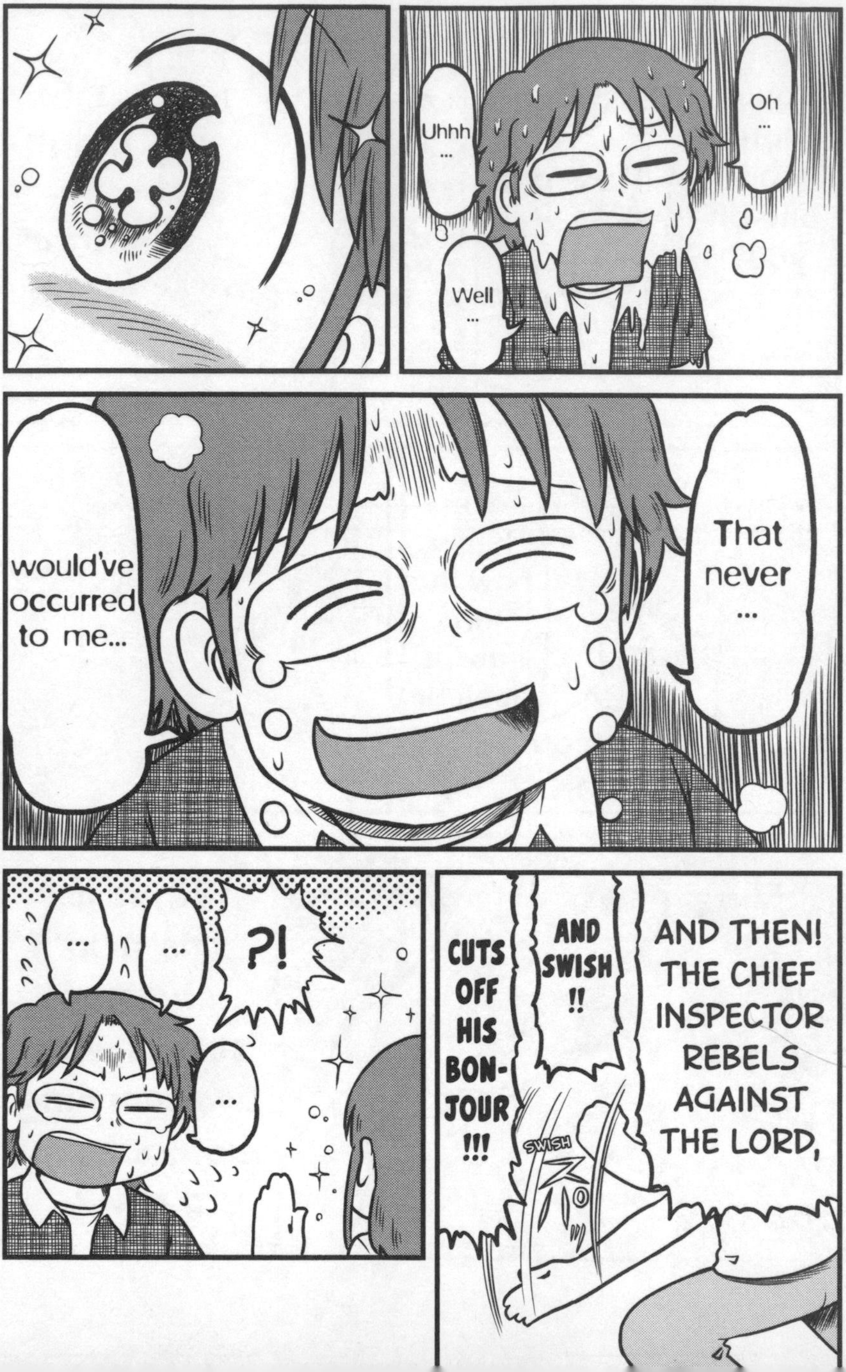
Oh ...
Uhhh ...
Well ...
That never ...
would've occurred to me...
AND THEN! THE CHIEF INSPECTOR REBELS AGAINST THE LORD,
AND SWISH !!
CUTS OFF HIS BON-JOUR !!!
SWISH
?!
...
...
...

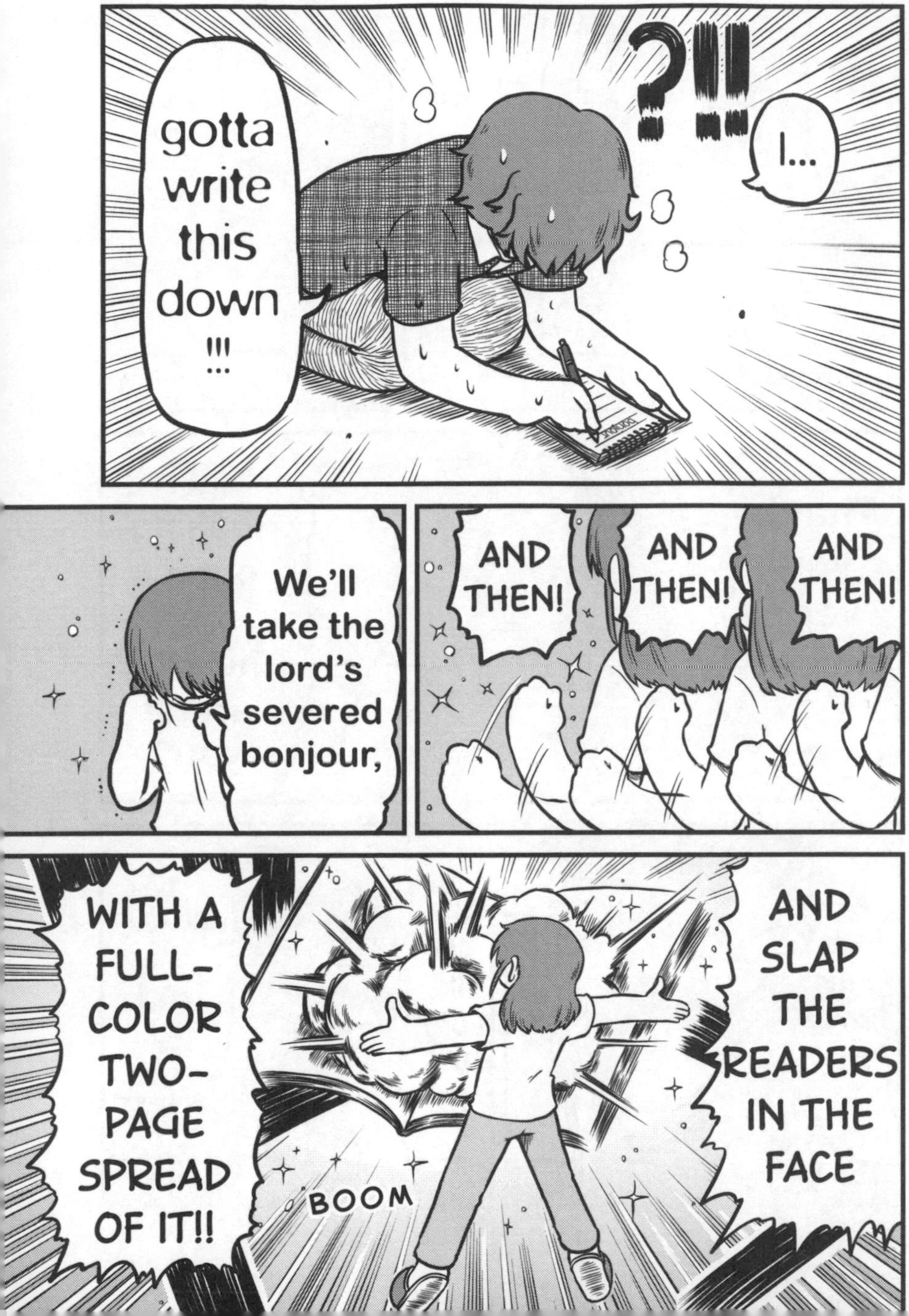
I...
?!!
gotta write this down !!! ...
AND THEN!
AND THEN!
AND THEN!
We'll take the lord's severed bonjour,
AND SLAP THE READERS IN THE FACE
BOOM
WITH A FULL-COLOR TWO-PAGE SPREAD OF IT!!

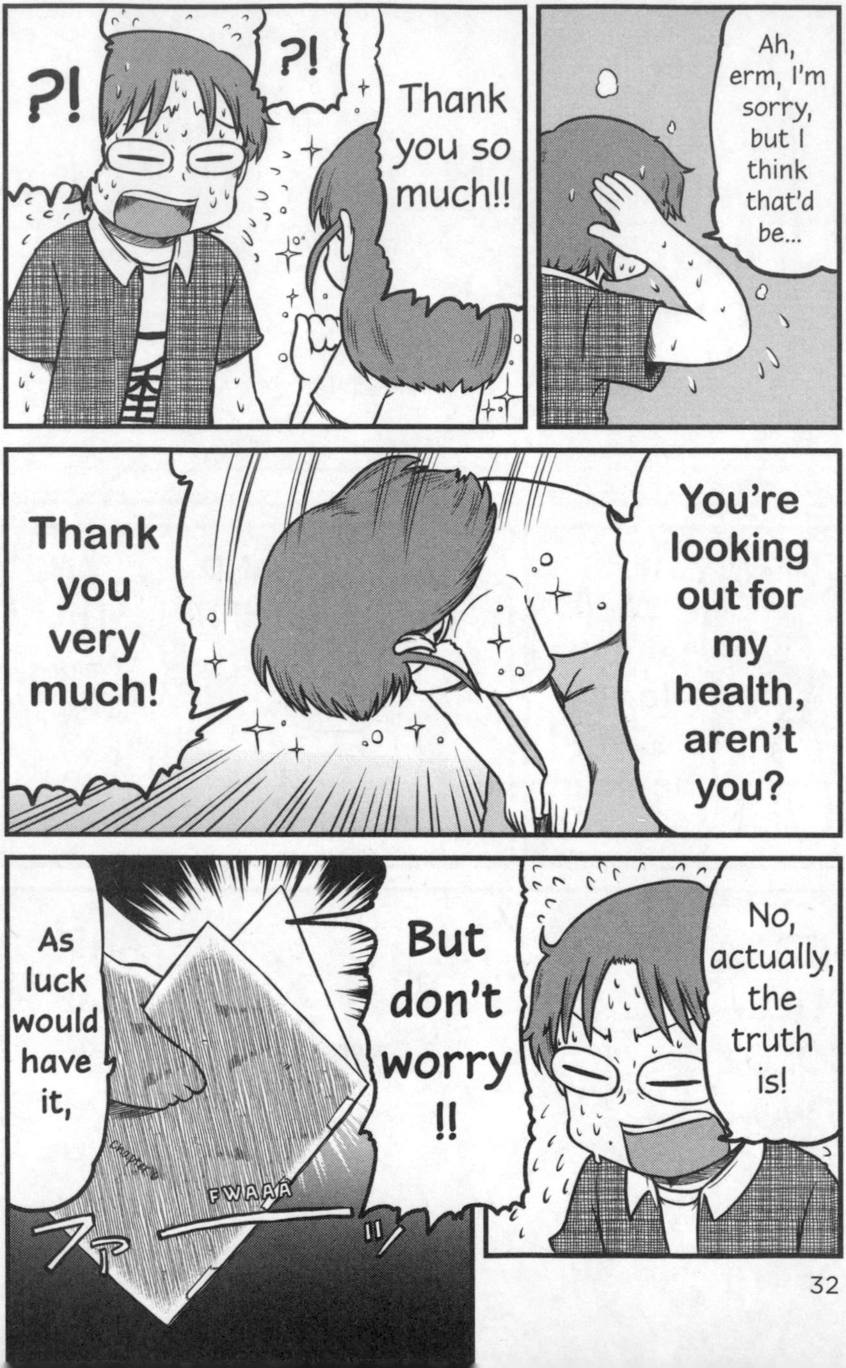
Ah, erm, I'm sorry, but I think that'd be...
Thank you so much!!
?!
?!
You're looking out for my health, aren't you?
Thank you very much!
No, actually, the truth is!
But don't worry!!
As luck would have it,
FWAAAA
ファー!!

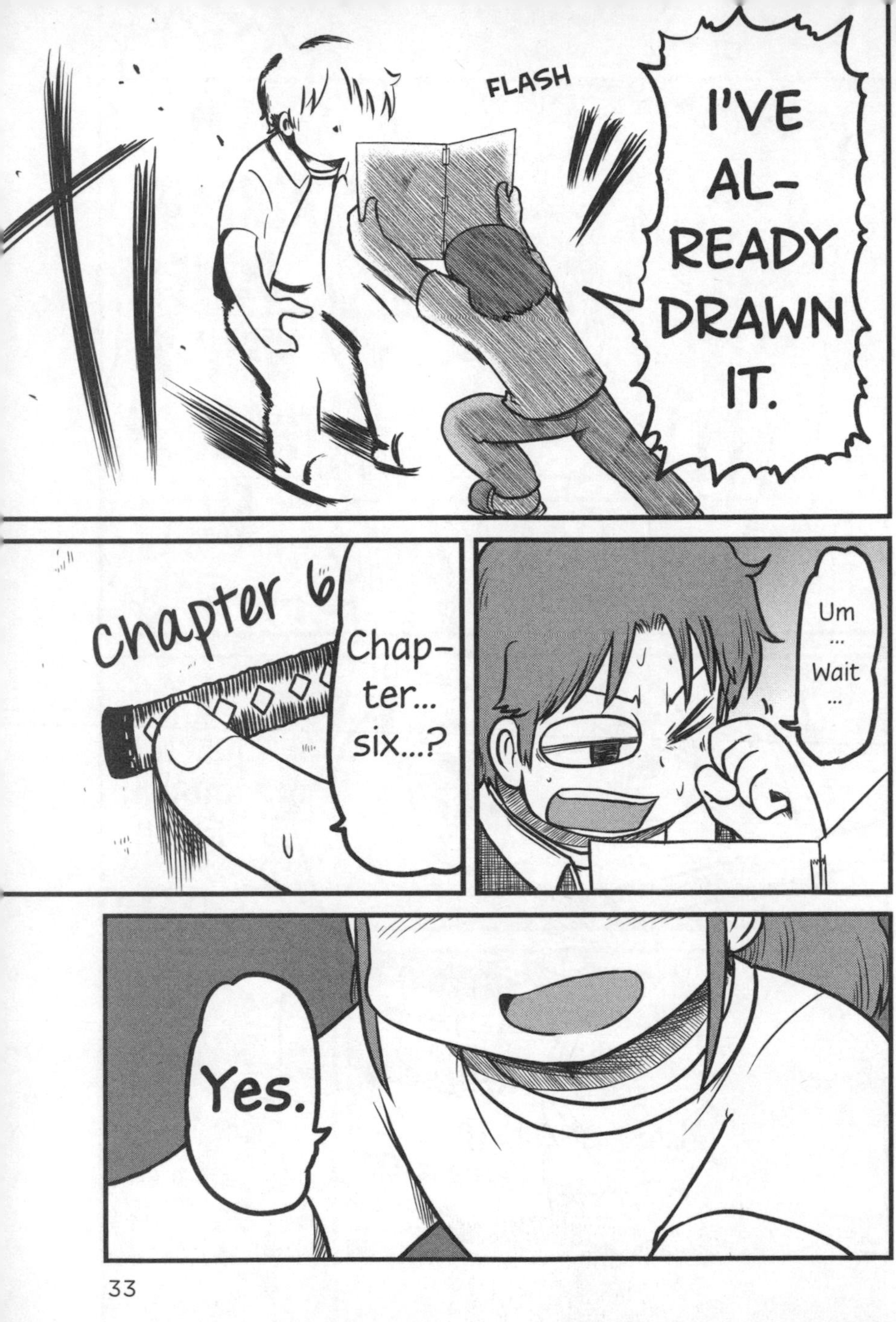
FLASH
I'VE AL-READY DRAWN IT.
Um ... Wait ...
Chapter 6
Chap-ter... six...?
Yes.

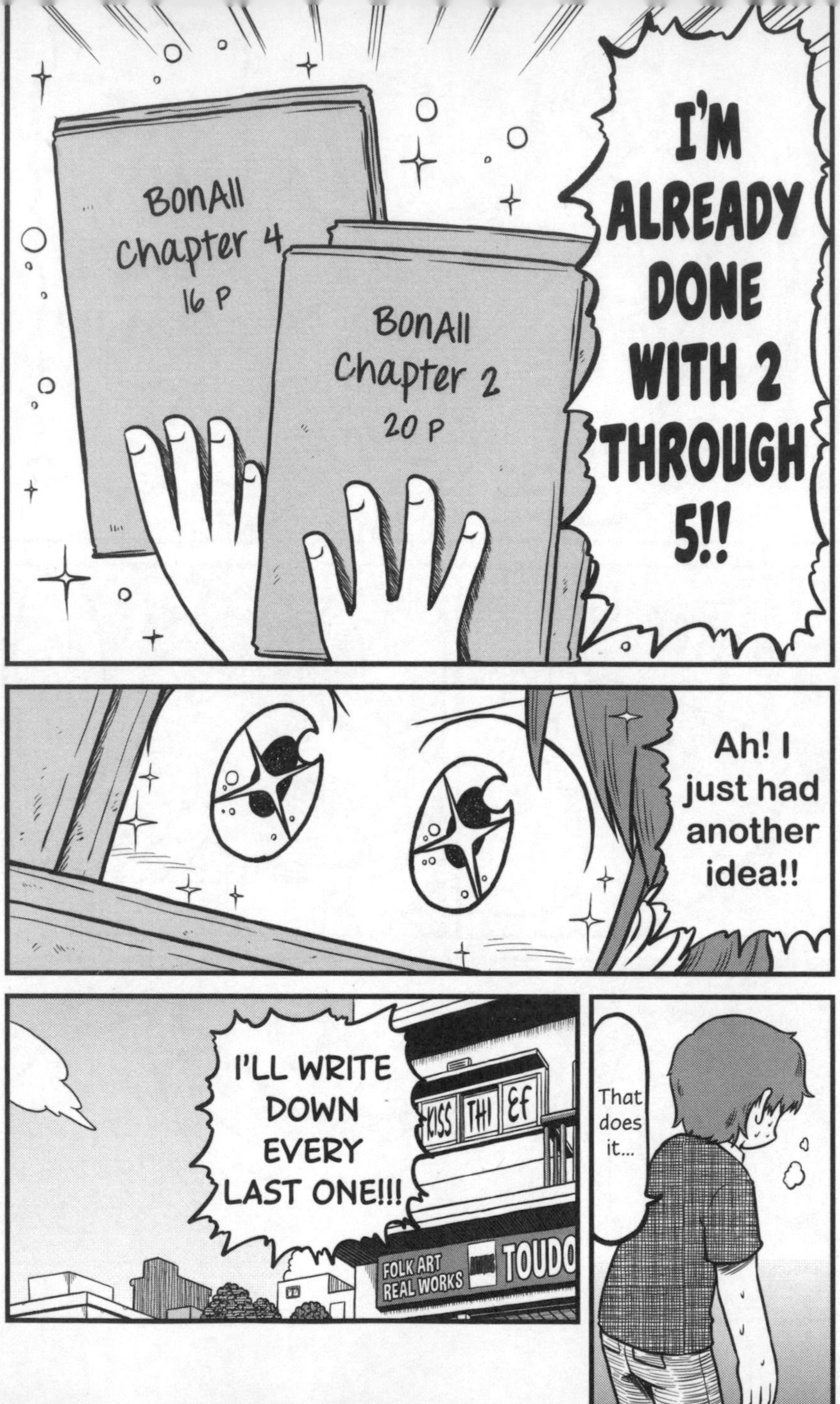
I'M ALREADY DONE WITH 2 THROUGH 5!!
BonAll Chapter 2 20 P
BonAll Chapter 4 16 P
Ah! I just had another idea!!
That does it...
I'LL WRITE DOWN EVERY LAST ONE!!!
KISS THI Ef
TOUDO
FOLK ART REAL WORKS

CITY

New
Mr. Bummer
32 P
BonAll
Chapter 2
20 P

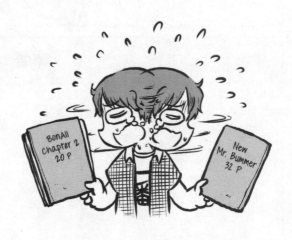

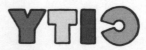

What's the first thing you do when you wake up?

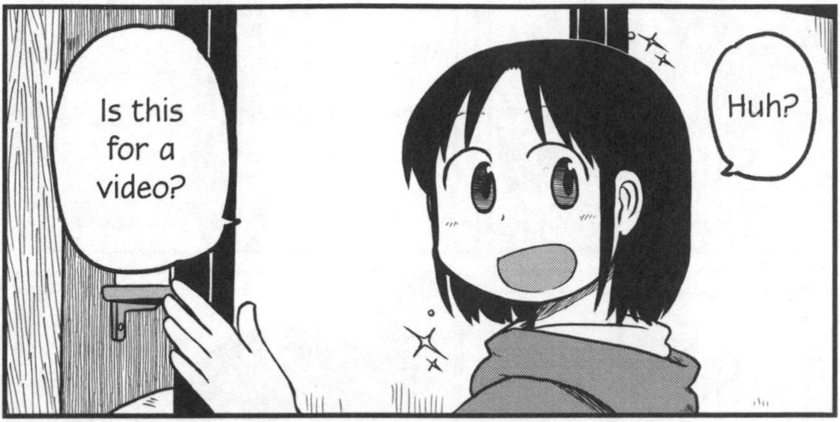
Huh?
Is this for a video?

Please tell us your morning routine, Ms. Wako.

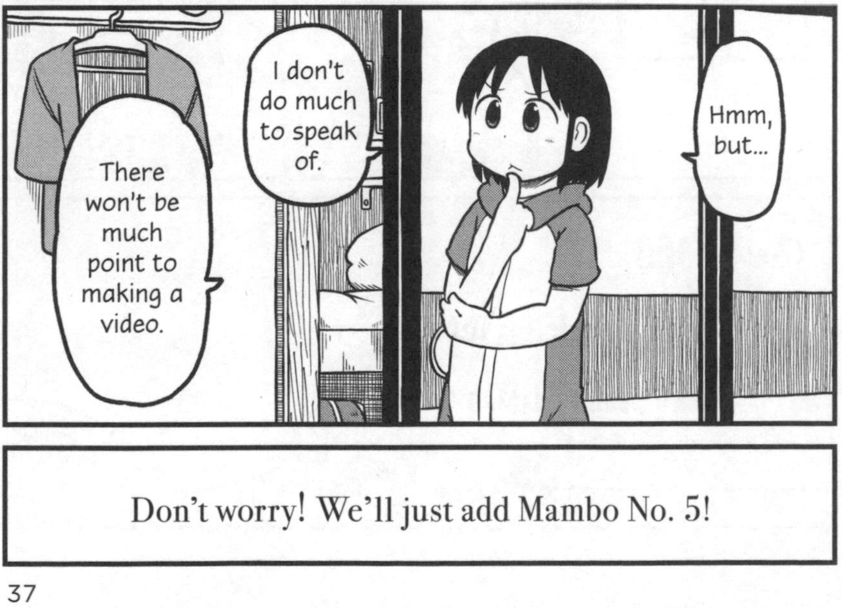
Hmm, but...
I don't do much to speak of.
There won't be much point to making a video.

Don't worry! We'll just add Mambo No. 5!

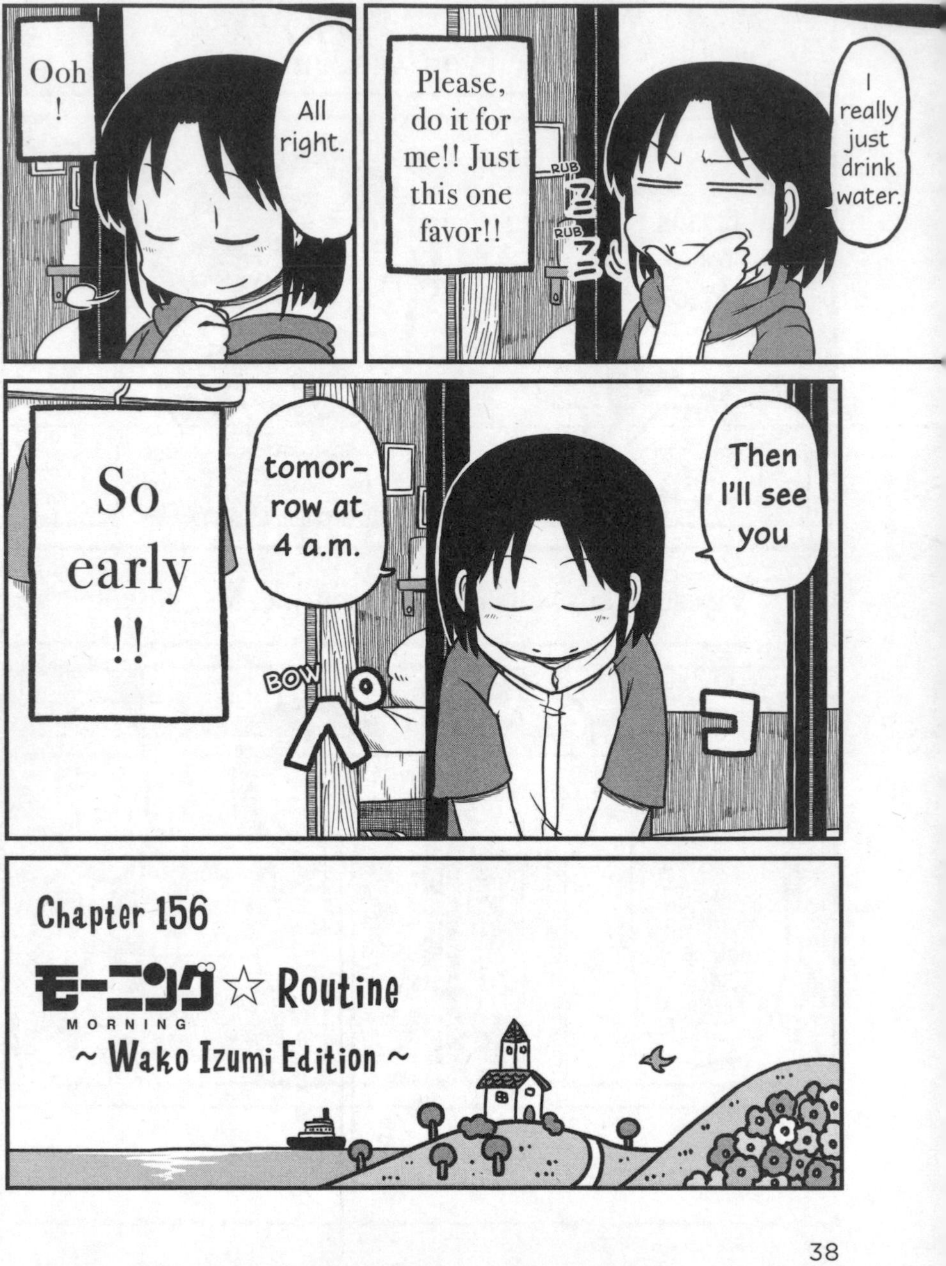
I really just drink water.
RUB
RUB
Please, do it for me!! Just this one favor!!
All right.
Ooh!
Then I'll see you
tomorrow at 4 a.m.
So early!!
BOW
Chapter 156
モーニング☆Routine
MORNING
~ Wako Izumi Edition ~

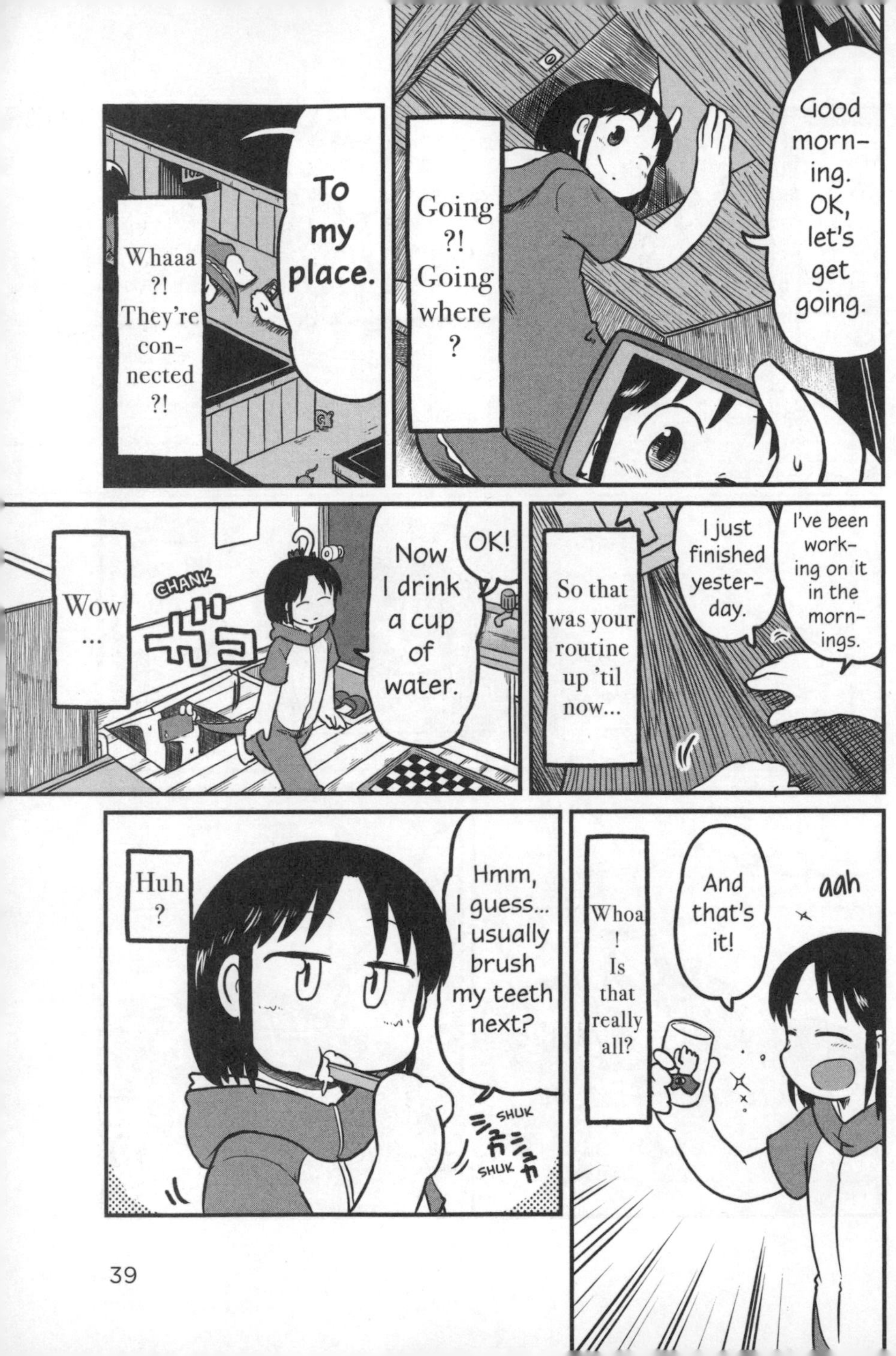
Good morn-ing. OK, let's get going.
Going?! Going where?
To my place.
Whaaa?! They're con-nected?!
I've been work-ing on it in the morn-ings.
I just finished yester-day.
So that was your routine up 'til now...
OK!
Now I drink a cup of water.
CHANK
Wow...
aah
And that's it!
Whoa! Is that really all?
Hmm, I guess... I usually brush my teeth next?
SHUK
SHUK
Huh?

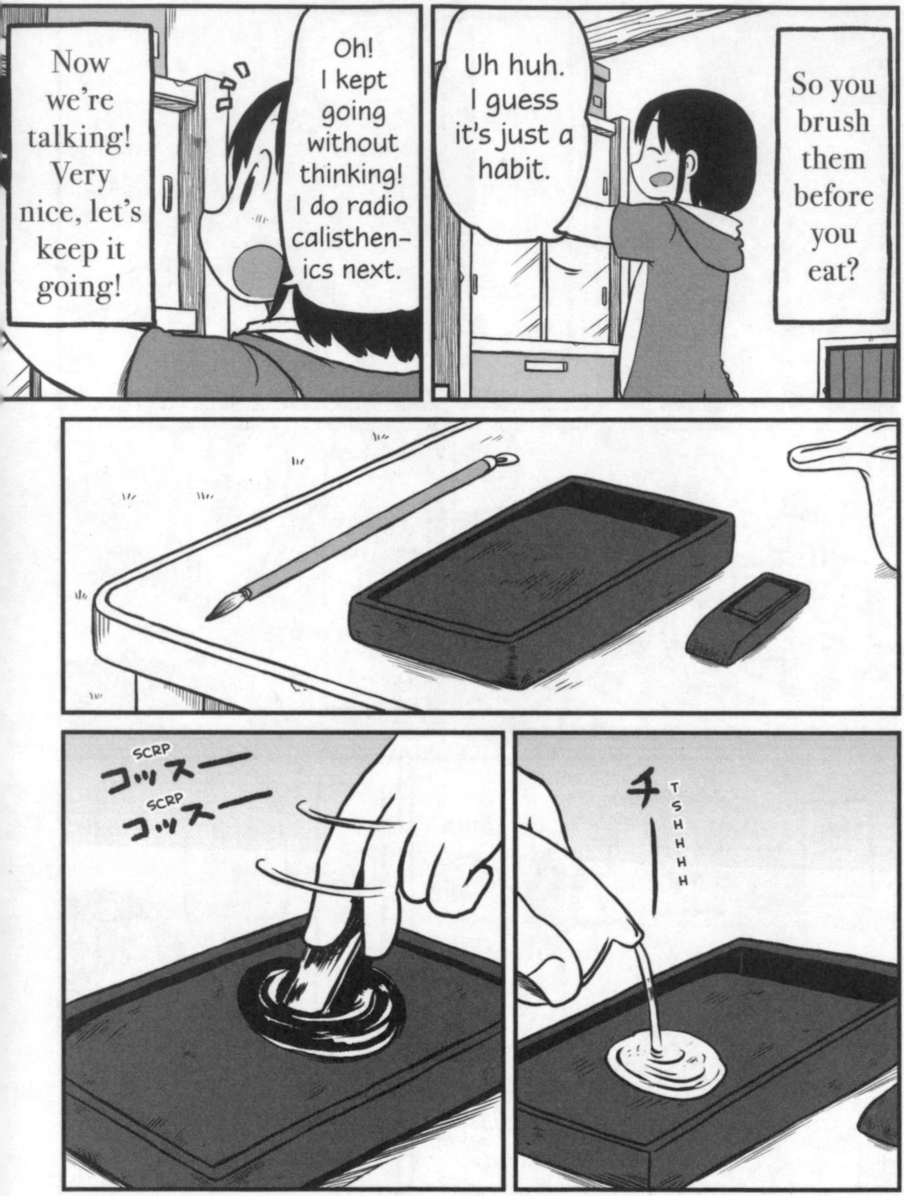
So you brush them before you eat?
Uh huh. I guess it's just a habit.
Oh! I kept going without thinking! I do radio calisthenics next.
Now we're talking! Very nice, let's keep it going!
チー
TSHHHH
SCRP
コッスー
SCRP
コッスー

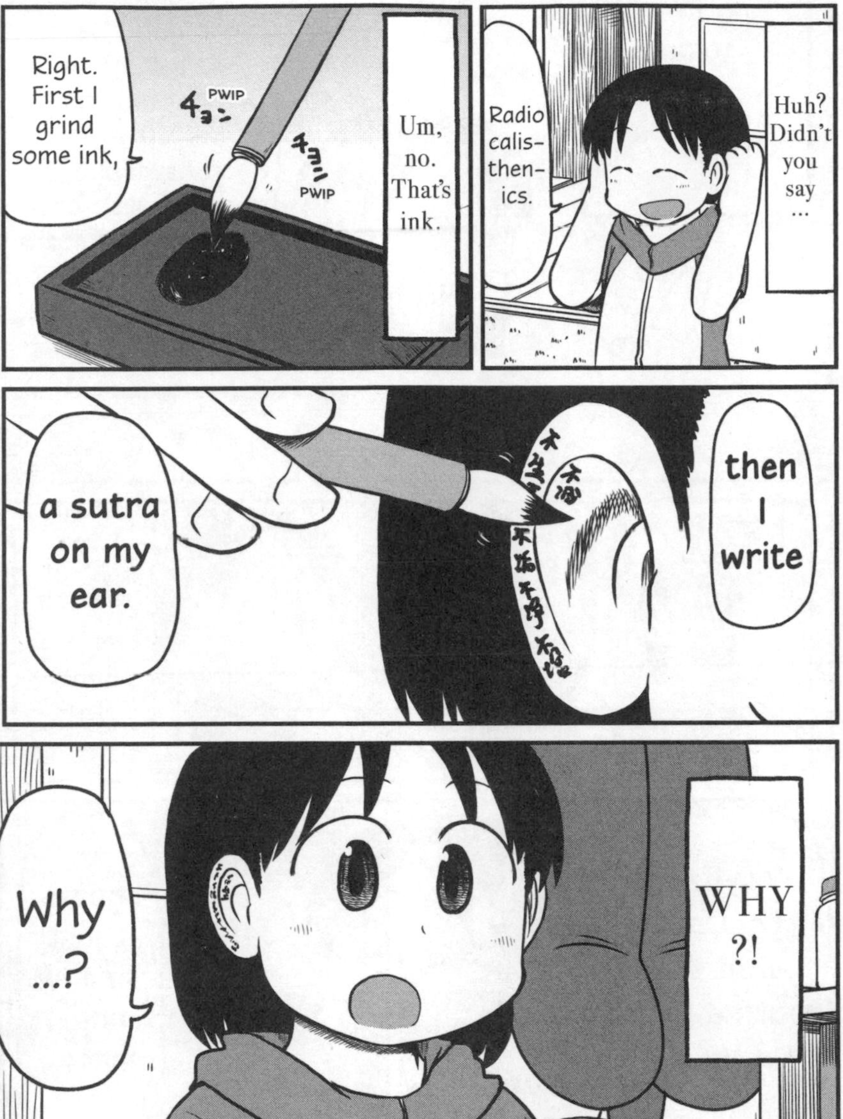
Huh? Didn't you say ...
Radio calis-then-ics.
Um, no. That's ink.
PWIP
Right. First I grind some ink,
PWIP
then I write
a sutra on my ear.
WHY ?!
Why ...?

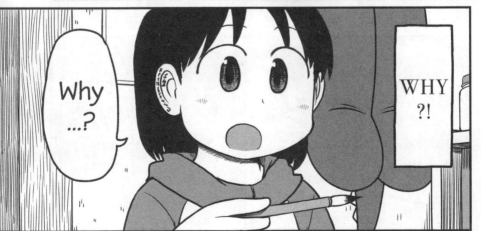

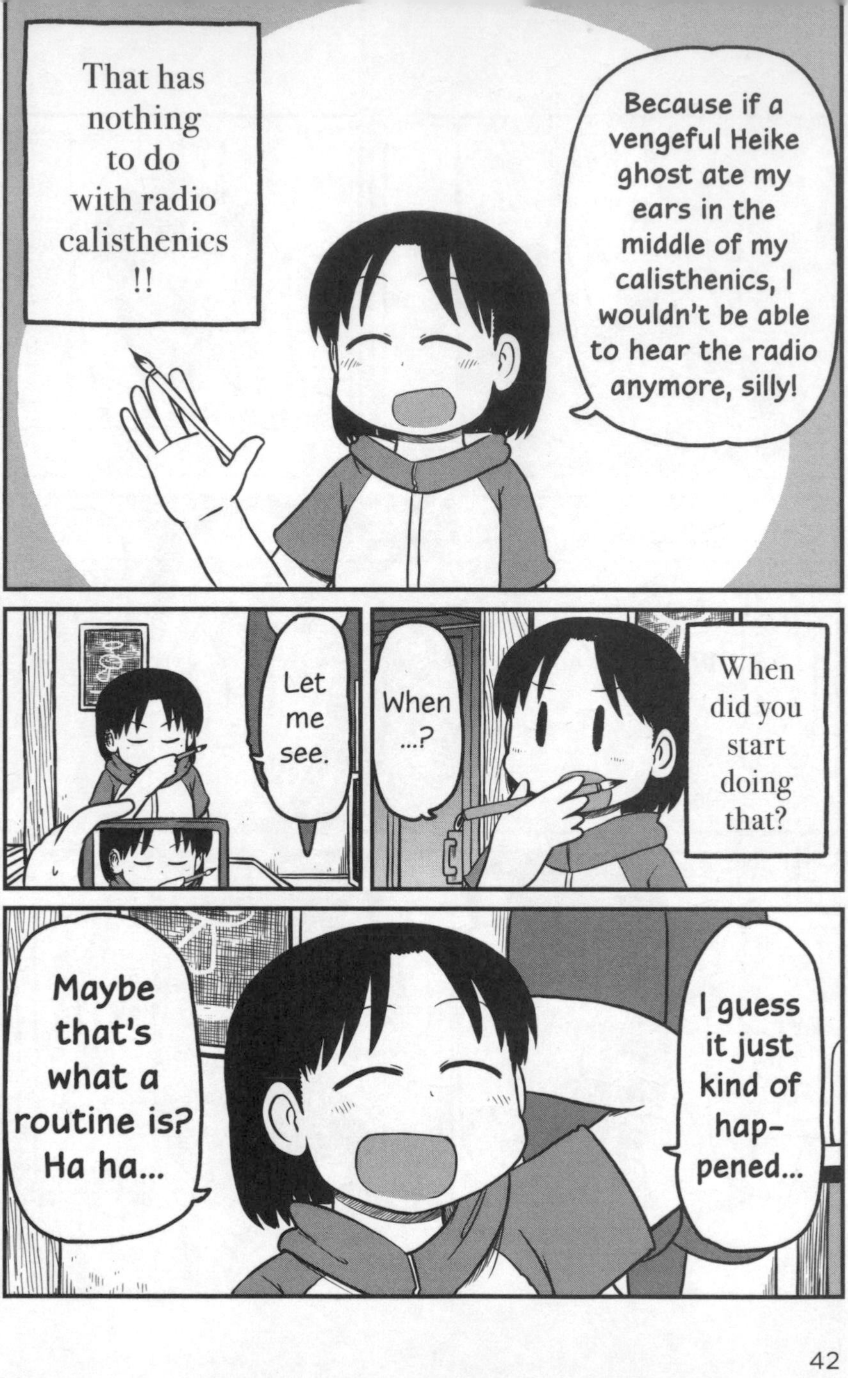
Because if a vengeful Heike ghost ate my ears in the middle of my calisthenics, I wouldn't be able to hear the radio anymore, silly!
That has nothing to do with radio calisthenics !!
When did you start doing that?
When ...?
Let me see.
I guess it just kind of hap-pened...
Maybe that's what a routine is? Ha ha...

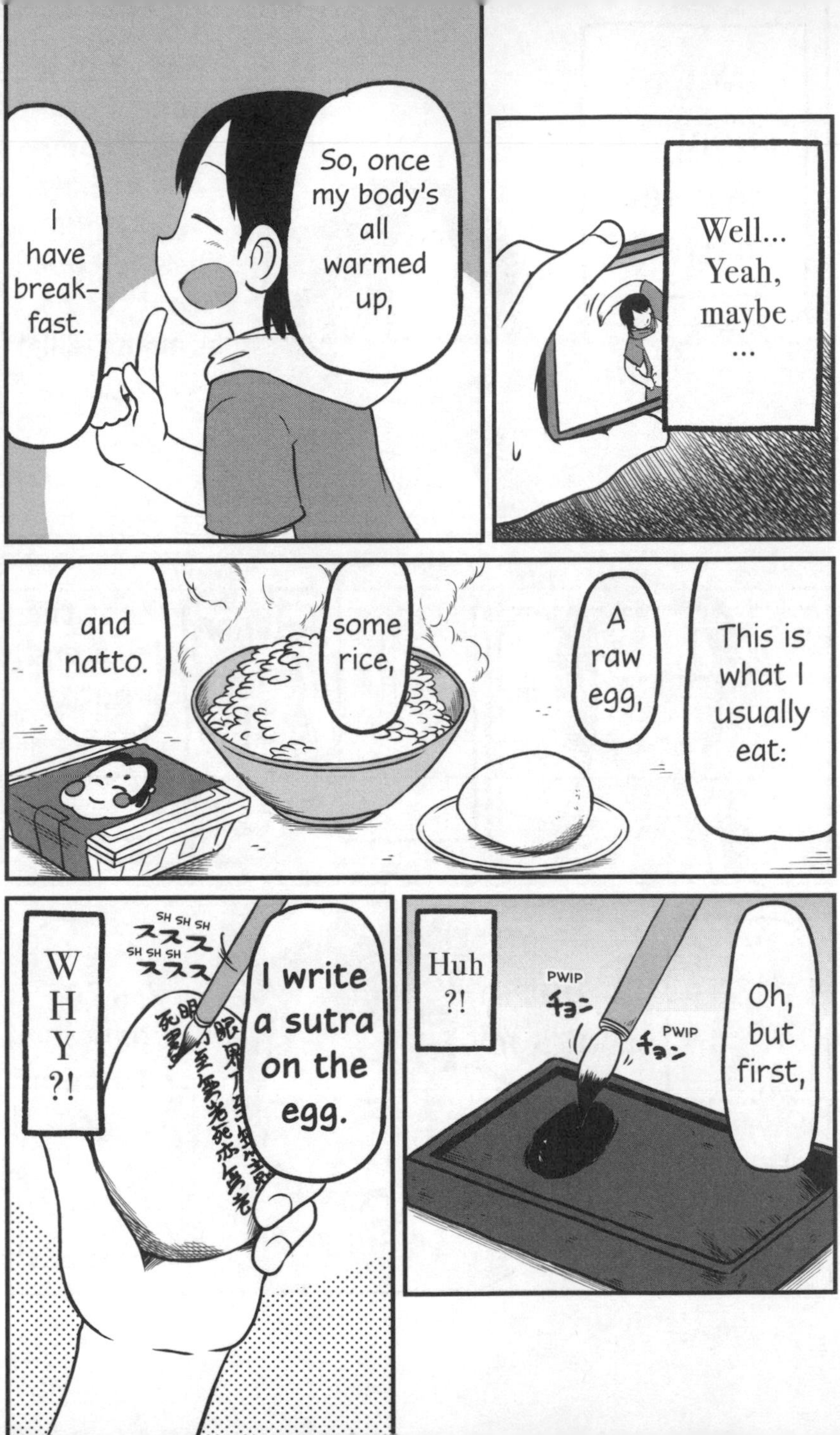
Well... Yeah, maybe ...
So, once my body's all warmed up,
I have break-fast.
This is what I usually eat:
A raw egg,
some rice,
and natto.
Oh, but first,
PWIP チョン
PWIP チョン
Huh ?!
I write a sutra on the egg.
SH SH SH ススス
SH SH SH ススス
WHY ?!

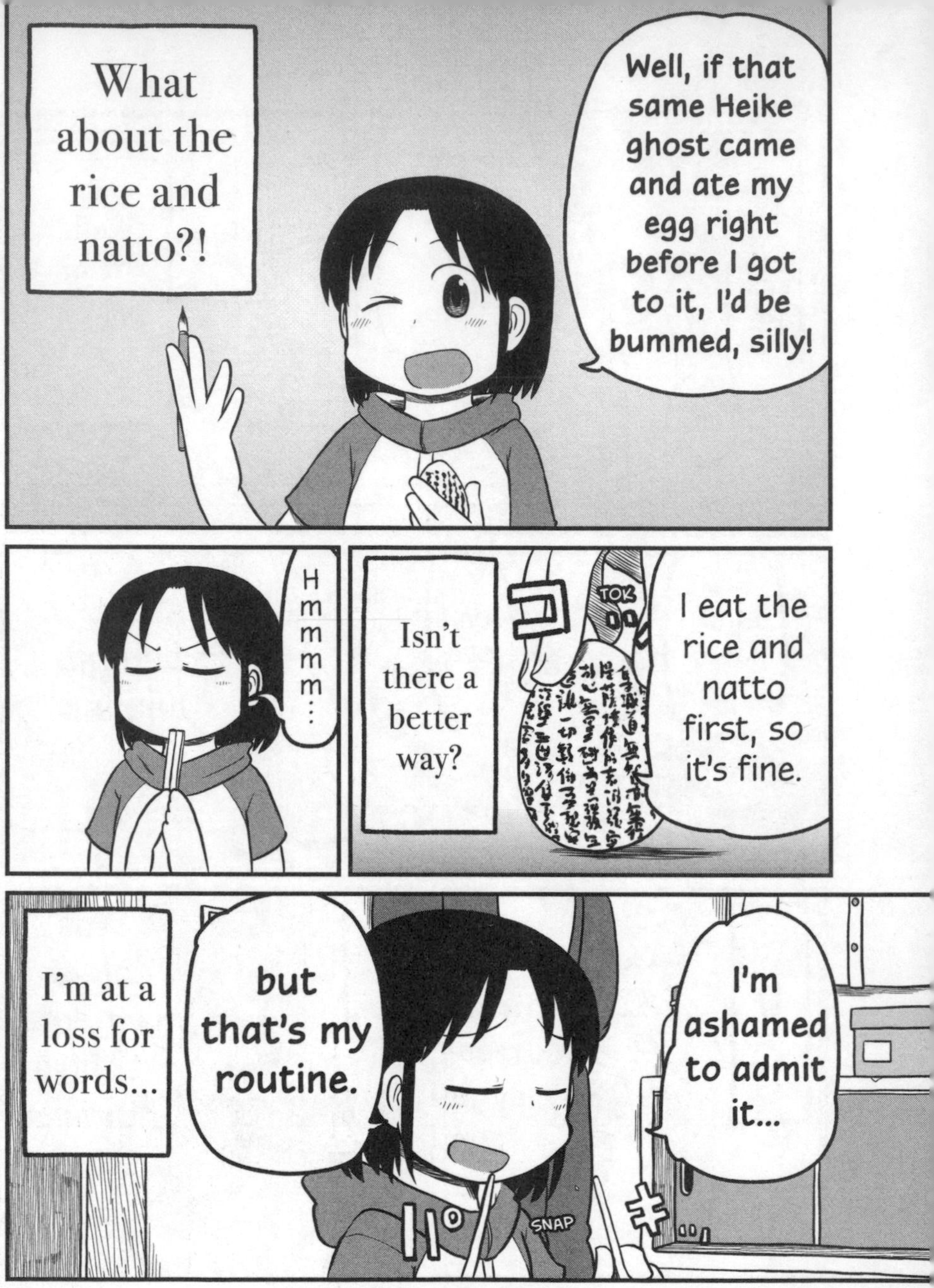
Well, if that same Heike ghost came and ate my egg right before I got to it, I'd be bummed, silly!
What about the rice and natto?!
TOK
I eat the rice and natto first, so it's fine.
Isn't there a better way?
Hmmmm...
I'm ashamed to admit it...
SNAP
but that's my routine.
I'm at a loss for words...

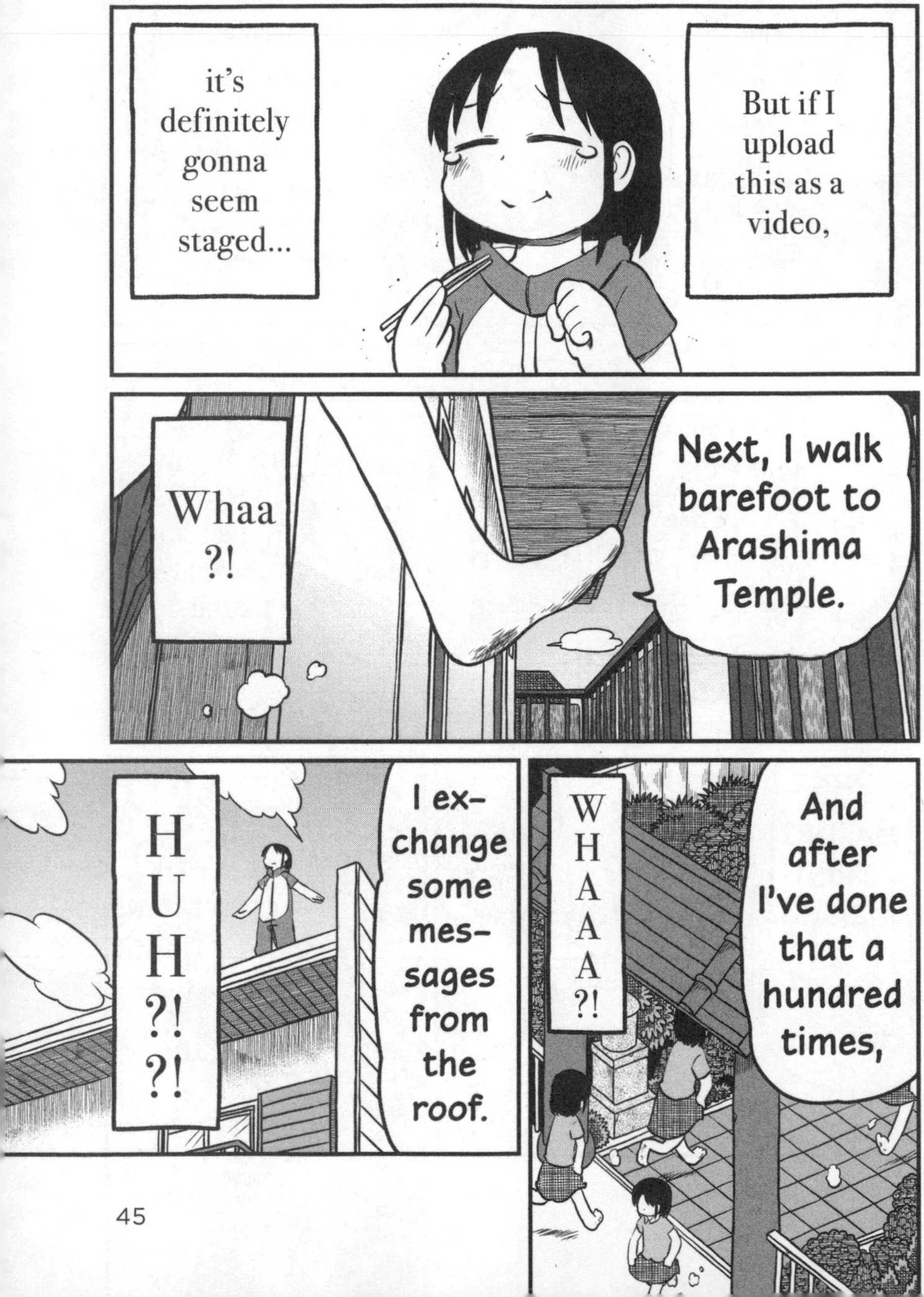
But if I upload this as a video,
it's definitely gonna seem staged...
Next, I walk barefoot to Arashima Temple.
Whaa?!
And after I've done that a hundred times,
WHAAA?!
I exchange some messages from the roof.
HUH?!?!

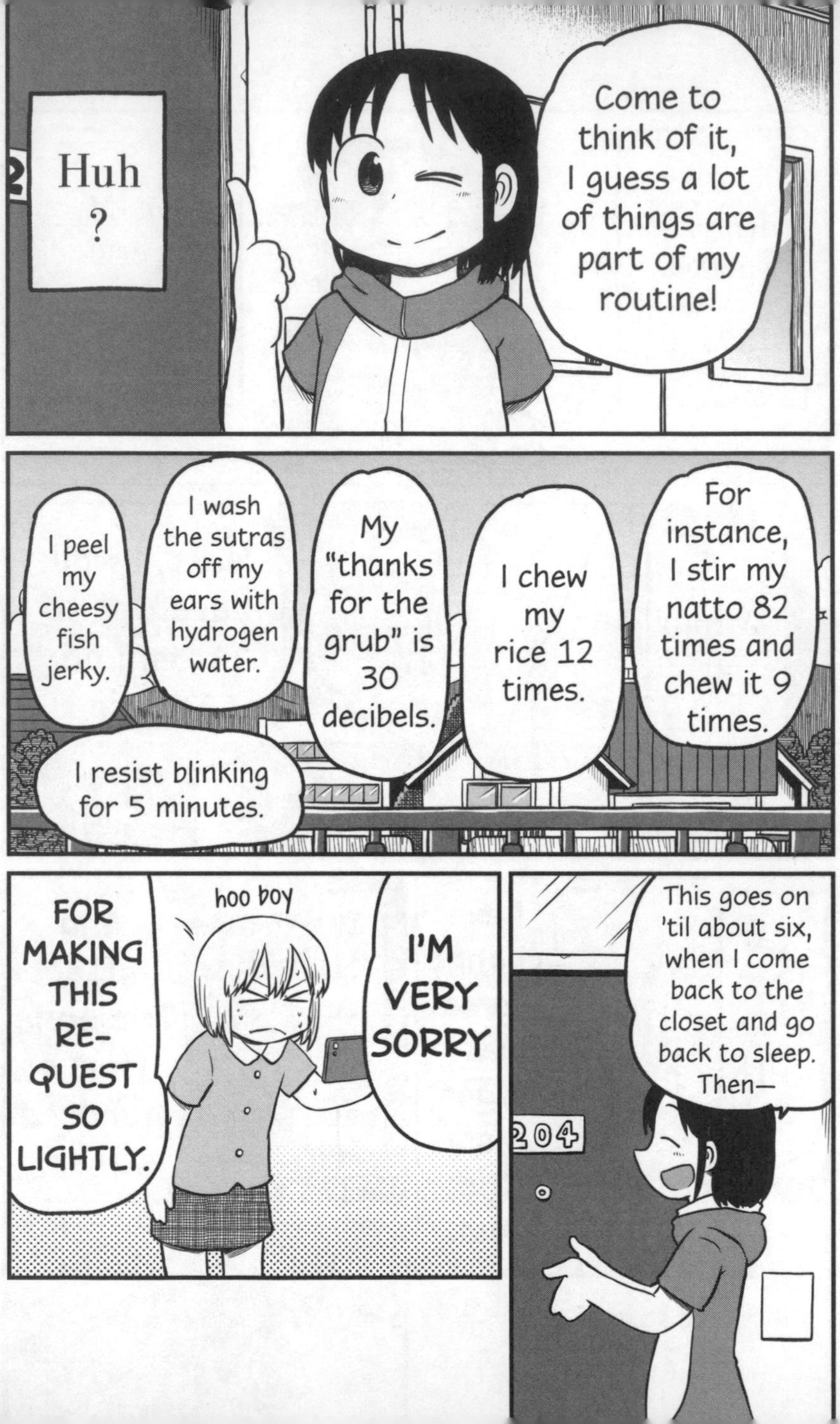
Come to think of it, I guess a lot of things are part of my routine!
Huh ?
For instance, I stir my natto 82 times and chew it 9 times.
I chew my rice 12 times.
My "thanks for the grub" is 30 decibels.
I wash the sutras off my ears with hydrogen water.
I peel my cheesy fish jerky.
I resist blinking for 5 minutes.
This goes on 'til about six, when I come back to the closet and go back to sleep. Then—
204
I'M VERY SORRY
hoo boy
FOR MAKING THIS RE-QUEST SO LIGHTLY.

What’s the first thing you do when you wake up?

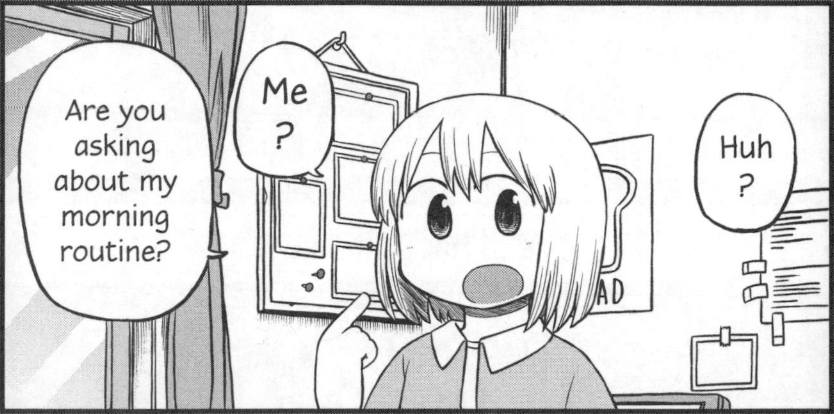
Huh ?
Me ?
Are you asking about my morning routine?

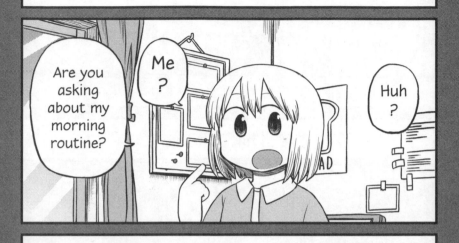

Yes, I want to post a video of it.

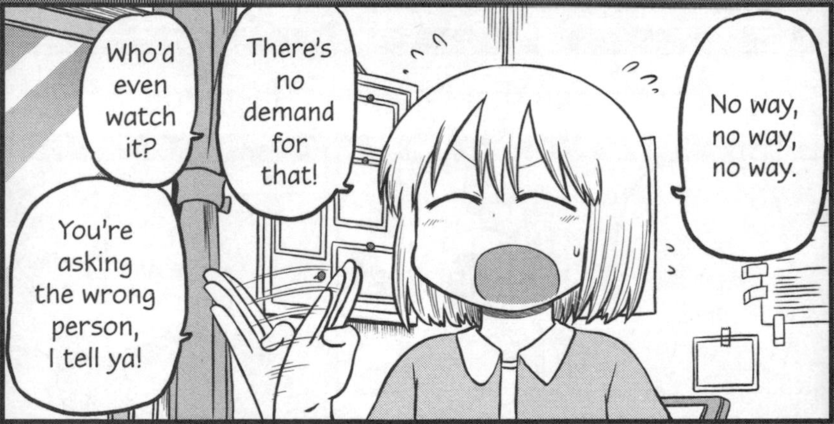
No way, no way, no way.
There's no demand for that!
Who'd even watch it?
You're asking the wrong person, I tell ya!

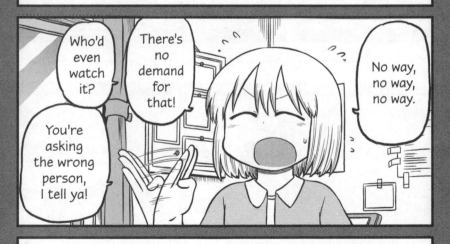

It’ll definitely go viral!

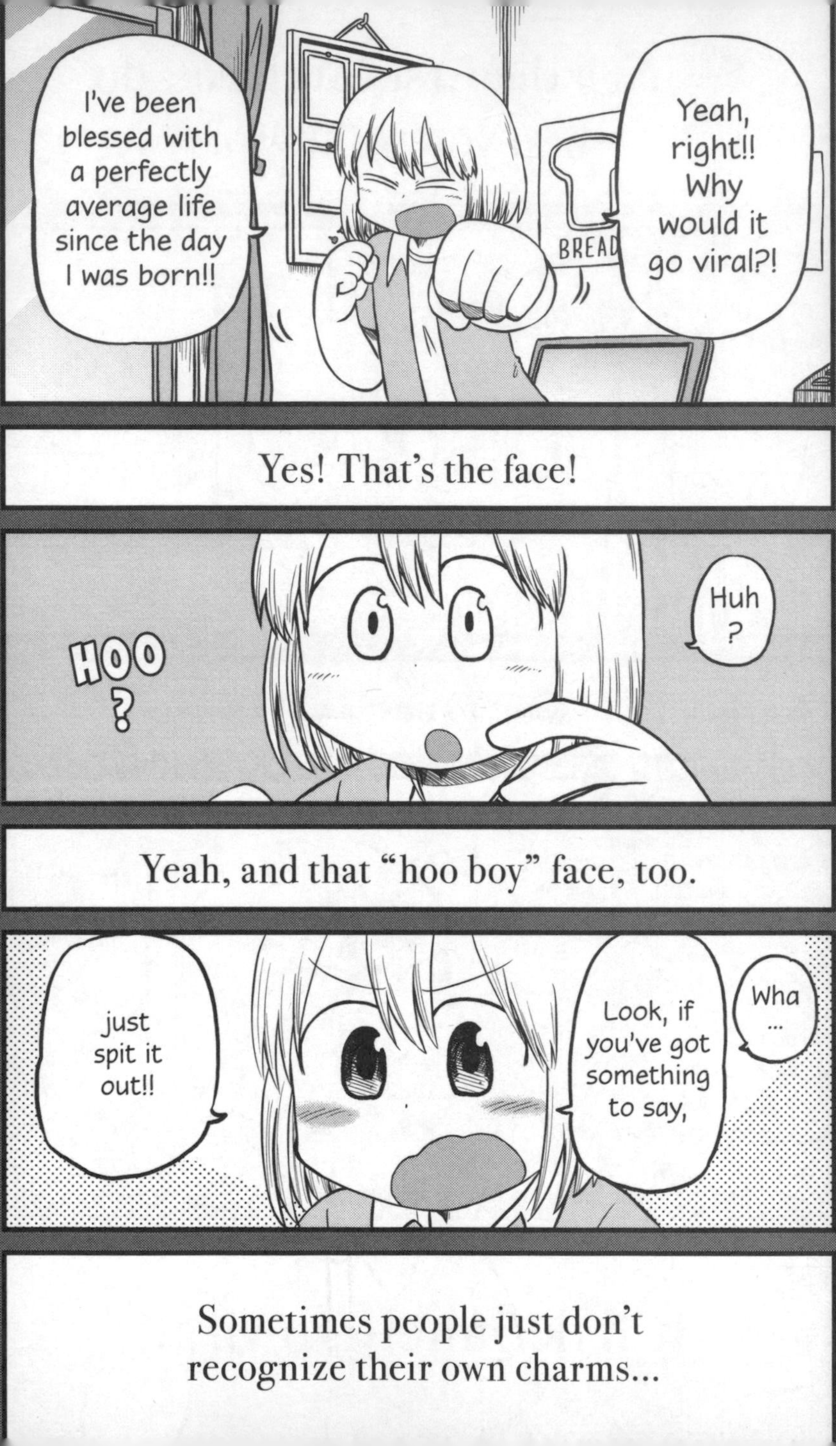
Yeah, right!! Why would it go viral?!
BREAD
I've been blessed with a perfectly average life since the day I was born!!
Yes! That's the face!
Huh ?
HOO ?
Yeah, and that "hoo boy" face, too.
Wha ...
Look, if you've got something to say,
just spit it out!!
Sometimes people just don't recognize their own charms...

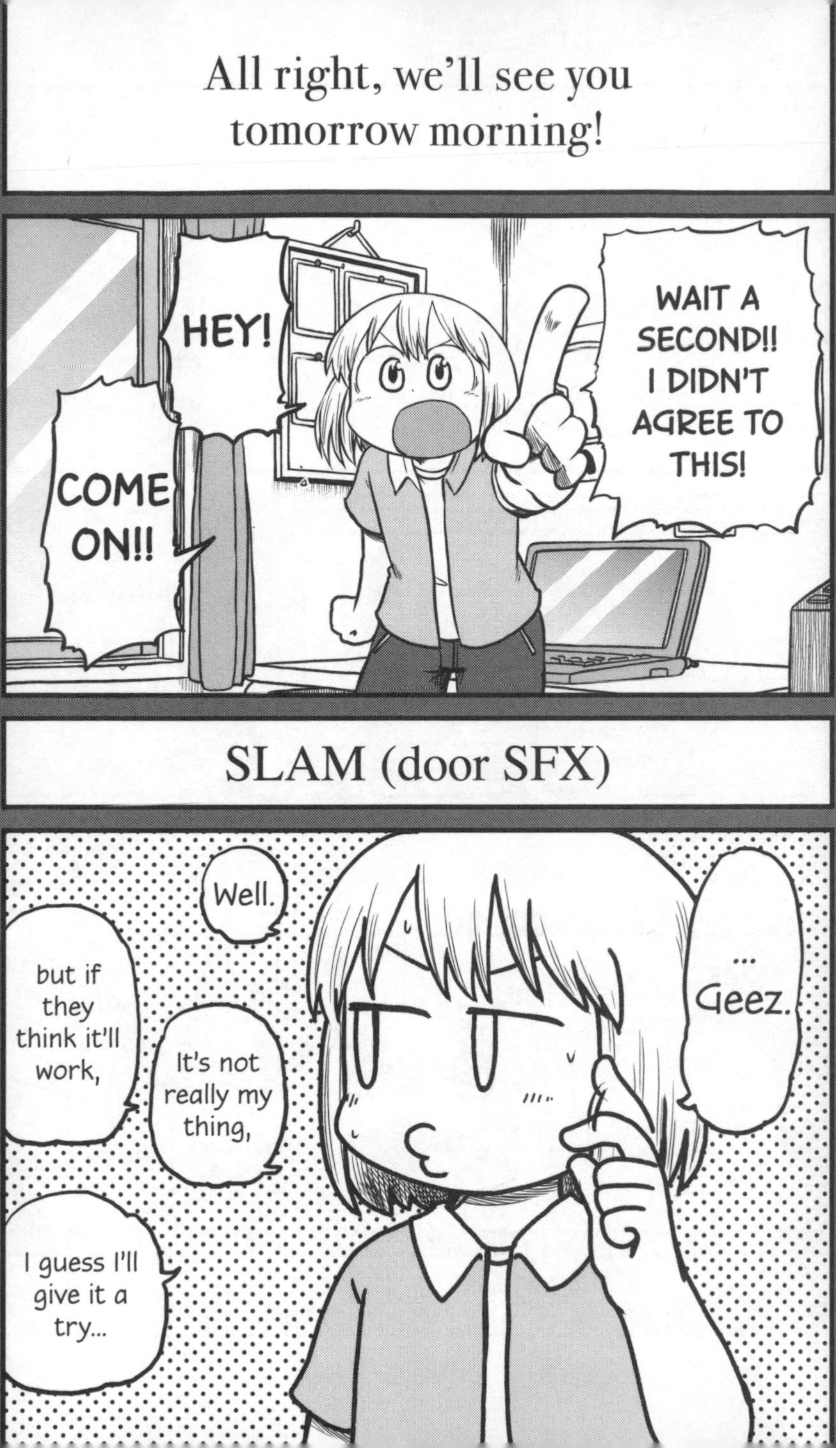
All right, we'll see you tomorrow morning!
WAIT A SECOND!! I DIDN'T AGREE TO THIS!
HEY!
COME ON!!
SLAM (door SFX)
... Geez.
Well.
It's not really my thing,
but if they think it'll work,
I guess I'll give it a try...

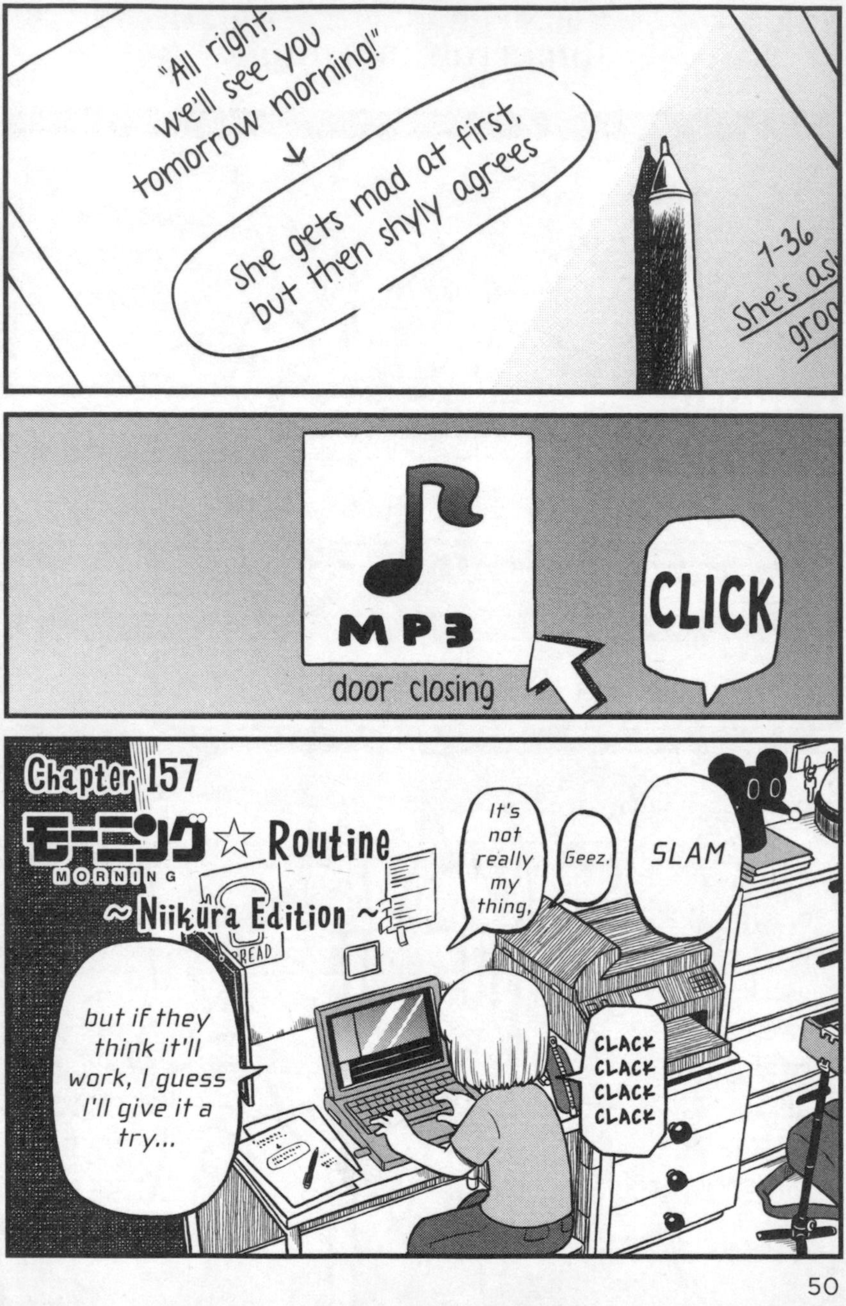
"All right, we'll see you tomorrow morning!"
↓
She gets mad at first, but then shyly agrees
1-36
MP3
door closing
CLICK
SLAM
Geez.
It's not really my thing,
Chapter 157
モーニング☆Routine
MORNING
~ Niikura Edition ~
CLACK CLACK CLACK CLACK
but if they think it'll work, I guess I'll give it a try...

Good morniiing! Wait! You're still asleep?!

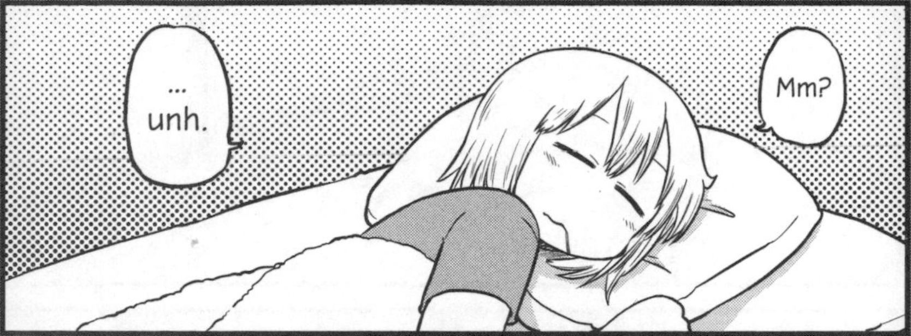
Mm?
... unh.

Thanks for the HapMorn!

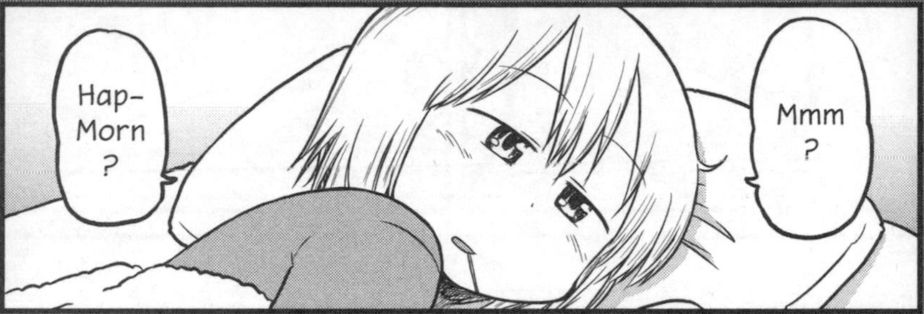
Mmm ?
Hap-Morn ?

※ Short for "Happening Morning."

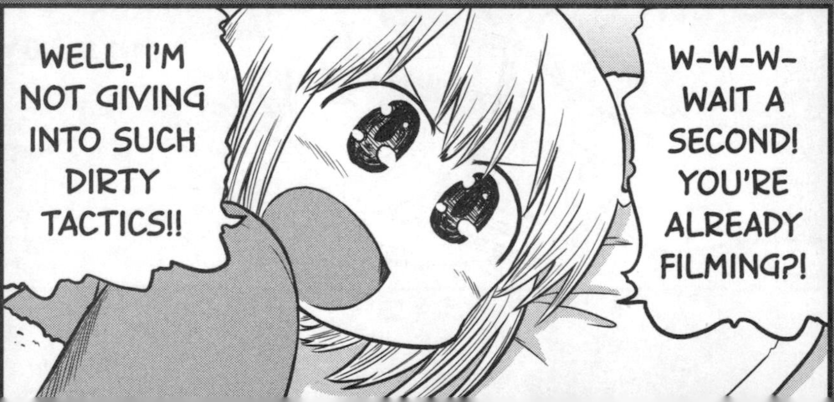
W-W-W-WAIT A SECOND! YOU'RE ALREADY FILMING?!
WELL, I'M NOT GIVING INTO SUCH DIRTY TACTICS!!

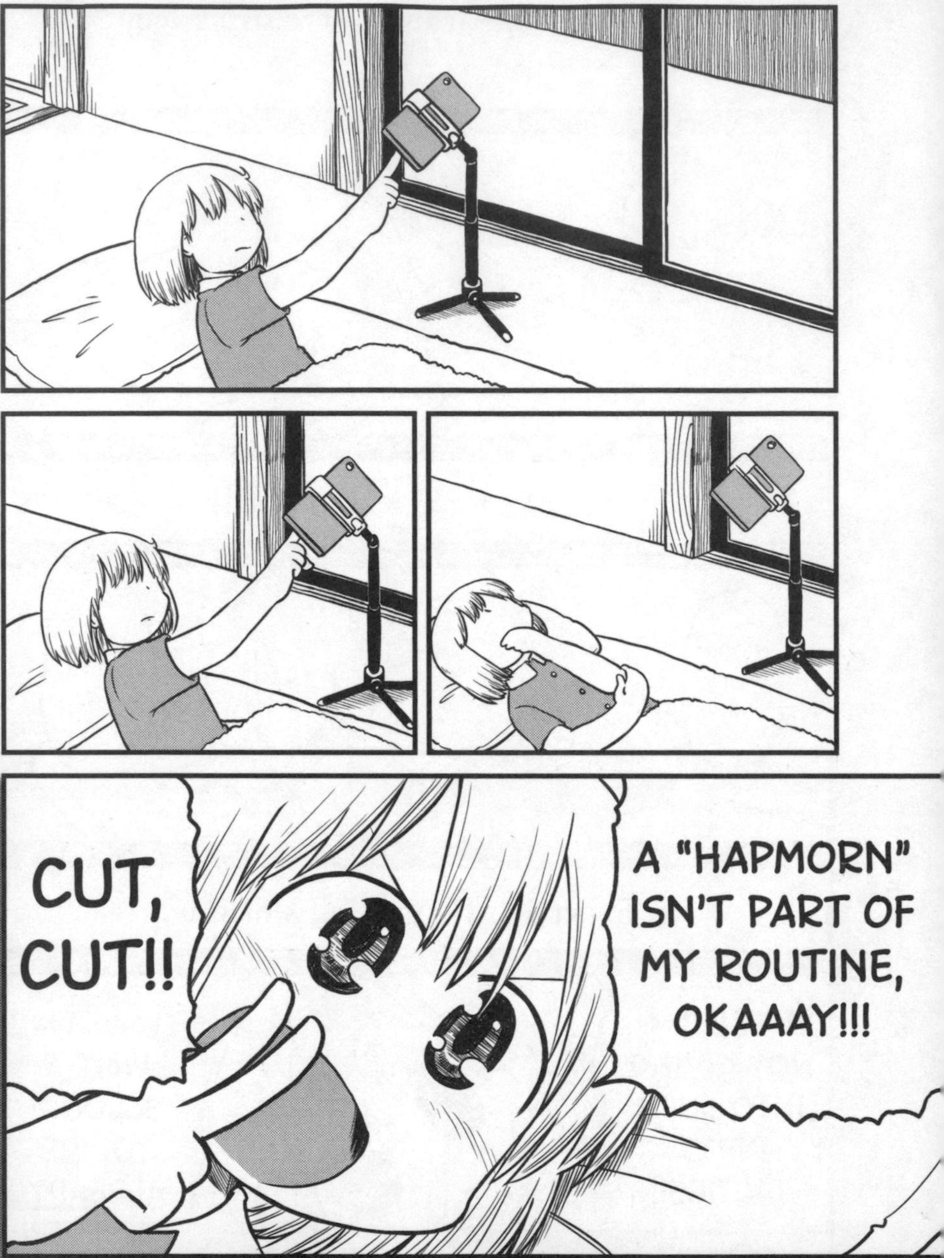
A "HAPMORN" ISN'T PART OF MY ROUTINE, OKAAAY!!!
CUT, CUT!!

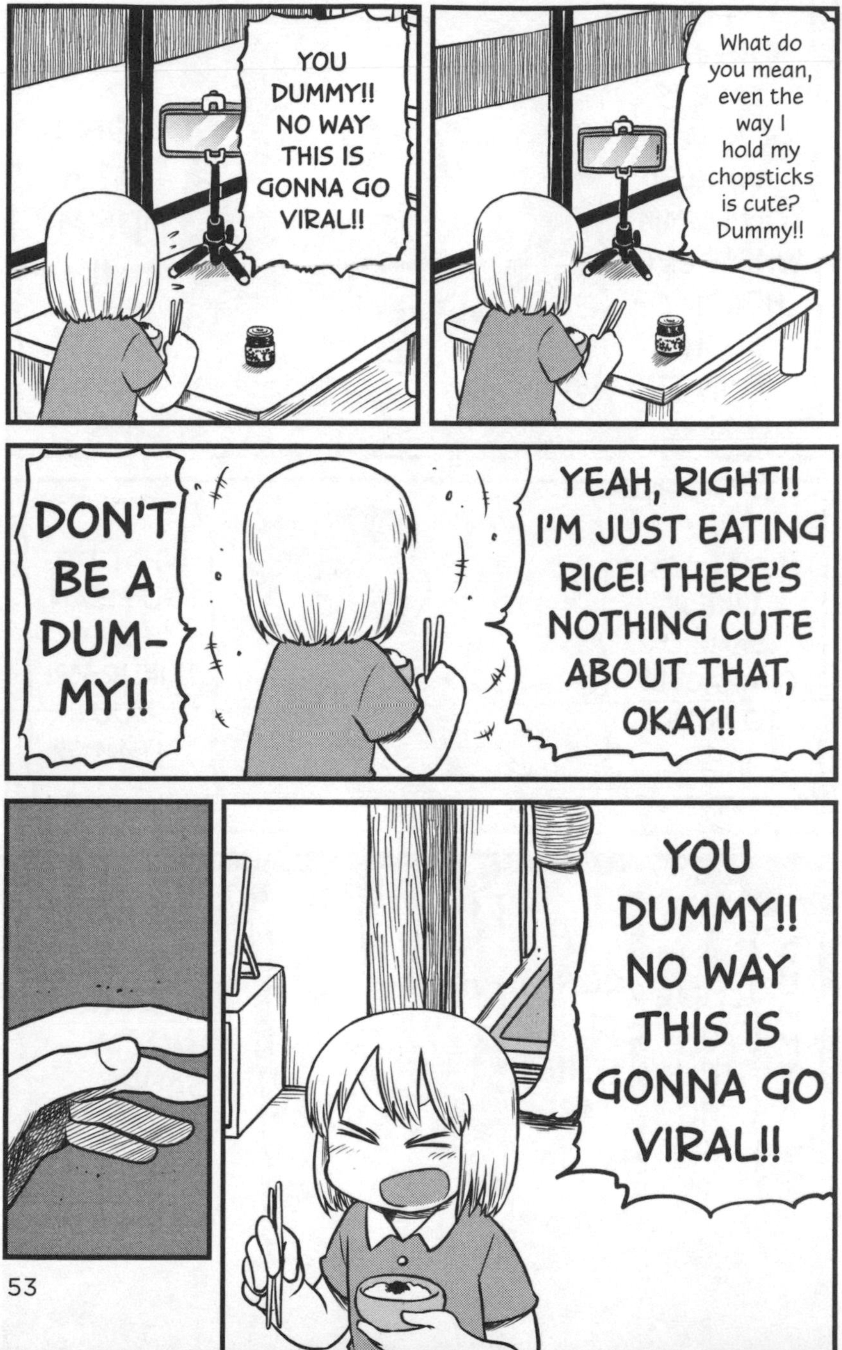
What do you mean, even the way I hold my chopsticks is cute? Dummy!!
YOU DUMMY!! NO WAY THIS IS GONNA GO VIRAL!!
YEAH, RIGHT!! I'M JUST EATING RICE! THERE'S NOTHING CUTE ABOUT THAT, OKAY!!
DON'T BE A DUM-MY!!
YOU DUMMY!! NO WAY THIS IS GONNA GO VIRAL!!

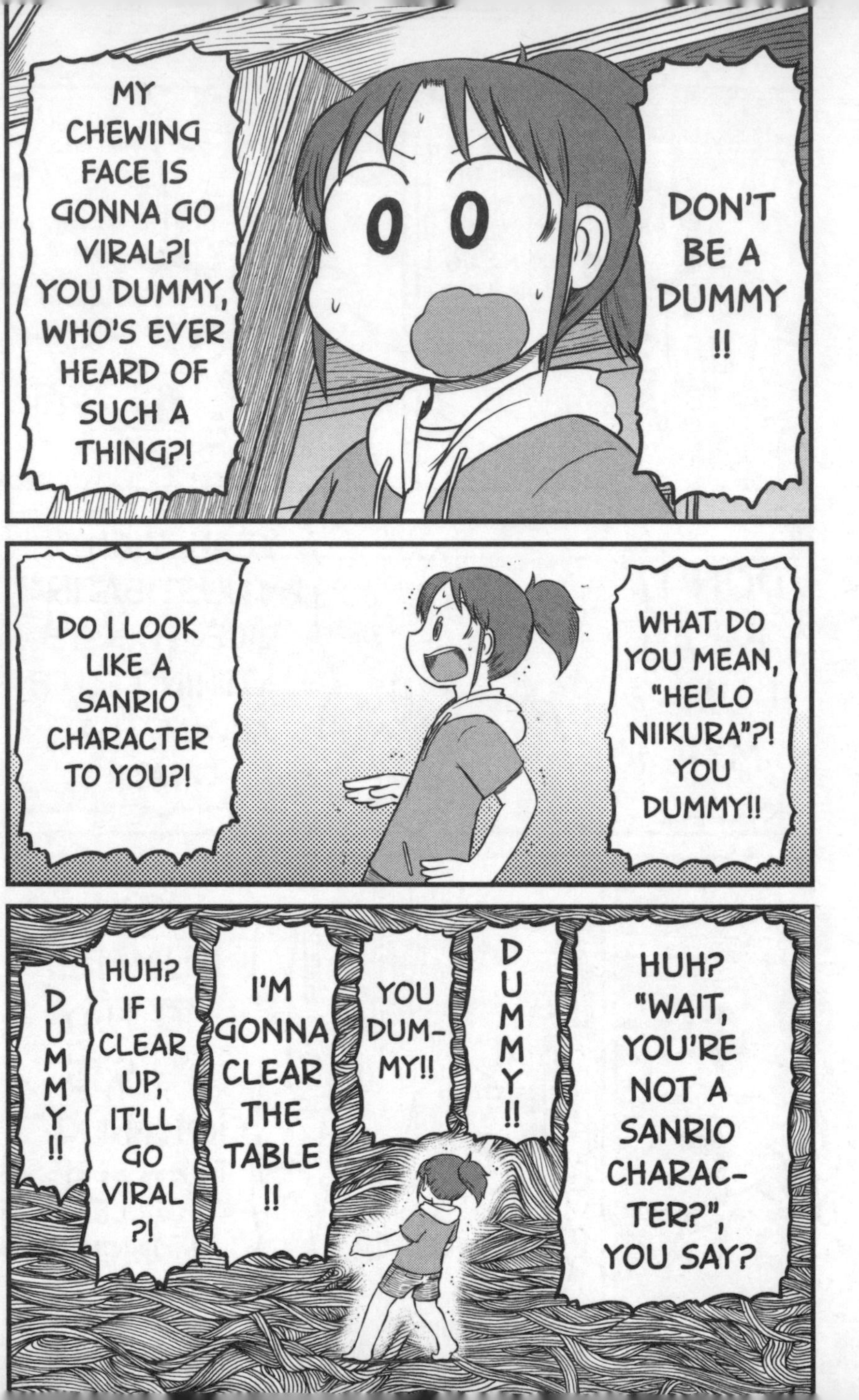

DON'T BE A DUMMY!!
MY CHEWING FACE IS GONNA GO VIRAL?! YOU DUMMY, WHO'S EVER HEARD OF SUCH A THING?!
WHAT DO YOU MEAN, "HELLO NIIKURA"?! YOU DUMMY!!
DO I LOOK LIKE A SANRIO CHARACTER TO YOU?!
HUH? "WAIT, YOU'RE NOT A SANRIO CHARAC-TER?", YOU SAY?
DUMMY!!
YOU DUM-MY!!
I'M GONNA CLEAR THE TABLE!!
HUH? IF I CLEAR UP, IT'LL GO VIRAL?!
DUMMY!!

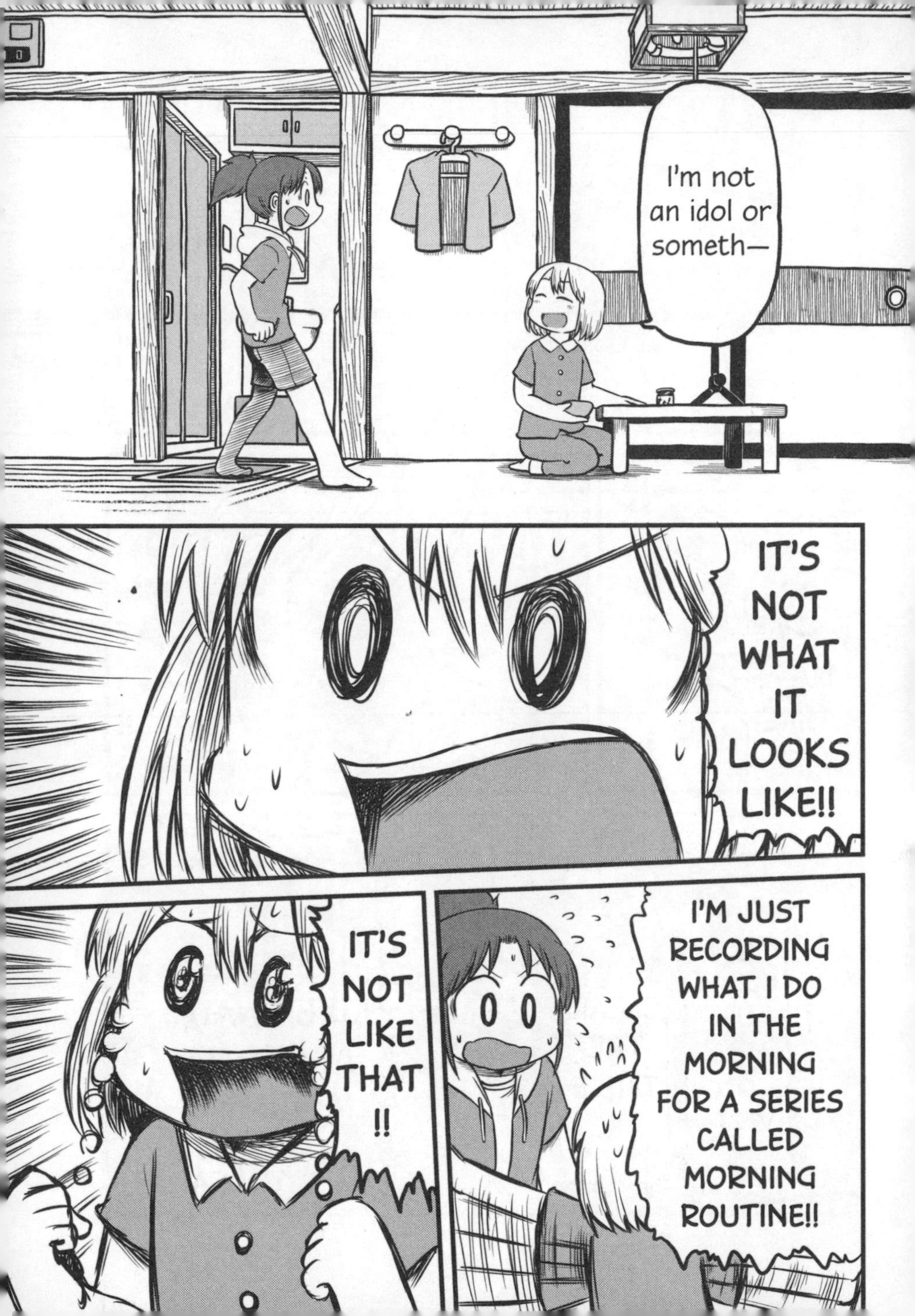
I'm not an idol or someth—
IT'S NOT WHAT IT LOOKS LIKE!!
I'M JUST RECORDING WHAT I DO IN THE MORNING FOR A SERIES CALLED MORNING ROUTINE!!
IT'S NOT LIKE THAT!!

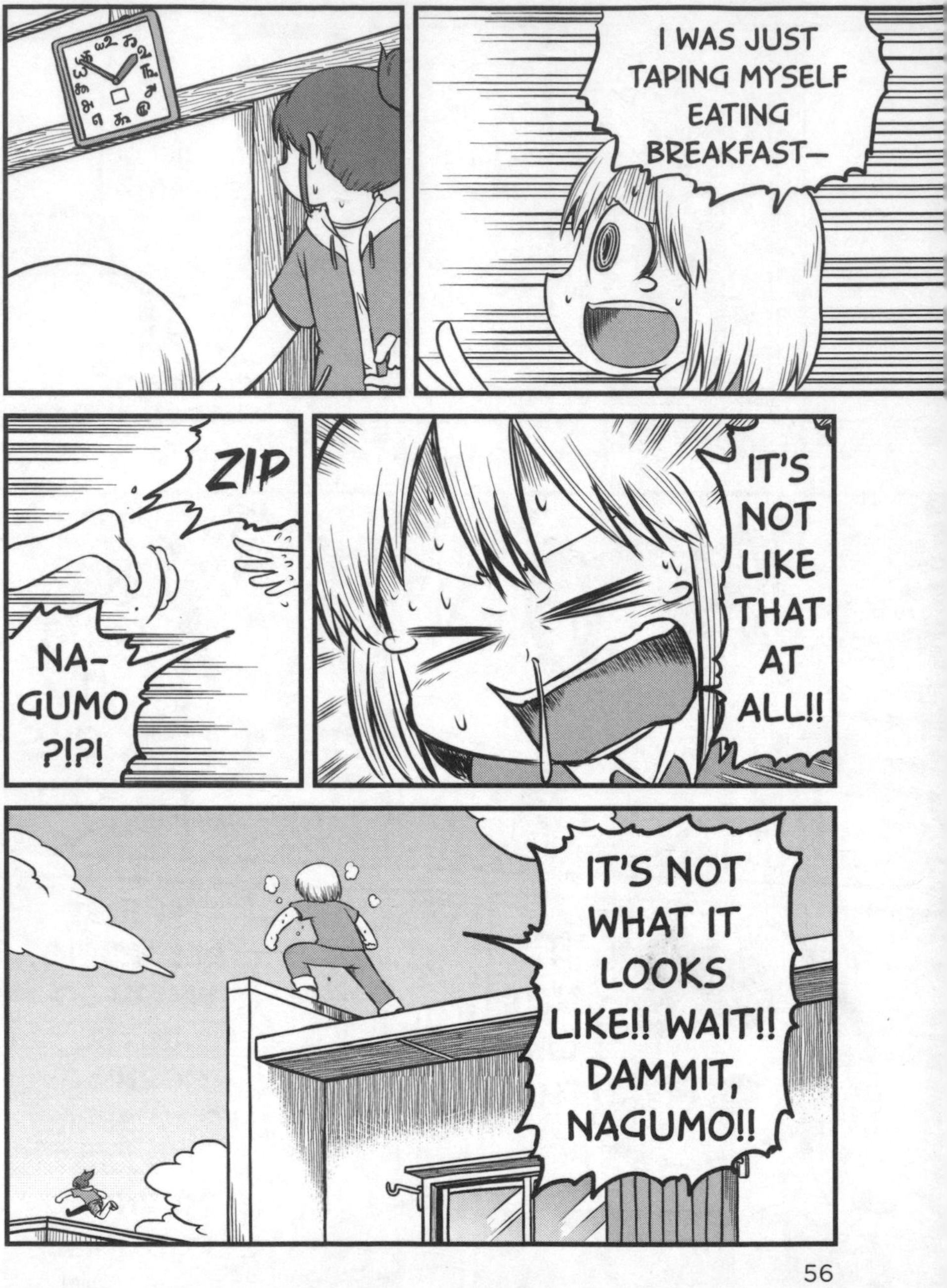
I WAS JUST TAPING MYSELF EATING BREAKFAST—
IT'S NOT LIKE THAT AT ALL!!
ZIP
NA-GUMO?!?!
IT'S NOT WHAT IT LOOKS LIKE!! WAIT!! DAMMIT, NAGUMO!!

 Nagumon's channel
3 subscribers

Michael J. Niikura channel
1 subscriber

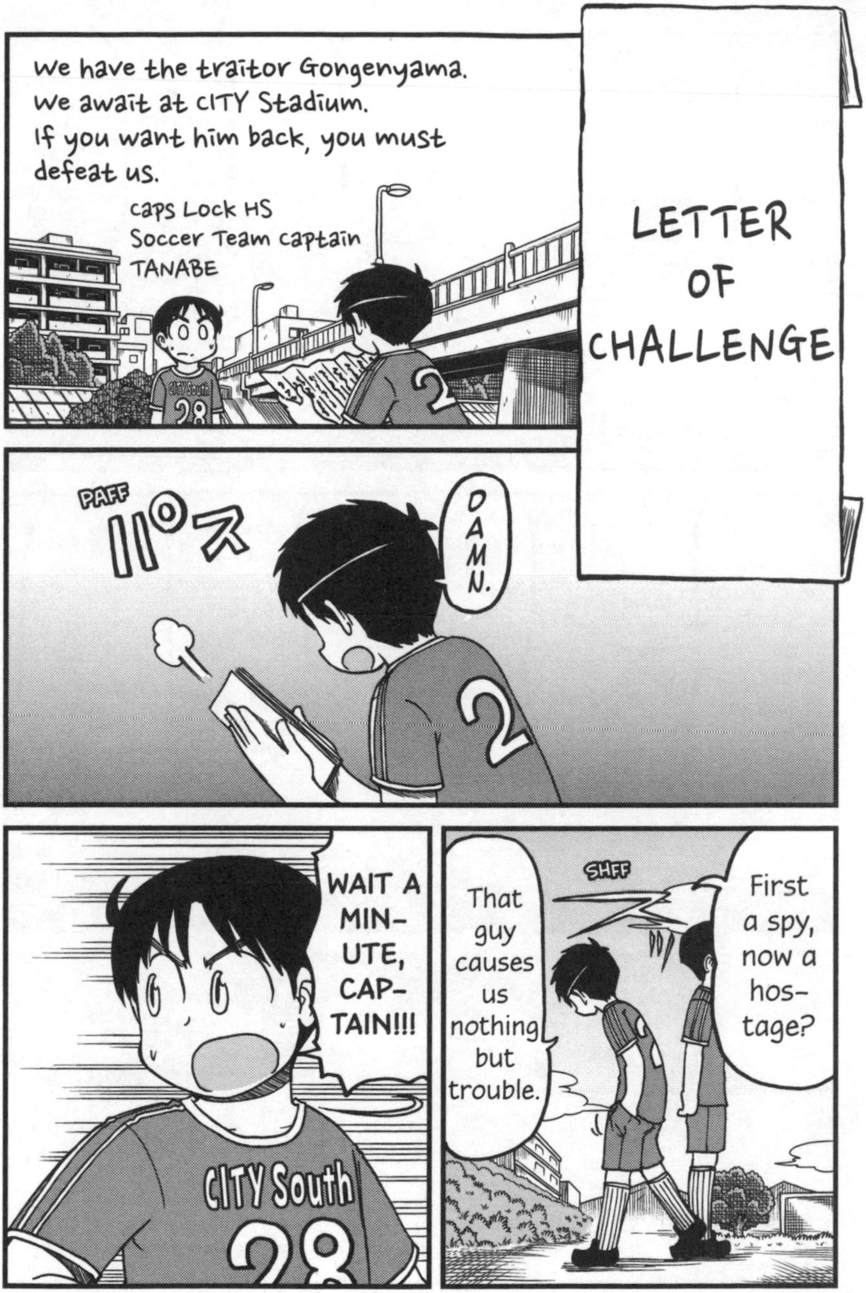
LETTER OF CHALLENGE
We have the traitor Gongenyama.
We await at CITY Stadium.
If you want him back, you must defeat us.
Caps Lock HS
Soccer Team captain
TANABE
PAFF
パス
DAMN.
First a spy, now a hos-tage?
SHFF
That guy causes us nothing but trouble.
WAIT A MIN-UTE, CAP-TAIN!!!
CITY South

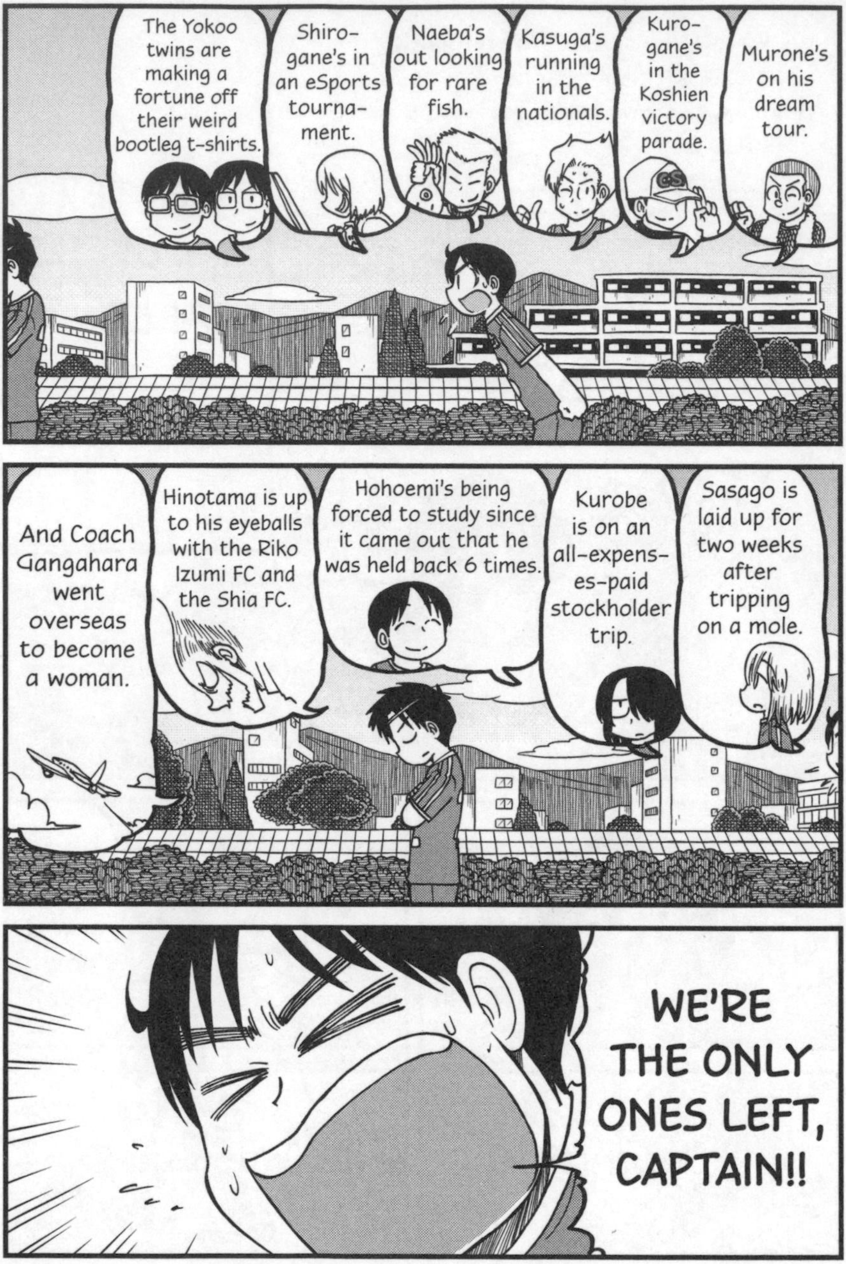
Murone's on his dream tour.
Kuro-gane's in the Koshien victory parade.
Kasuga's running in the nationals.
Naeba's out looking for rare fish.
Shiro-gane's in an eSports tourna-ment.
The Yokoo twins are making a fortune off their weird bootleg t-shirts.
Sasago is laid up for two weeks after tripping on a mole.
Kurobe is on an all-expens-es-paid stockholder trip.
Hohoemi's being forced to study since it came out that he was held back 6 times.
Hinotama is up to his eyeballs with the Riko Izumi FC and the Shia FC.
And Coach Gangahara went overseas to become a woman.
WE'RE THE ONLY ONES LEFT, CAPTAIN!!

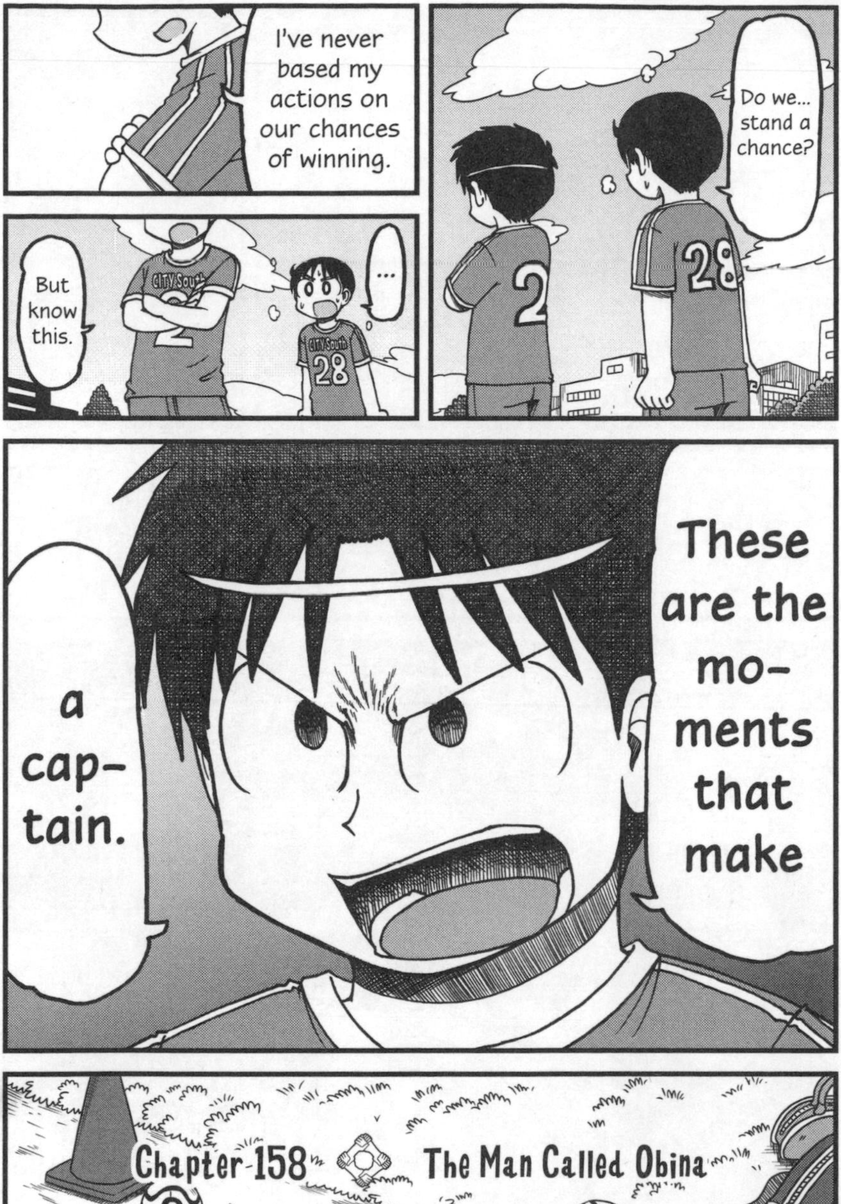
Do we... stand a chance?
I've never based my actions on our chances of winning.
...
But know this.
These are the mo-ments that make
a cap-tain.
Chapter 158 The Man Called Obina

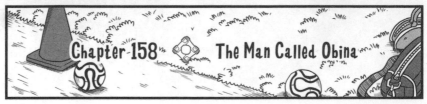

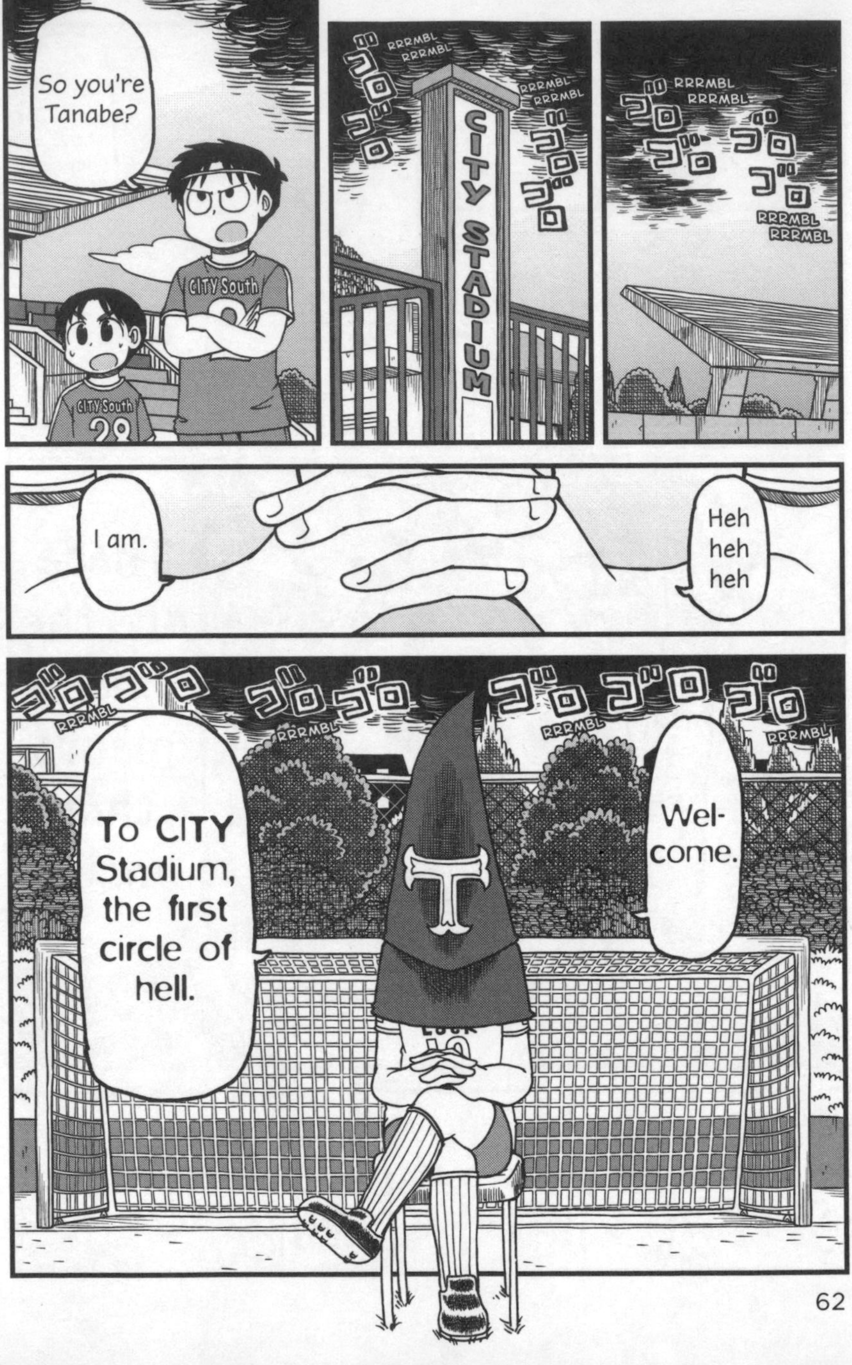
ゴロ RRRMBL RRRMBL
ゴロ ゴロ
RRRMBL RRRMBL
ゴロゴロ RRRMBL RRRMBL
RRRMBL RRRMBL ゴロゴロ
CITY STADIUM
So you're Tanabe?
CITY South 8
CITY South 28
Heh heh heh
I am.
ゴロゴロ RRRMBL
ゴロゴロ RRRMBL
ゴロゴロ RRRMBL
ゴロゴロ RRRMBL
Wel- come.
To CITY Stadium, the first circle of hell.

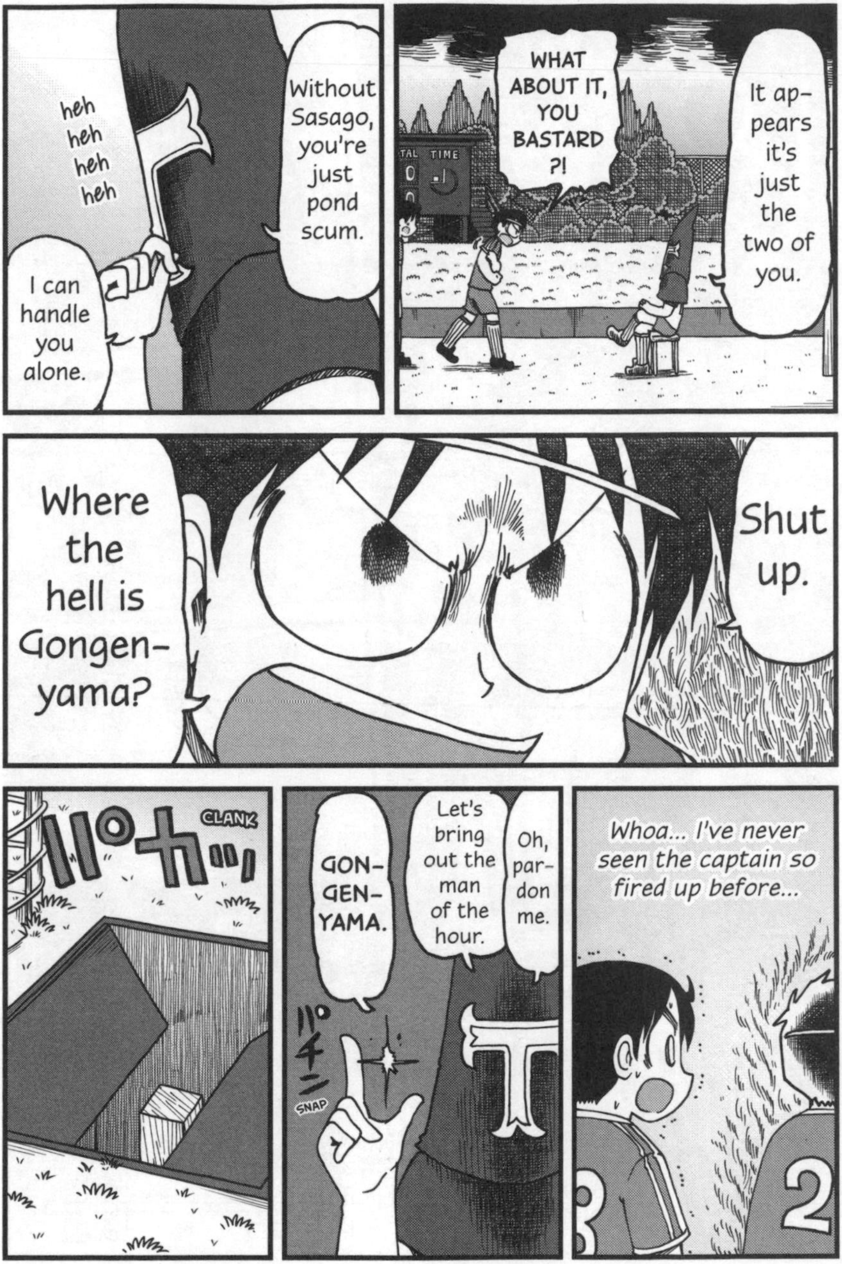
It appears it's just the two of you.
WHAT ABOUT IT, YOU BASTARD?!
Without Sasago, you're just pond scum.
heh heh heh heh
I can handle you alone.
Shut up.
Where the hell is Gongenyama?
Whoa... I've never seen the captain so fired up before...
Oh, pardon me.
Let's bring out the man of the hour.
GONGENYAMA.
SNAP
CLANK

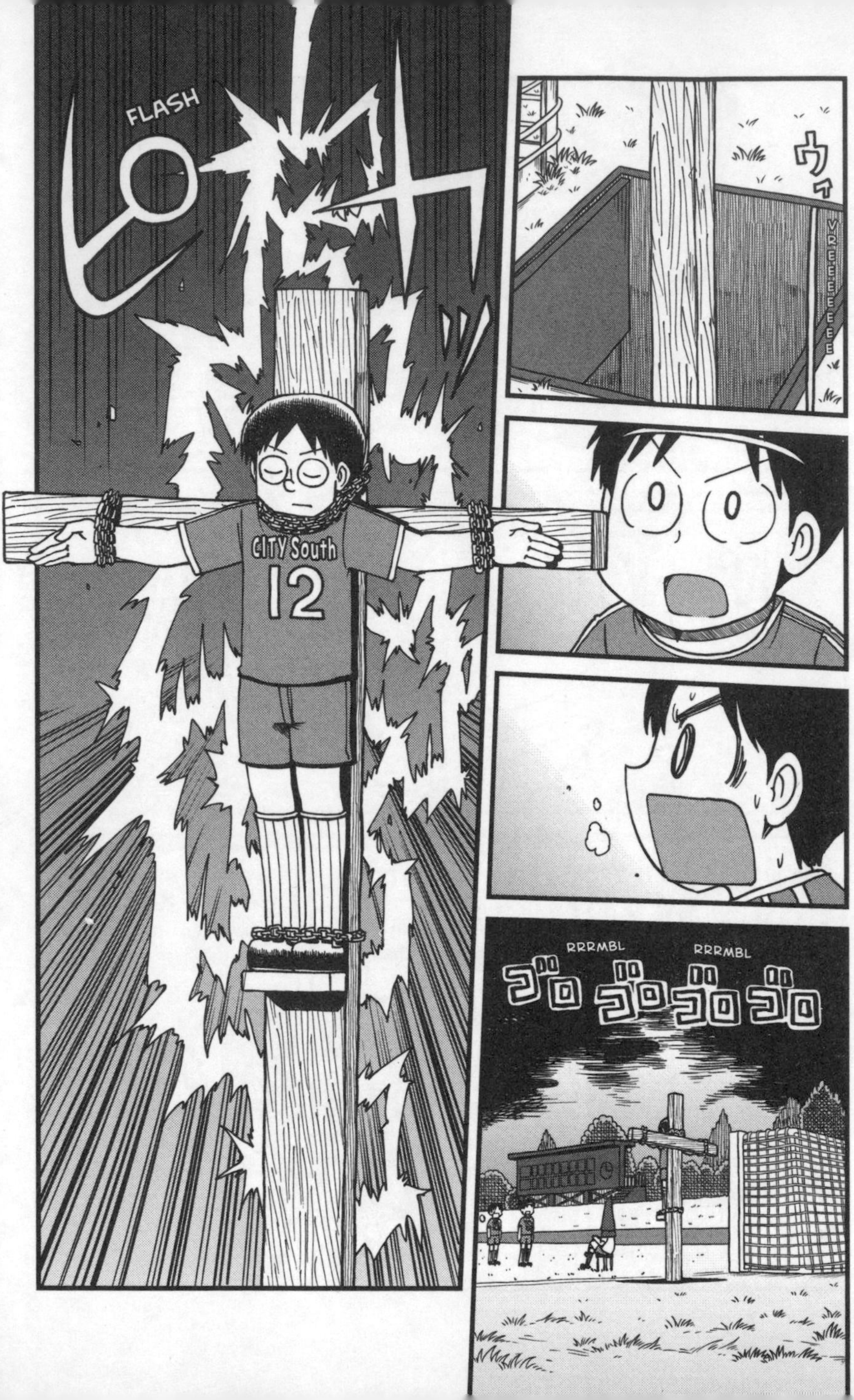
ウィ
VREEEEEEE
RRRMBL
ゴロ
RRRMBL
ゴロゴロゴロ
FLASH
ピカッ
CITY South
12

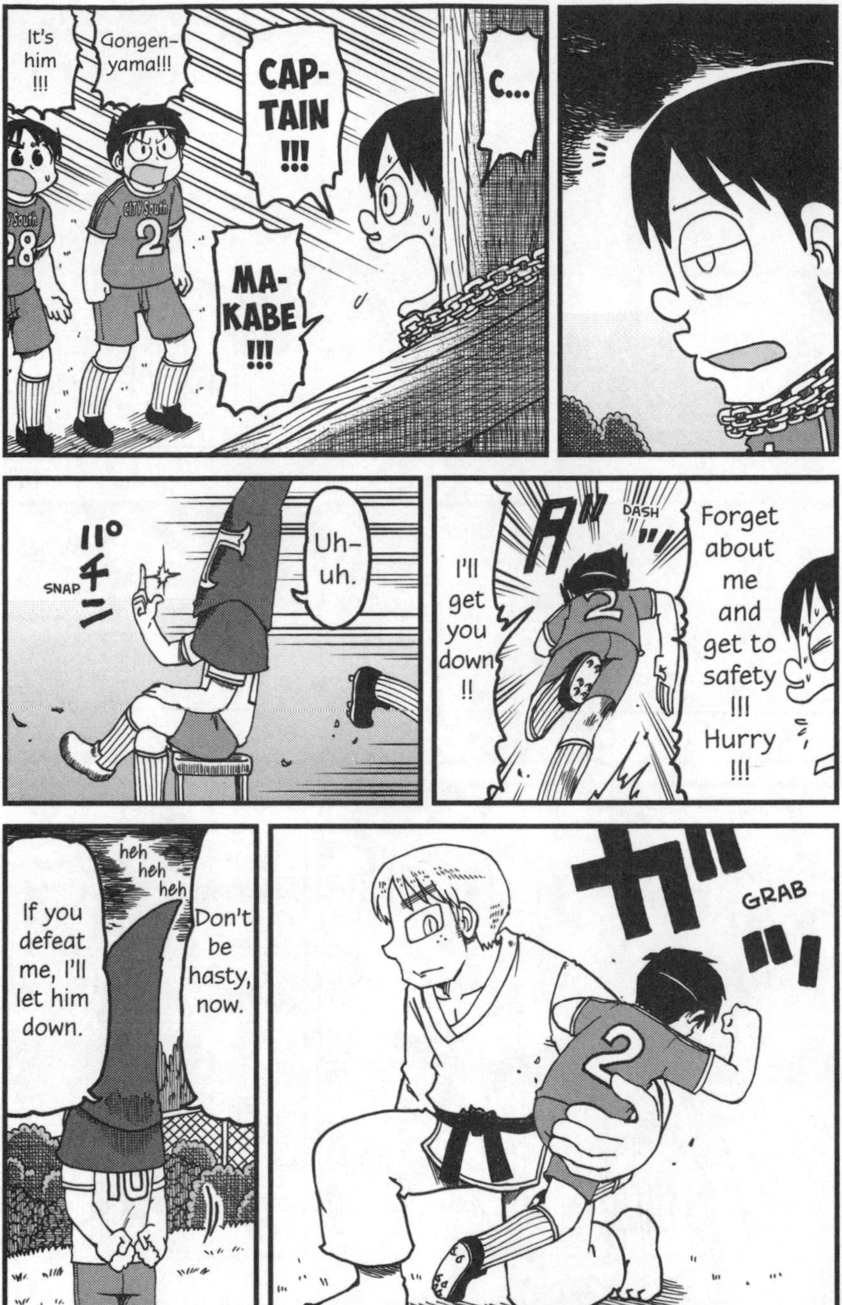
C...
CAP-TAIN!!!
MA-KABE!!!
Gongen-yama!!!
It's him!!!
Forget about me and get to safety!!! Hurry!!!
DASH
I'll get you down!!
Uh-uh.
パチン
SNAP
GRAB
heh heh heh
Don't be hasty, now.
If you defeat me, I'll let him down.

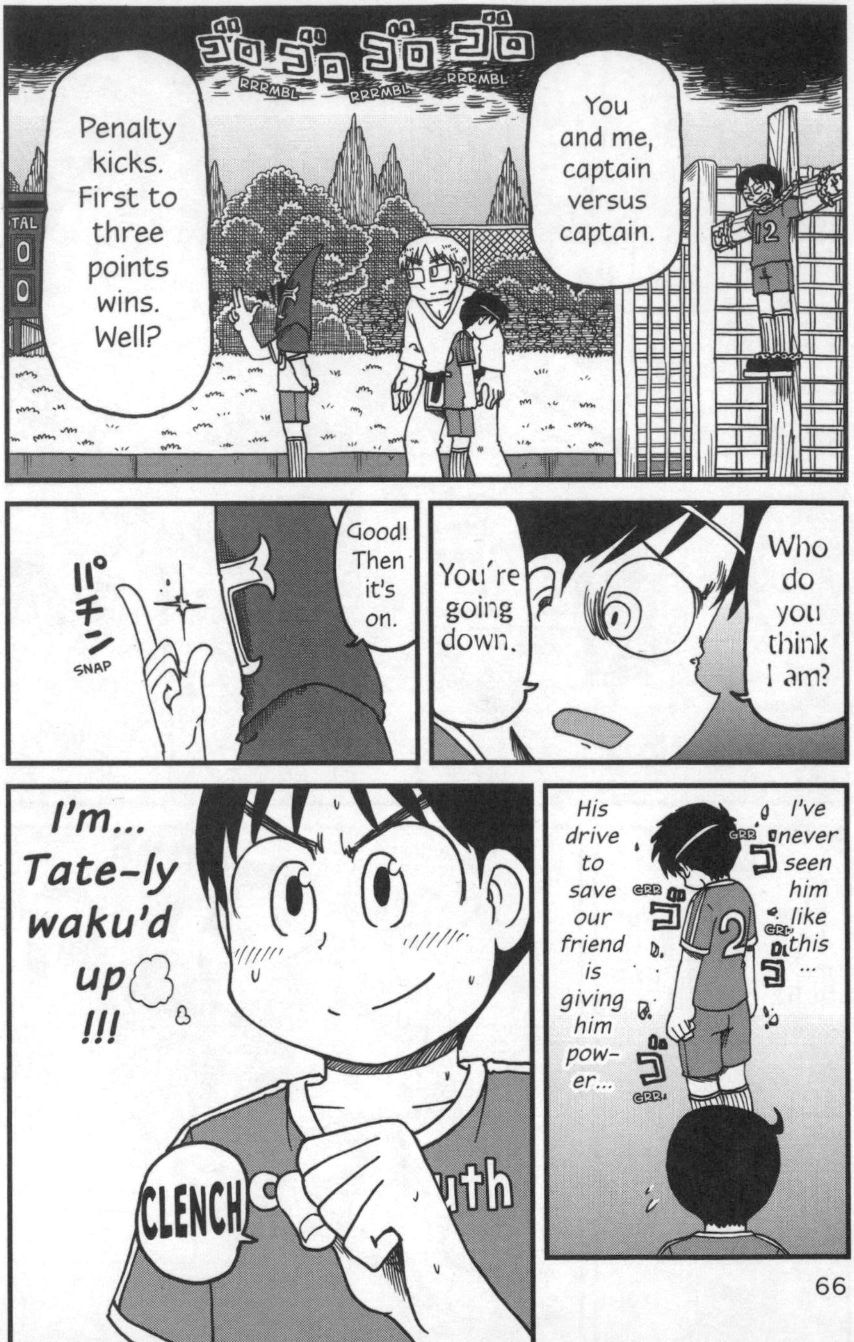
ゴロゴロゴロゴロ
RRRMBL RRRMBL RRRMBL
You and me, captain versus captain.
Penalty kicks. First to three points wins. Well?
Who do you think I am?
You're going down.
Good! Then it's on.
パチン
SNAP
I've never seen him like this...
His drive to save our friend is giving him pow-er...
ゴ GRR ゴ GRR ゴ GRR ゴ GRR
I'm... Tate-ly waku'd up!!!
CLENCH

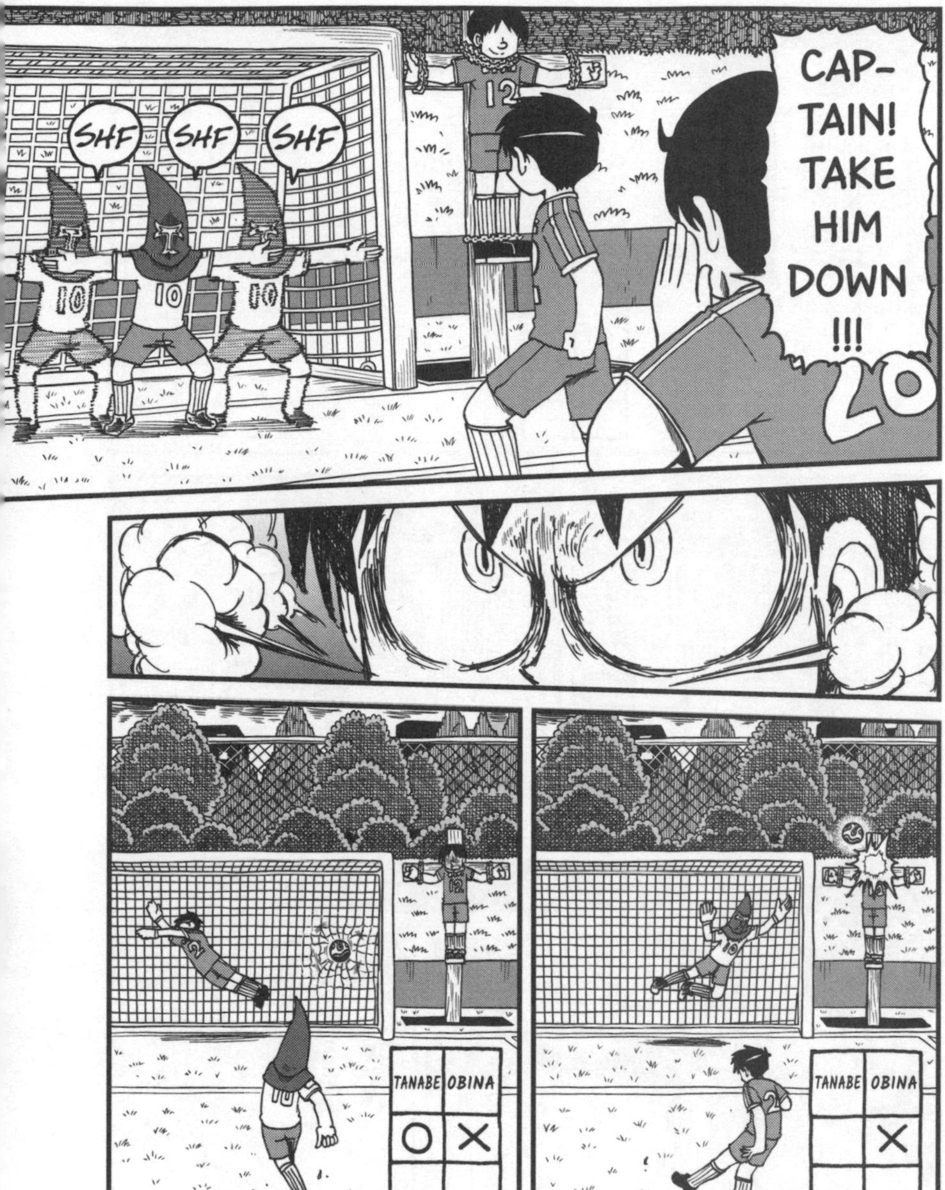
CAP-
TAIN!
TAKE
HIM
DOWN
!!!
SHF
SHF
SHF
TANABE OBINA
TANABE OBINA

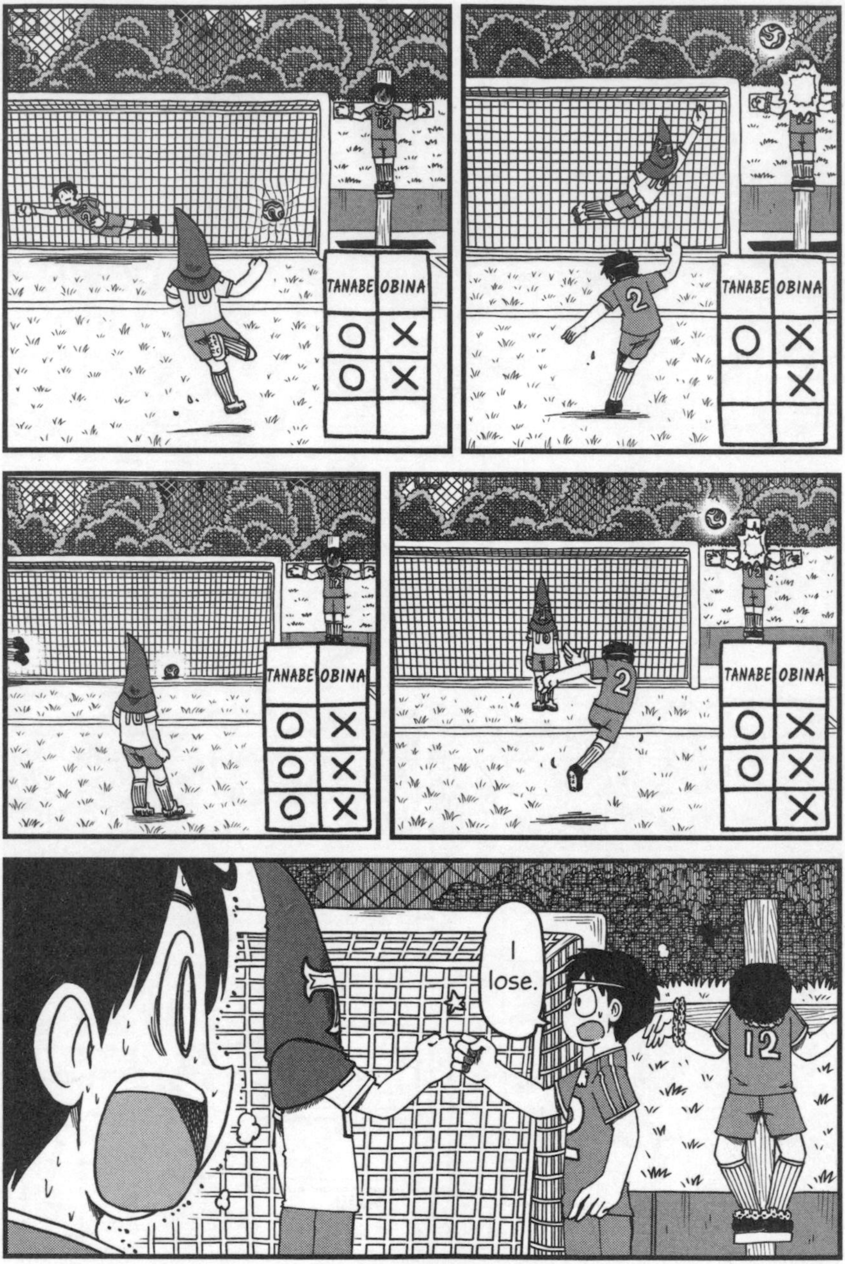
TANABE
OBINA
TANABE
OBINA
TANABE
OBINA
TANABE
OBINA
I lose.

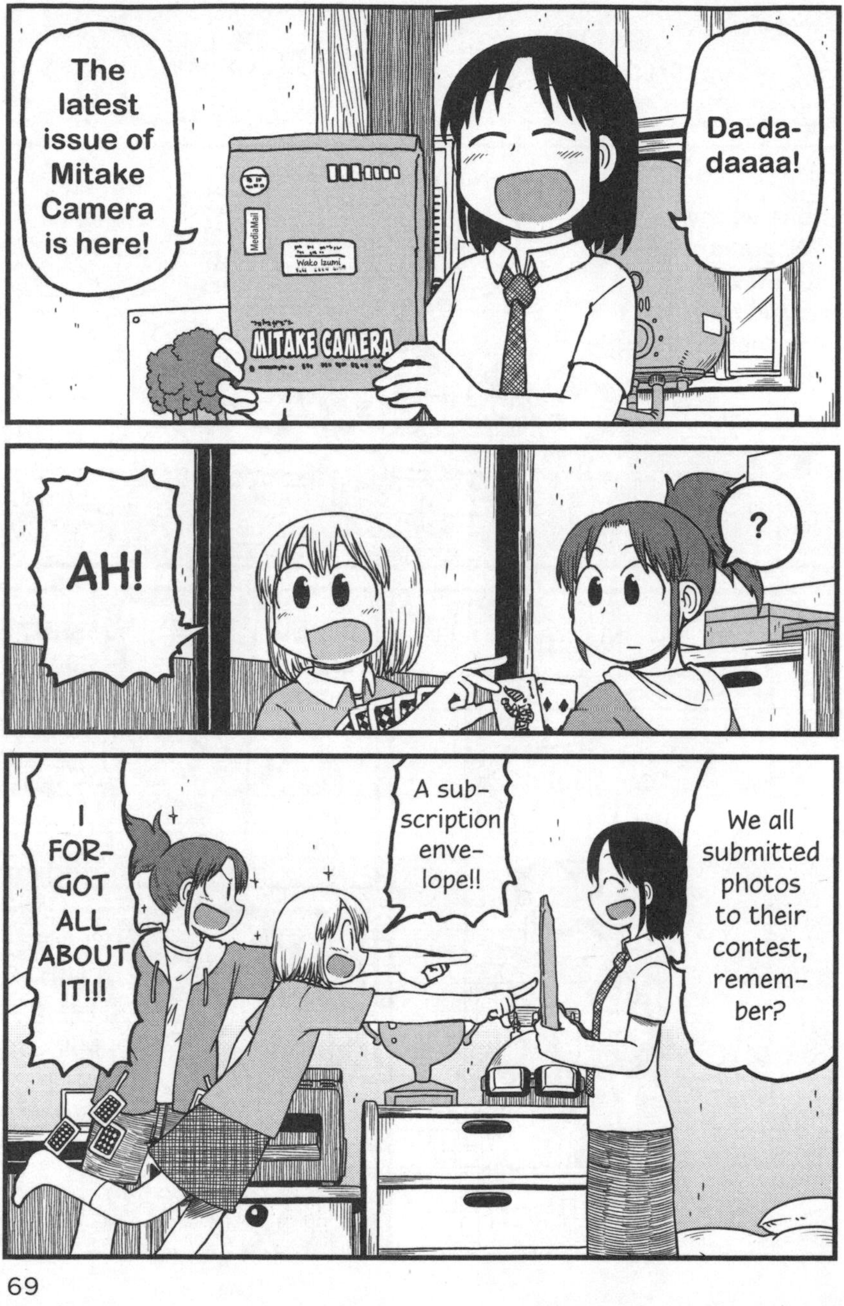
Da-da-daaaa!
The latest issue of Mitake Camera is here!
MediaMail
Wako Izumi
MITAKE CAMERA
?
AH!
We all submitted photos to their contest, remember?
A sub-scription enve-lope!!
I FOR-GOT ALL ABOUT IT!!!

Chapter 159 "Summer" Photo Contest

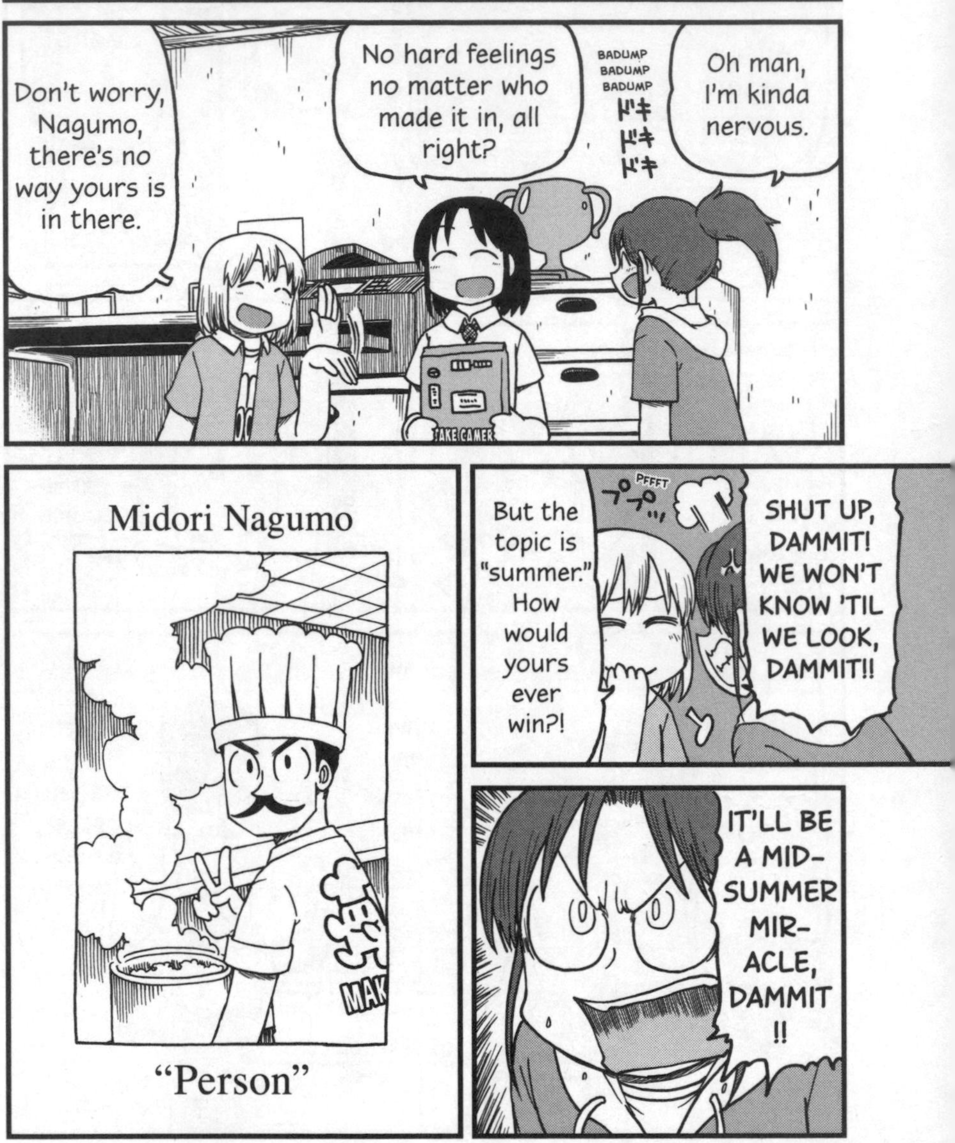
Oh man, I'm kinda nervous.
BADUMP BADUMP BADUMP
ドキ ドキ ドキ
No hard feelings no matter who made it in, all right?
Don't worry, Nagumo, there's no way yours is in there.
TAKE CAMER
SHUT UP, DAMMIT! WE WON'T KNOW 'TIL WE LOOK, DAMMIT!!
PFFFT
プ プ
But the topic is "summer." How would yours ever win?!
IT'LL BE A MID-SUMMER MIR-ACLE, DAMMIT !!
Midori Nagumo
MAK
"Person"

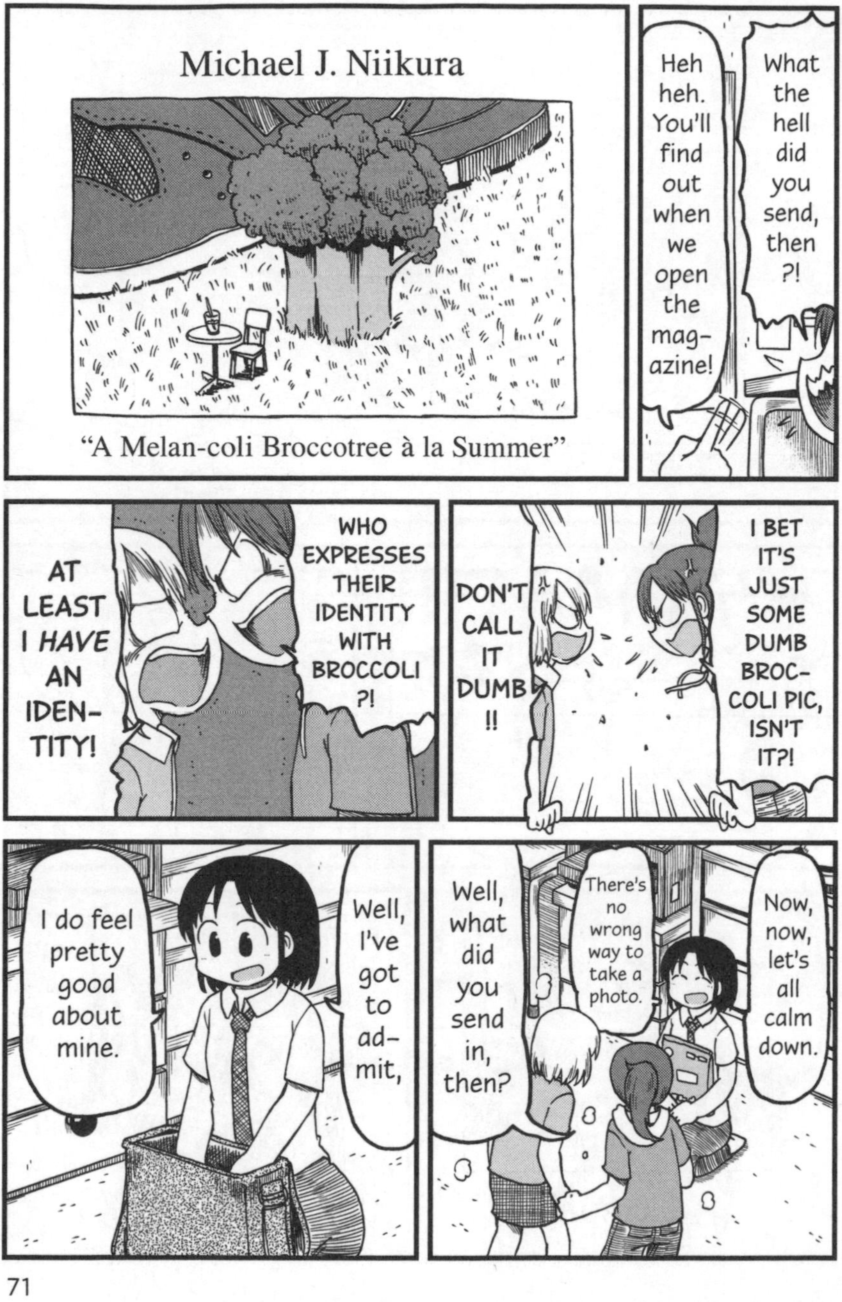
What the hell did you send, then?!
Heh heh. You'll find out when we open the magazine!
Michael J. Niikura
"A Melan-coli Broccotree à la Summer"
I BET IT'S JUST SOME DUMB BROCCOLI PIC, ISN'T IT?!
DON'T CALL IT DUMB!!
WHO EXPRESSES THEIR IDENTITY WITH BROCCOLI?!
AT LEAST I *HAVE* AN IDENTITY!
Now, now, let's all calm down.
There's no wrong way to take a photo.
Well, what did you send in, then?
Well, I've got to admit,
I do feel pretty good about mine.

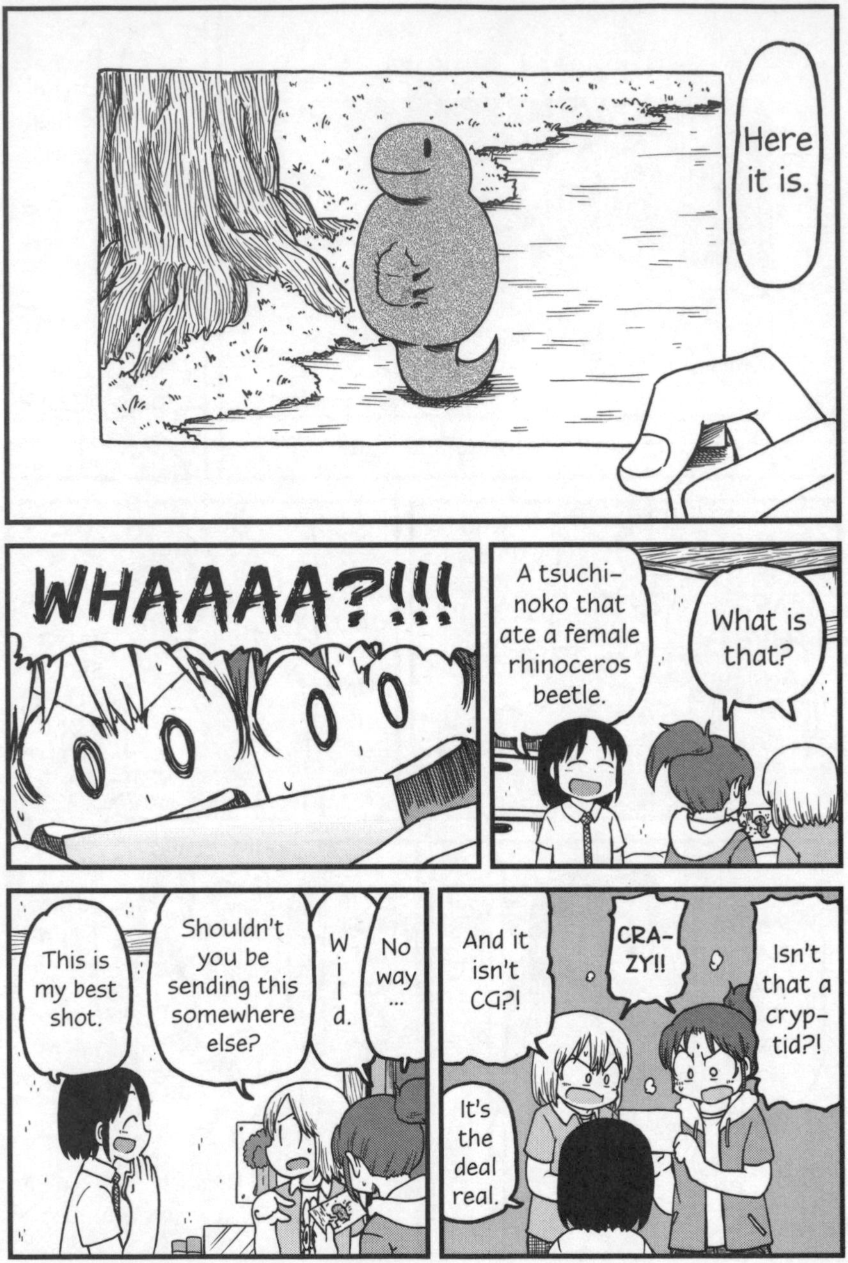

Here it is.
What is that?
A tsuchinoko that ate a female rhinoceros beetle.
WHAAAA?!!!
Isn't that a cryptid?!
CRA-ZY!!
And it isn't CG?!
It's the deal real.
No way...
Wild.
Shouldn't you be sending this somewhere else?
This is my best shot.

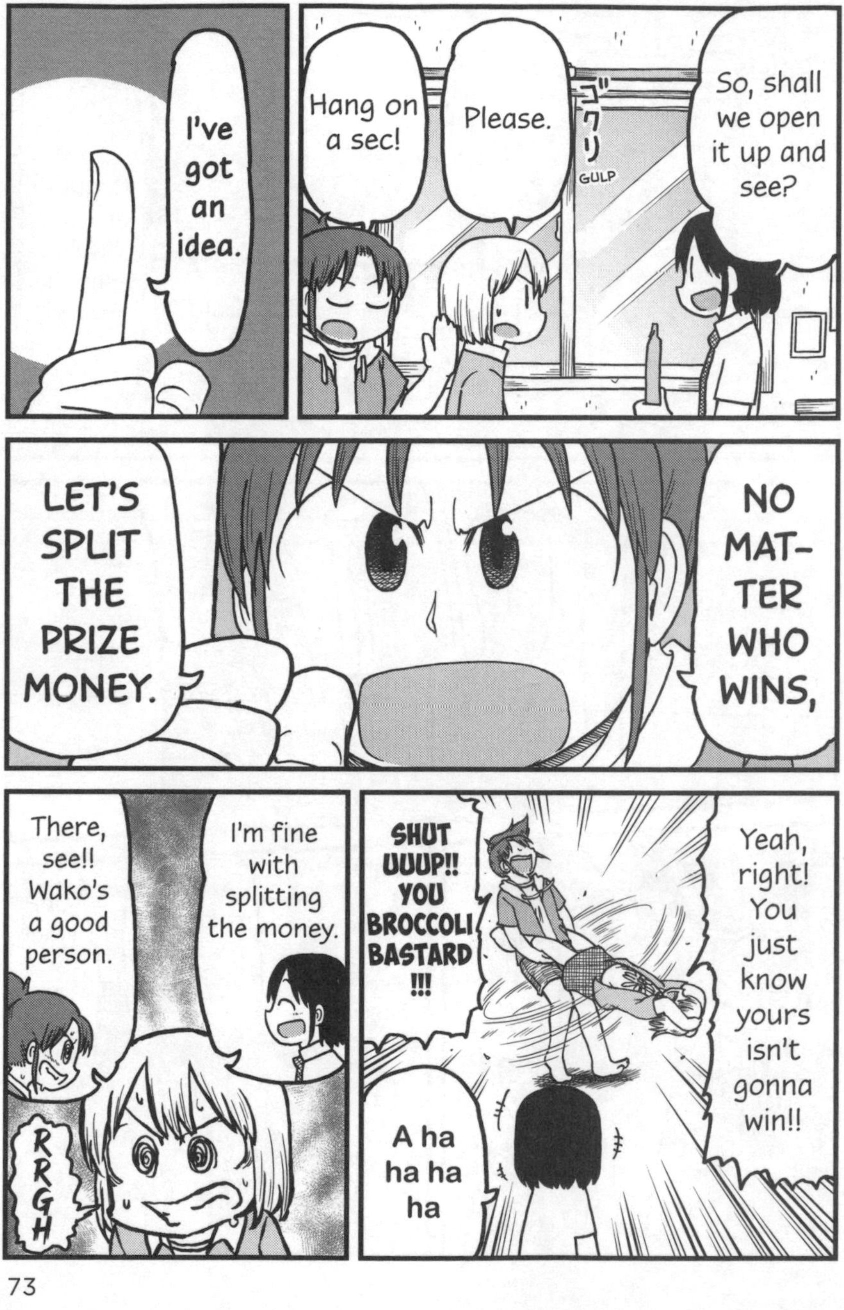
So, shall we open it up and see?
ゴクリ
GULP
Please.
Hang on a sec!
I've got an idea.
NO MATTER WHO WINS,
LET'S SPLIT THE PRIZE MONEY.
Yeah, right! You just know yours isn't gonna win!!
SHUT UUUP!! YOU BROCCOLI BASTARD!!!
A ha ha ha ha
I'm fine with splitting the money.
There, see!! Wako's a good person.
RRGH

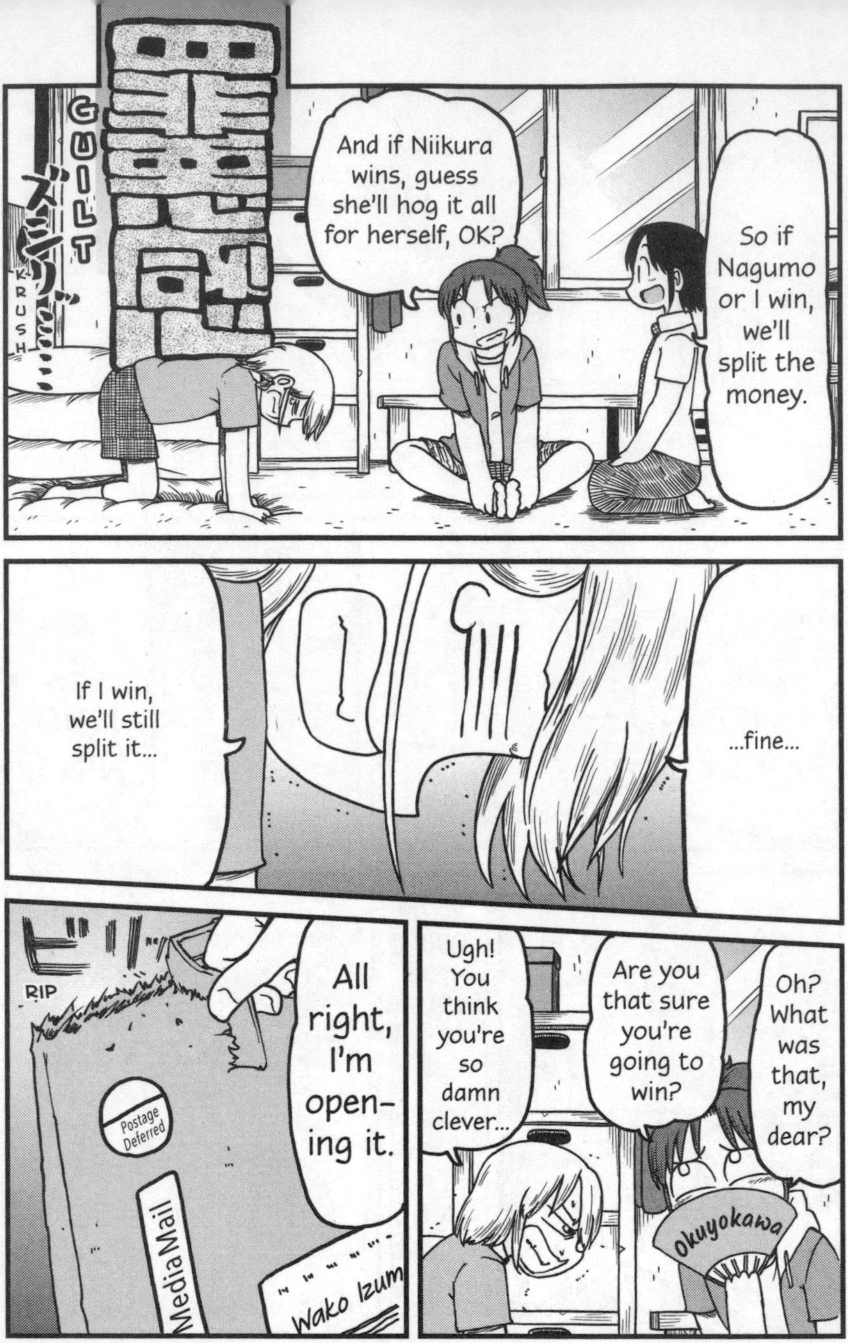
So if Nagumo or I win, we'll split the money.
And if Niikura wins, guess she'll hog it all for herself, OK?
GUILT
KRUSH
...fine...
If I win, we'll still split it...
Oh? What was that, my dear?
Are you that sure you're going to win?
Ugh! You think you're so damn clever...
Okuyokawa
All right, I'm open-ing it.
RIP
Postage Deferred
Media Mail
Wako Izum

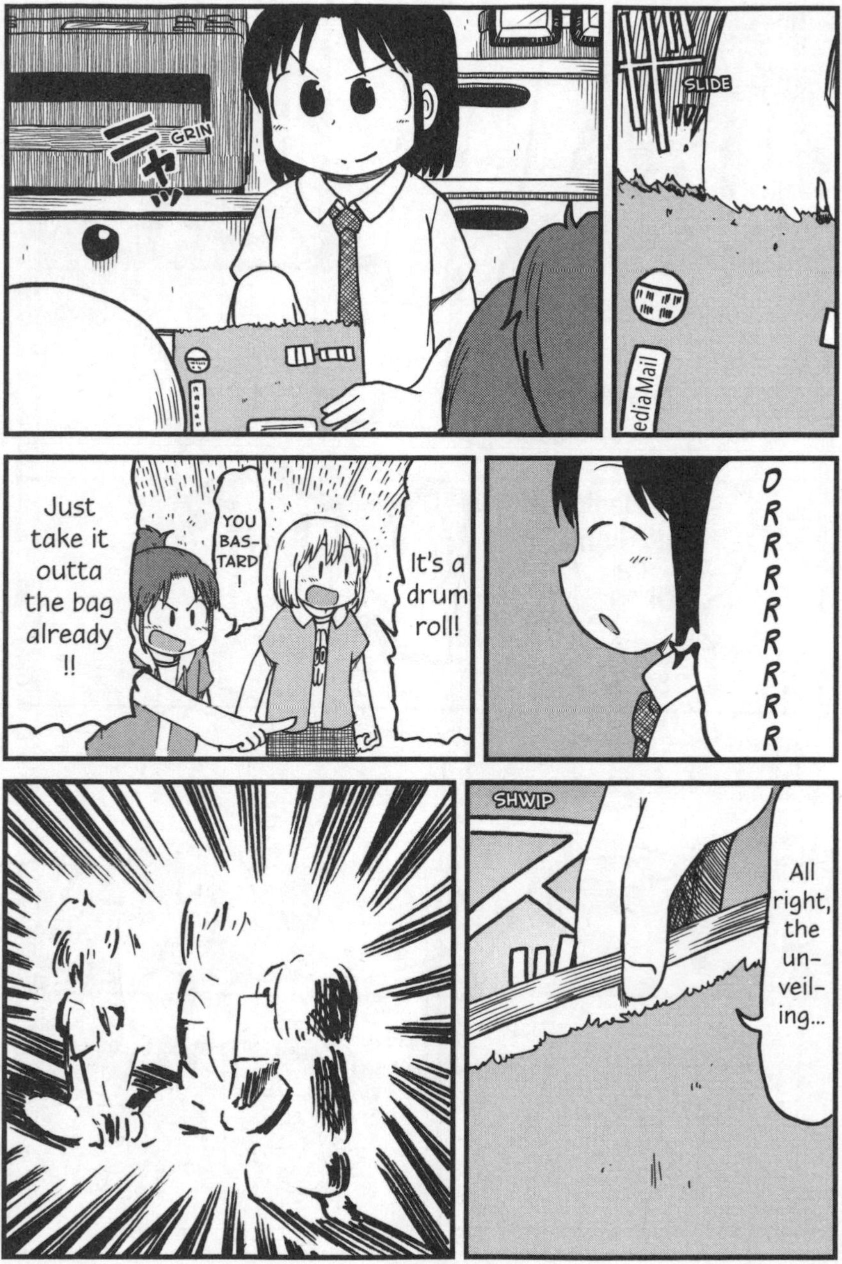
SLIDE
ediaMail
GRIN
ニヤッ
DRRRRRRRR
It's a drum roll!
YOU BASTARD!
Just take it outta the bag already!!
SHWIP
All right, the unveiling...

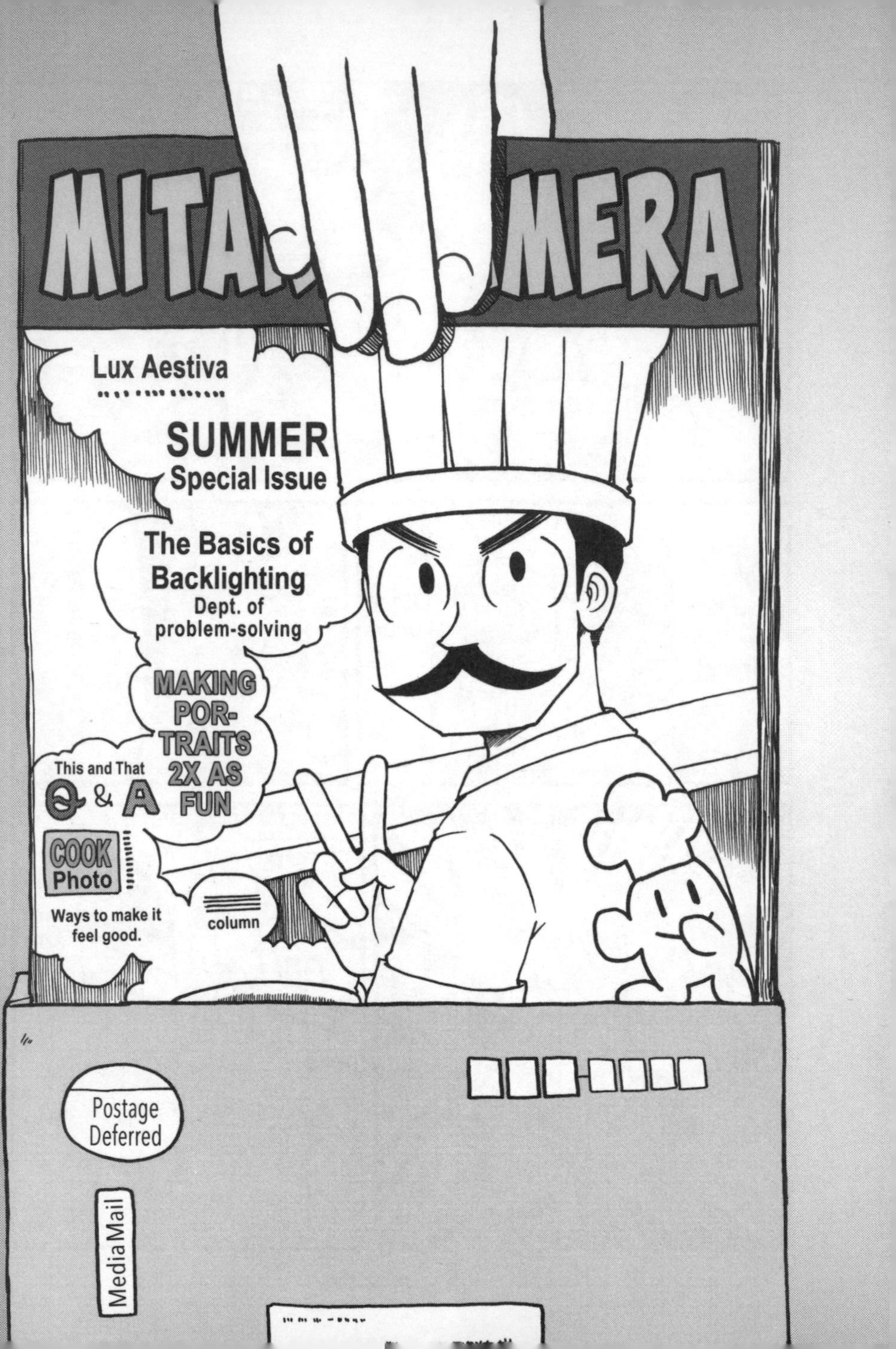

MITA MERA
Lux Aestiva
SUMMER
Special Issue
The Basics of
Backlighting
Dept. of
problem-solving
MAKING
POR-
TRAITS
2X AS
FUN
This and That
Q & A
COOK
Photo
Ways to make it
feel good.
column
Postage
Deferred
Media Mail

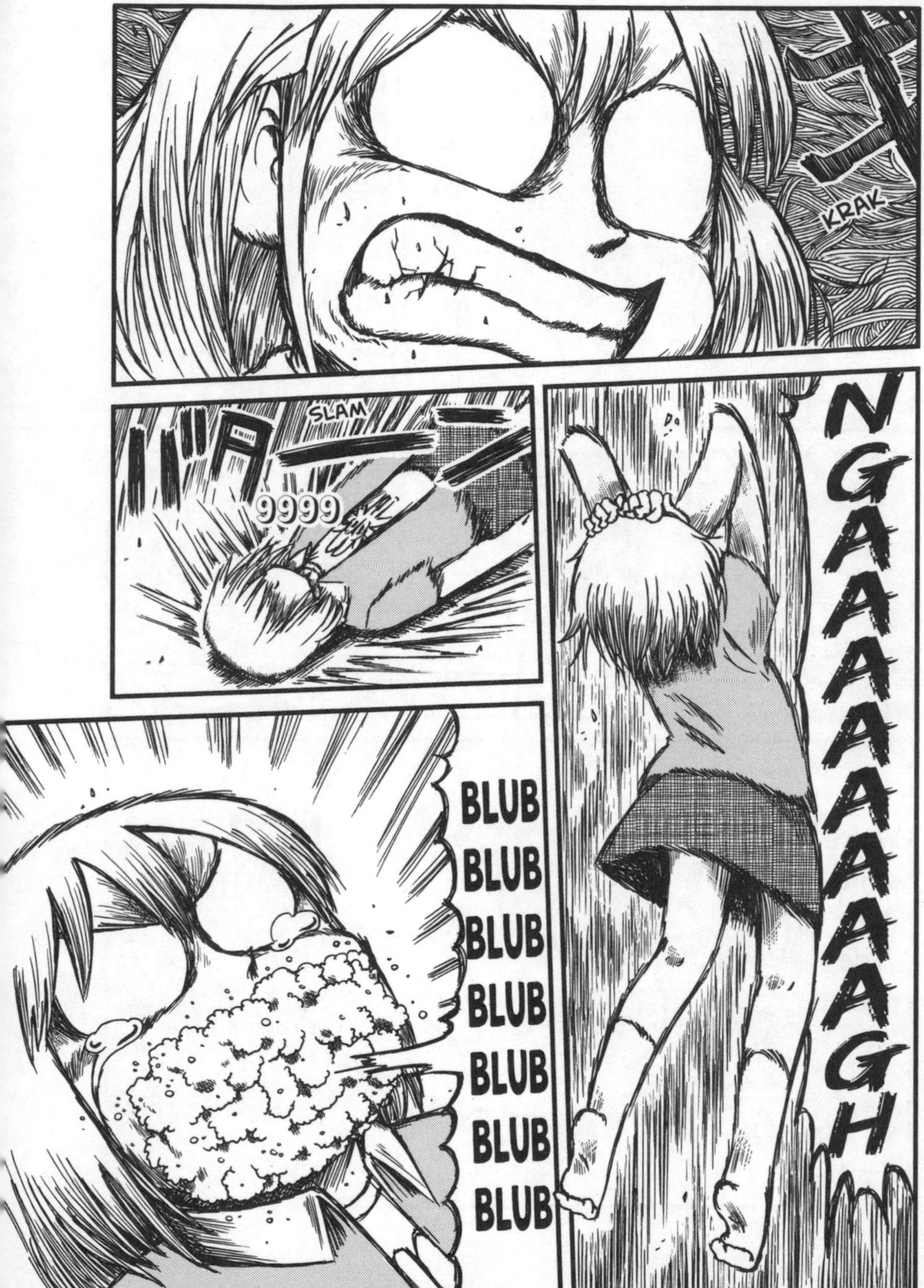
KRAK
NGAAAAAAAAGH
SLAM
9999
BLUB
BLUB
BLUB
BLUB
BLUB
BLUB
BLUB

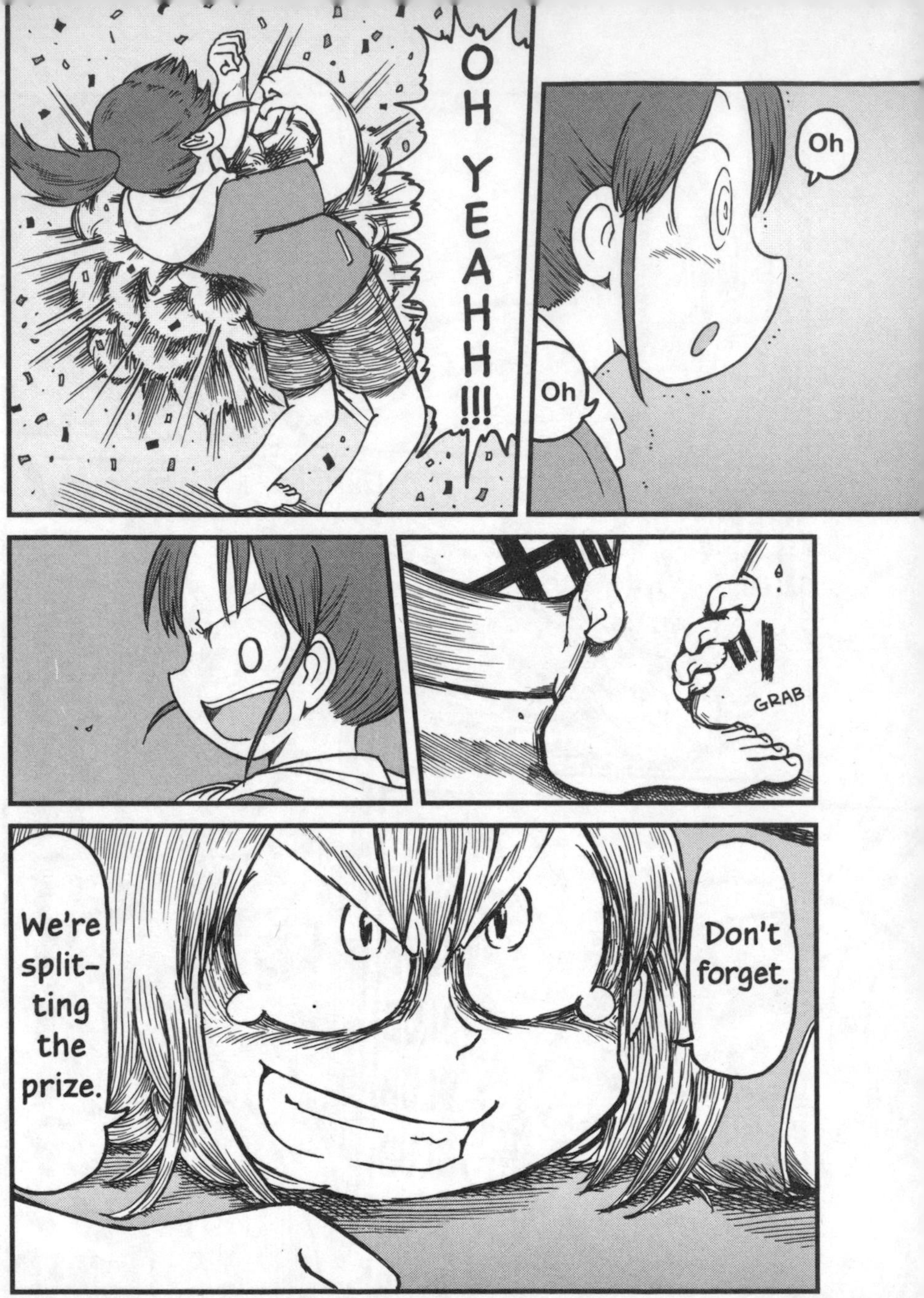
Oh
Oh
OH YEAHH!!!
GRAB
Don't forget.
We're split-ting the prize.

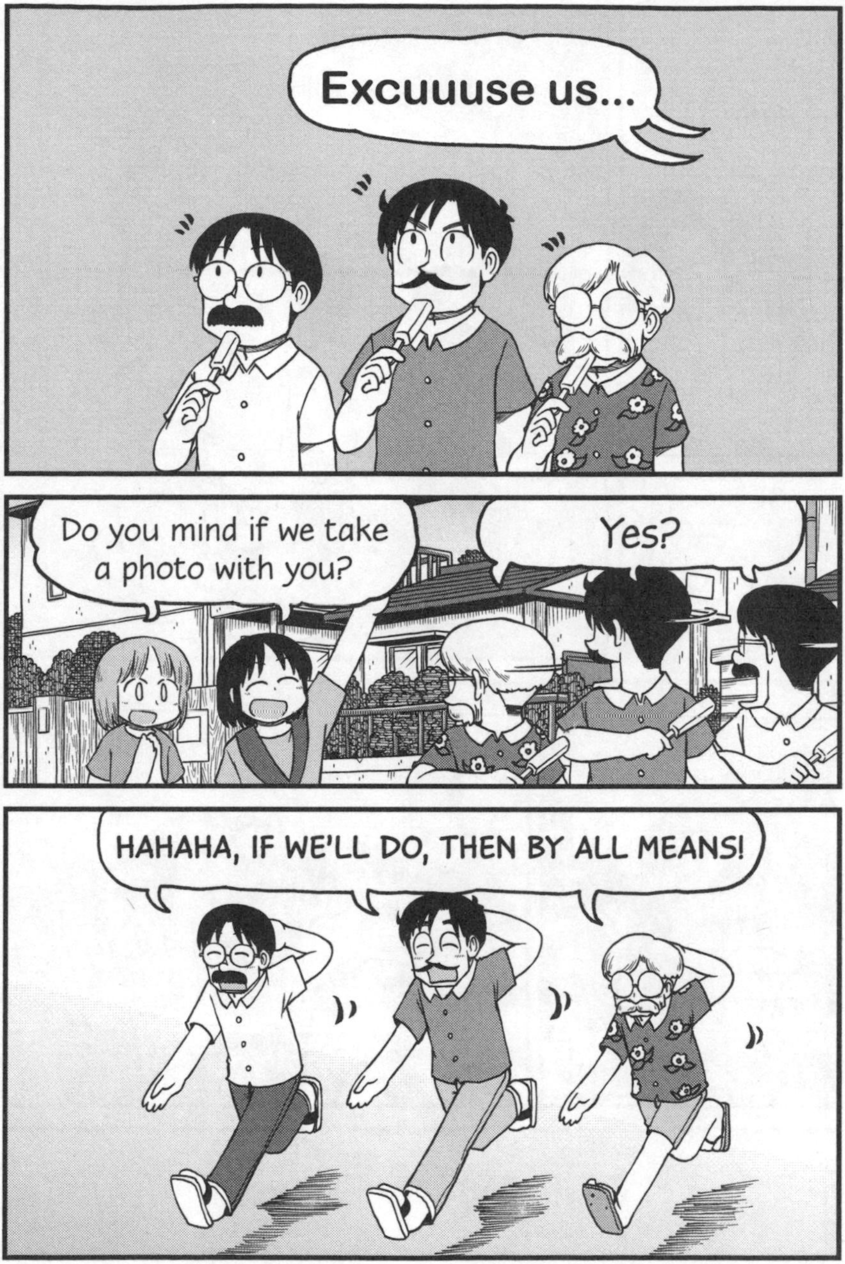
Excuuuse us...
Yes?
Do you mind if we take a photo with you?
HAHAHA, IF WE'LL DO, THEN BY ALL MEANS!

HUH?

SNAP

Chapter 160 Superstar

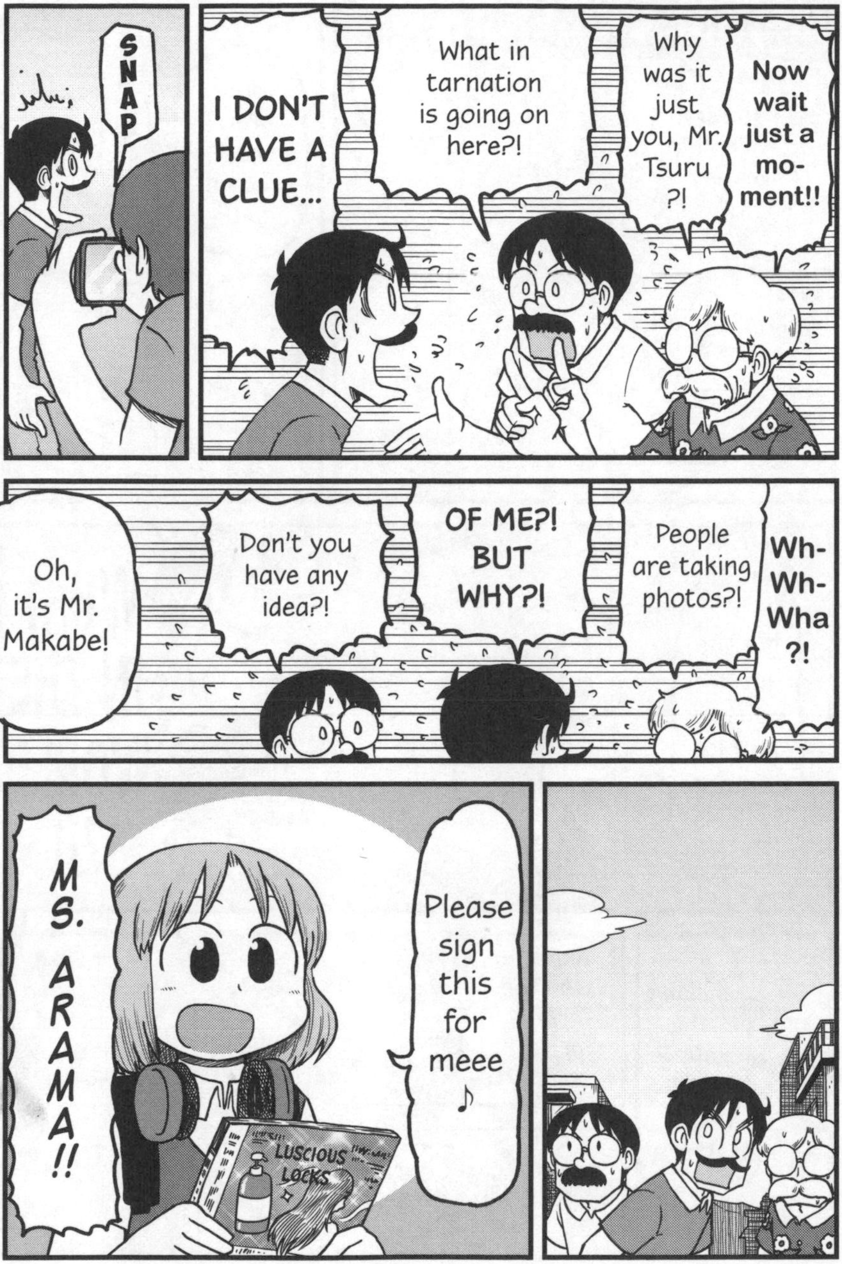
Now wait just a moment!!
Why was it just you, Mr. Tsuru?!
What in tarnation is going on here?!
I DON'T HAVE A CLUE...
SNAP
Wh-Wh-Wha?!
People are taking photos?!
OF ME?! BUT WHY?!
Don't you have any idea?!
Oh, it's Mr. Makabe!
Please sign this for meee ♪
MS. ARAMA!!
LUSCIOUS LOCKS

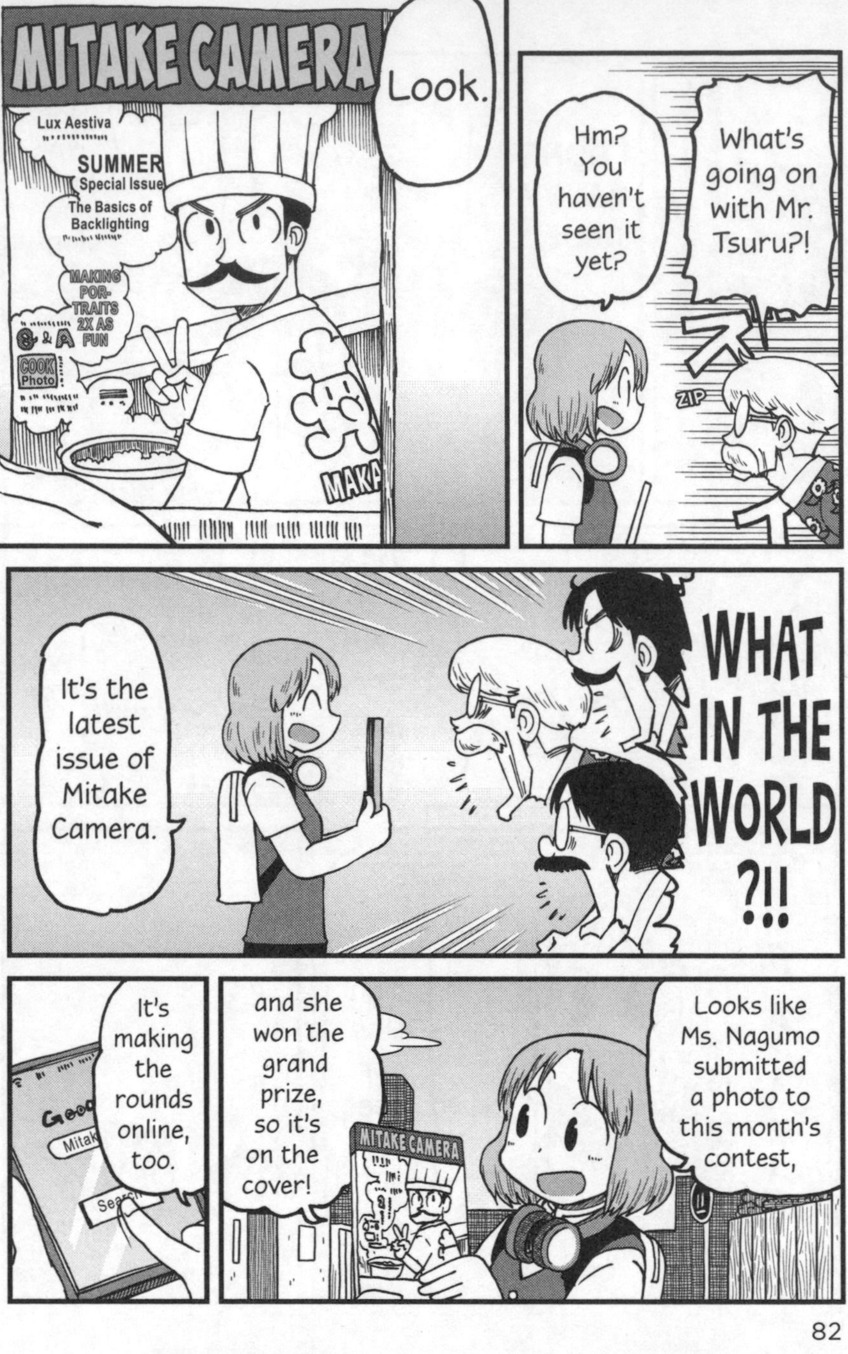
What's going on with Mr. Tsuru?!
Hm? You haven't seen it yet?
ZIP
Look.
MITAKE CAMERA
Lux Aestiva
SUMMER Special Issue
The Basics of Backlighting
MAKING POR-TRAITS 2X AS FUN
Q & A
COOK Photo
MAKA
WHAT IN THE WORLD ?!!
It's the latest issue of Mitake Camera.
Looks like Ms. Nagumo submitted a photo to this month's contest,
and she won the grand prize, so it's on the cover!
MITAKE CAMERA
It's making the rounds online, too.

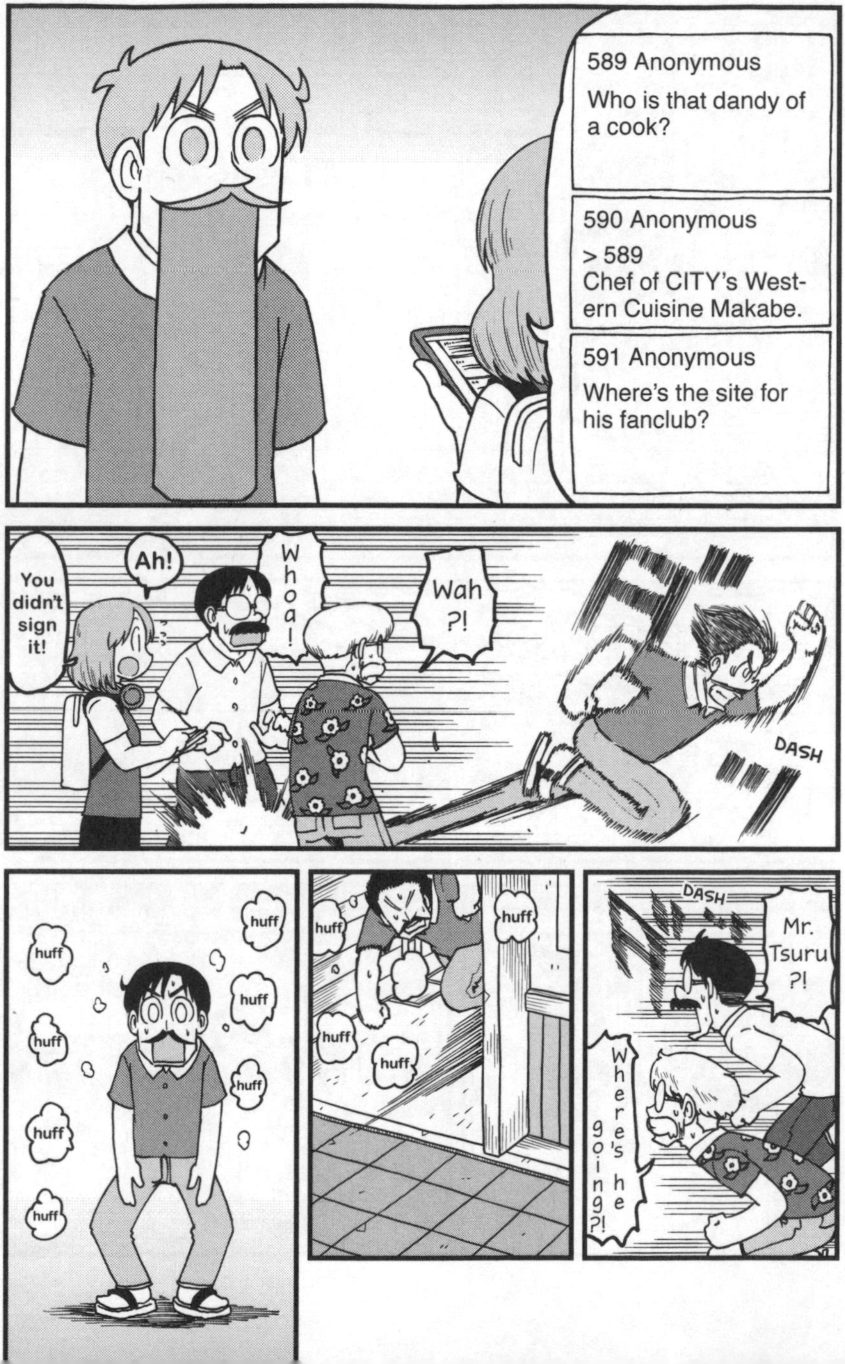
589 Anonymous
Who is that dandy of a cook?
590 Anonymous
> 589
Chef of CITY's Western Cuisine Makabe.
591 Anonymous
Where's the site for his fanclub?
DASH
Wah?!
Whoa!
Ah!
You didn't sign it!
DASH
Mr. Tsuru?!
Where's he going?!
huff
huff
huff
huff
huff
huff
huff
huff
huff
huff
huff

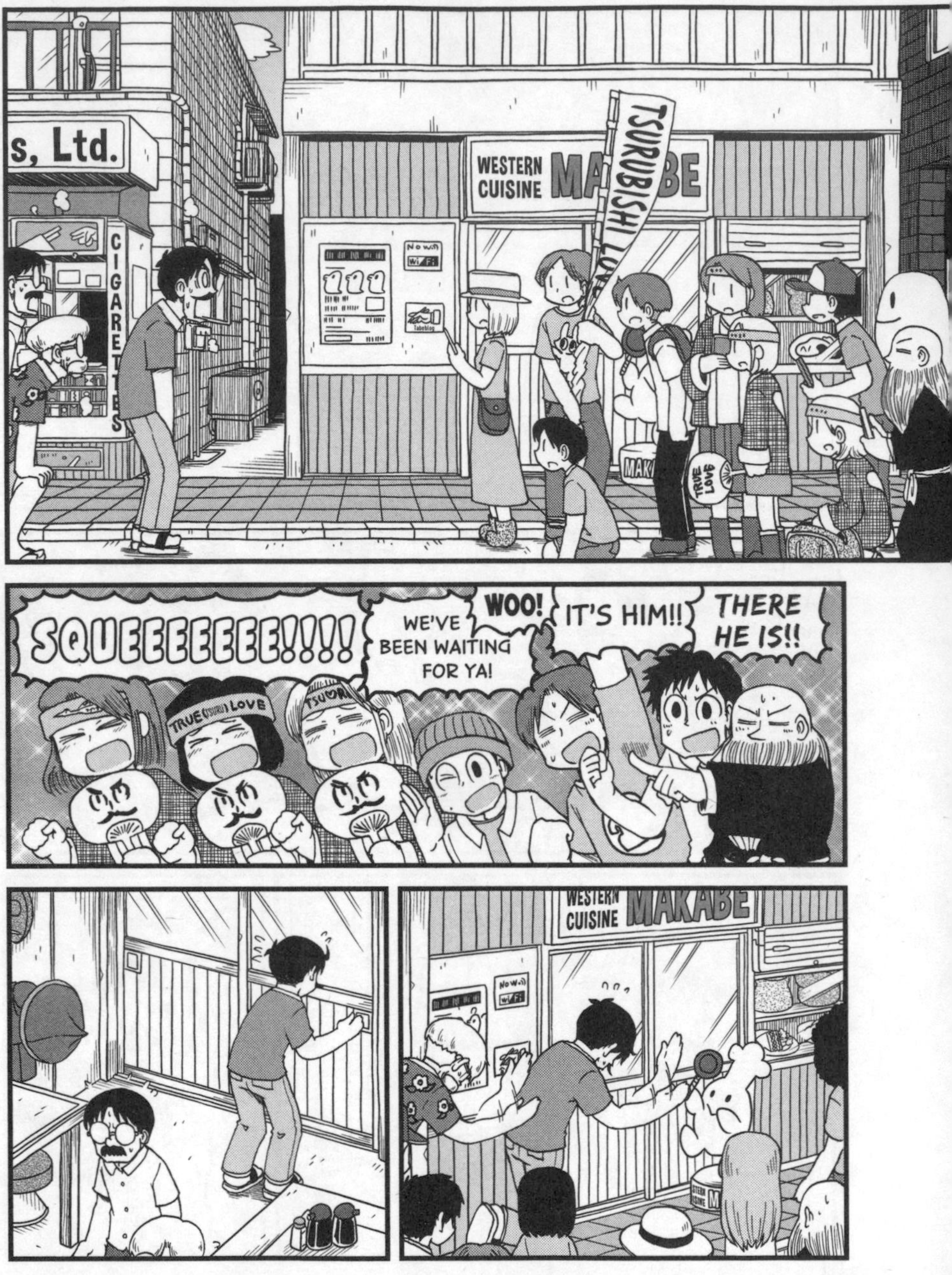
s, Ltd.
CIGARETTES
WESTERN CUISINE
TSURUBISHI LOVE
Tabeblog
TRUE LOVE
THERE HE IS!!
IT'S HIM!!
WOO!
WE'VE BEEN WAITING FOR YA!
SQUEEEEEEEE!!!!
TRUE (TSURU) LOVE
WESTERN CUISINE MAKABE

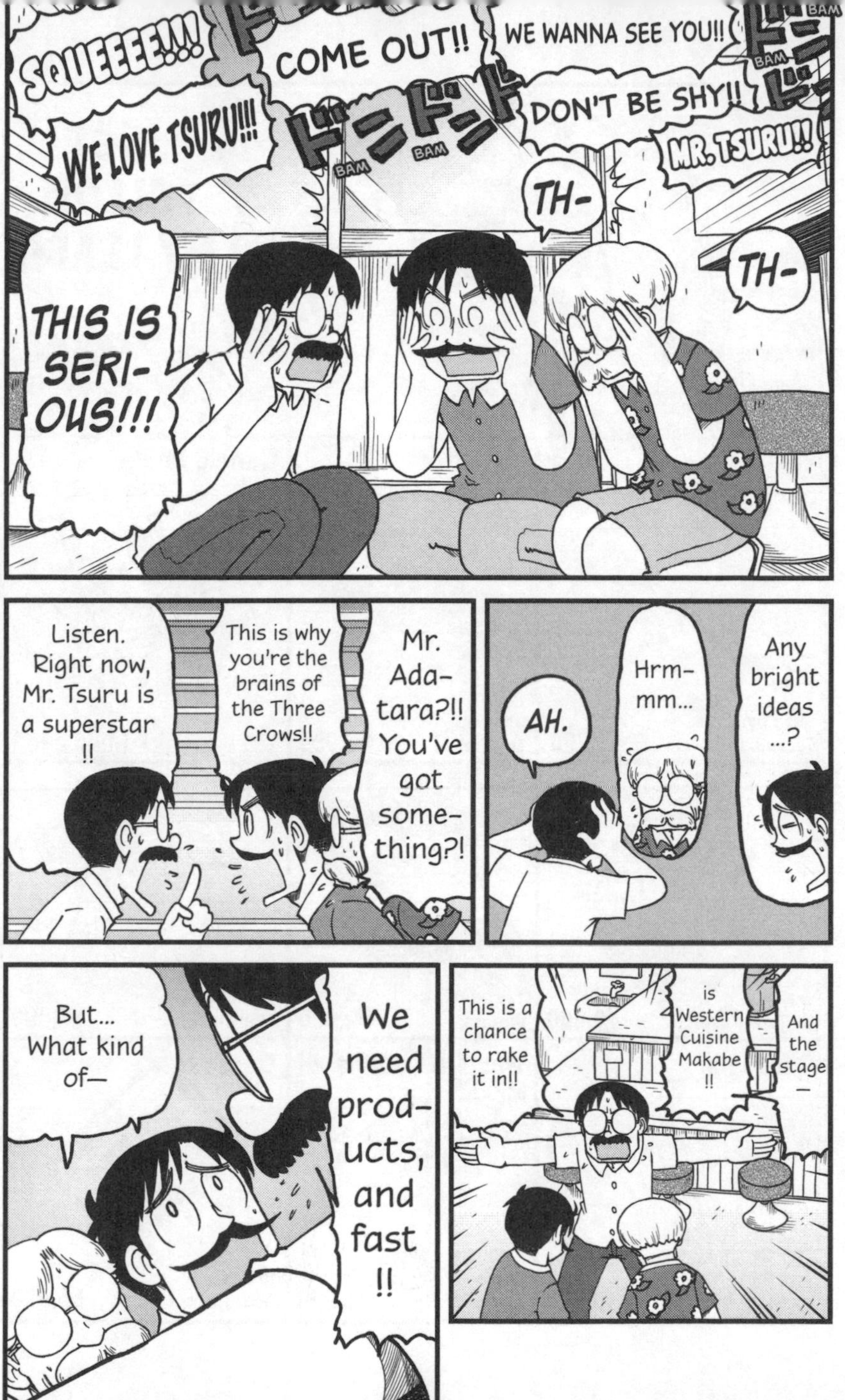
BAM
BAM
WE WANNA SEE YOU!!
COME OUT!!
SQUEEEEE!!!
DON'T BE SHY!!
BAM
BAM
MR. TSURU!!
WE LOVE TSURU!!!
TH-
TH-
THIS IS SERI-OUS!!!
Any bright ideas ...?
Hrm-mm...
AH.
Mr. Ada-tara?!! You've got some-thing?!
This is why you're the brains of the Three Crows!!
Listen. Right now, Mr. Tsuru is a superstar !!
And the stage —
is Western Cuisine Makabe !!
This is a chance to rake it in!!
We need prod-ucts, and fast !!
But... What kind of—

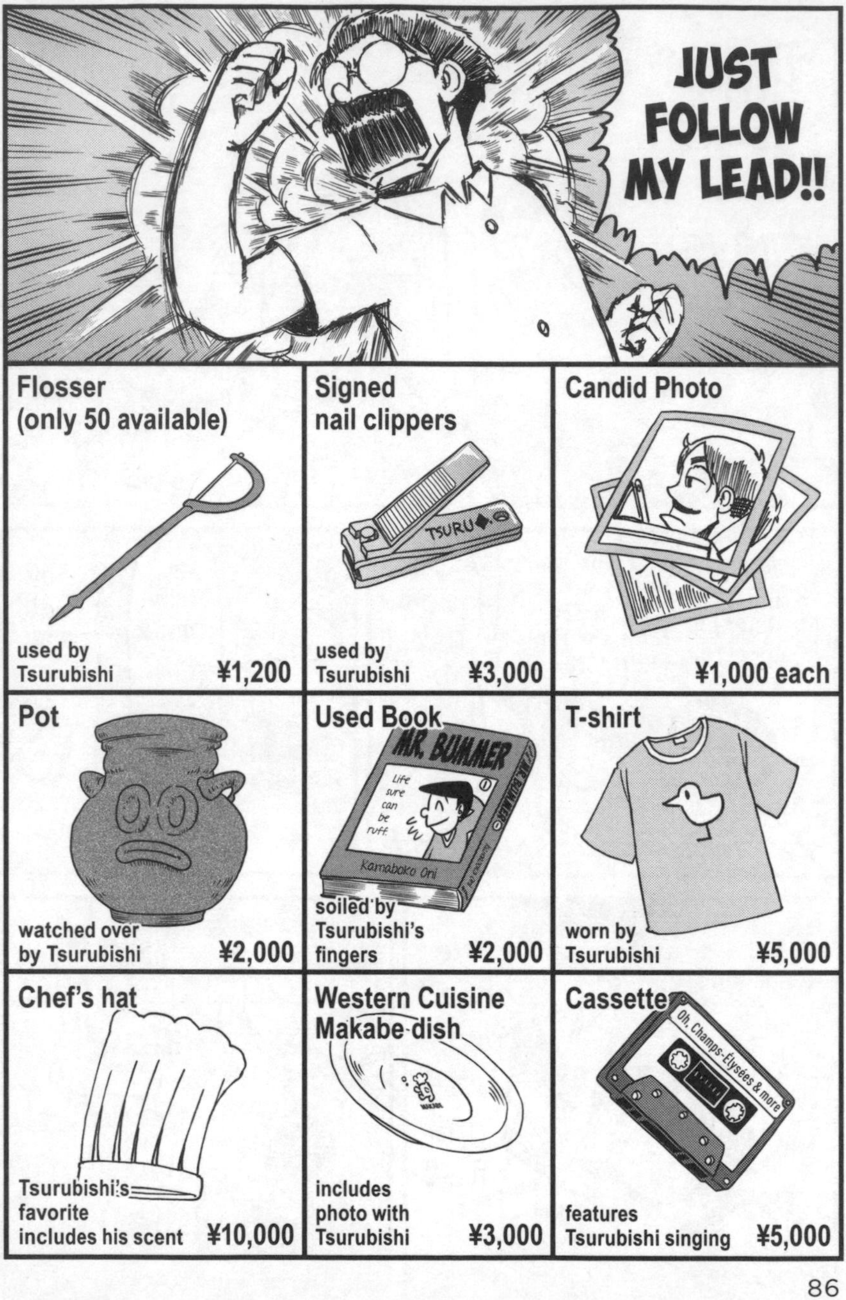
JUST FOLLOW MY LEAD!!
Candid Photo
¥1,000 each
Signed nail clippers
TSURU
used by Tsurubishi
¥3,000
Flosser (only 50 available)
used by Tsurubishi
¥1,200
T-shirt
worn by Tsurubishi
¥5,000
Used Book
MR. BUMMER
Life sure can be ruff.
Kamaboko Oni
soiled by Tsurubishi's fingers
¥2,000
Pot
watched over by Tsurubishi
¥2,000
Cassette
Oh, Champs-Élysées & more
features Tsurubishi singing
¥5,000
Western Cuisine Makabe dish
includes photo with Tsurubishi
¥3,000
Chef's hat
Tsurubishi's favorite
includes his scent
¥10,000

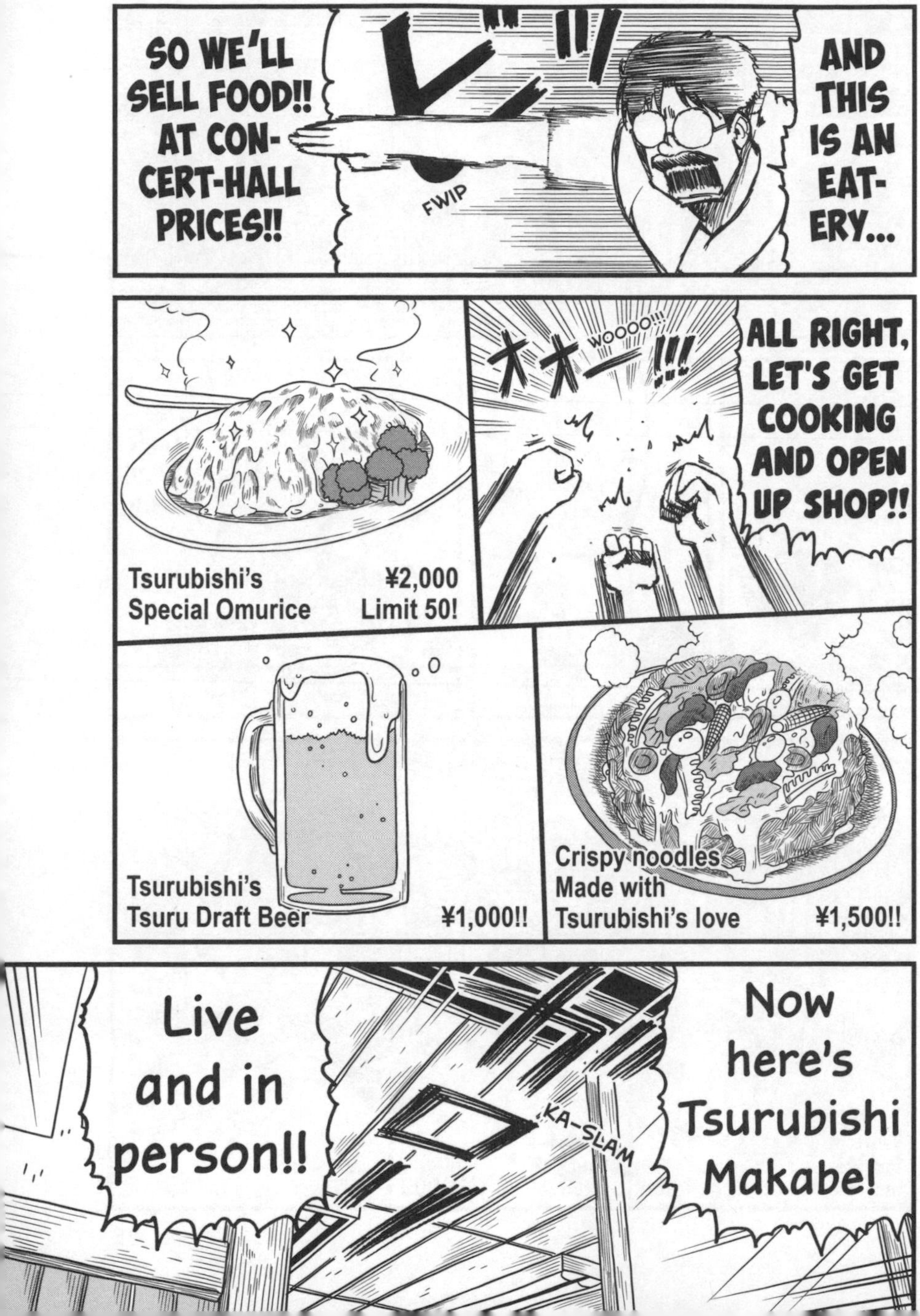
AND THIS IS AN EATERY...
SO WE'LL SELL FOOD!! AT CONCERT-HALL PRICES!!
FWIP
ALL RIGHT, LET'S GET COOKING AND OPEN UP SHOP!!
オオー!!!
WOOOO!!!
Tsurubishi's Special Omurice
¥2,000 Limit 50!
Crispy noodles Made with Tsurubishi's love
¥1,500!!
Tsurubishi's Tsuru Draft Beer
¥1,000!!
Now here's Tsurubishi Makabe!
KA-SLAM
Live and in person!!

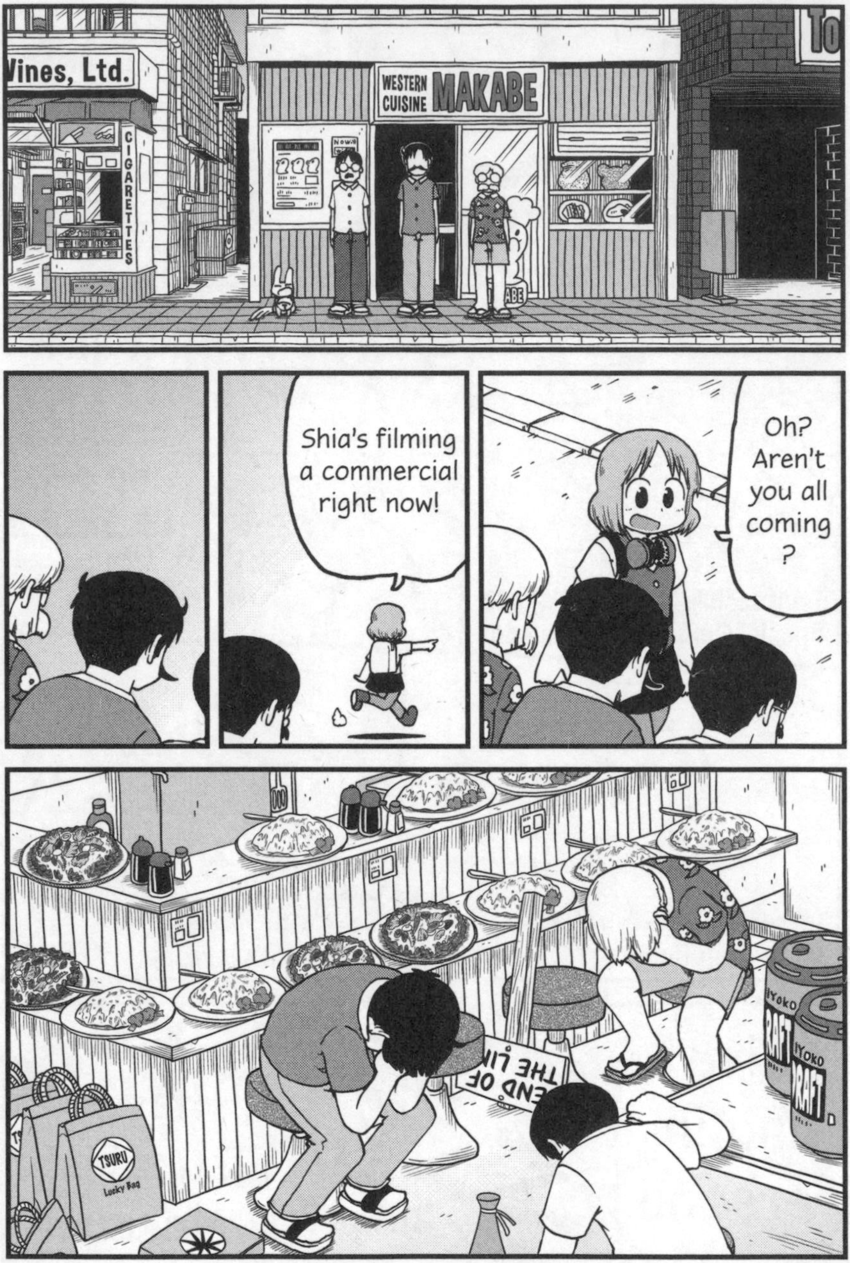
Wines, Ltd.
CIGARETTES
WESTERN CUISINE MAKABE
Oh? Aren't you all coming ?
Shia's filming a commercial right now!
TSURU
Lucky Bag

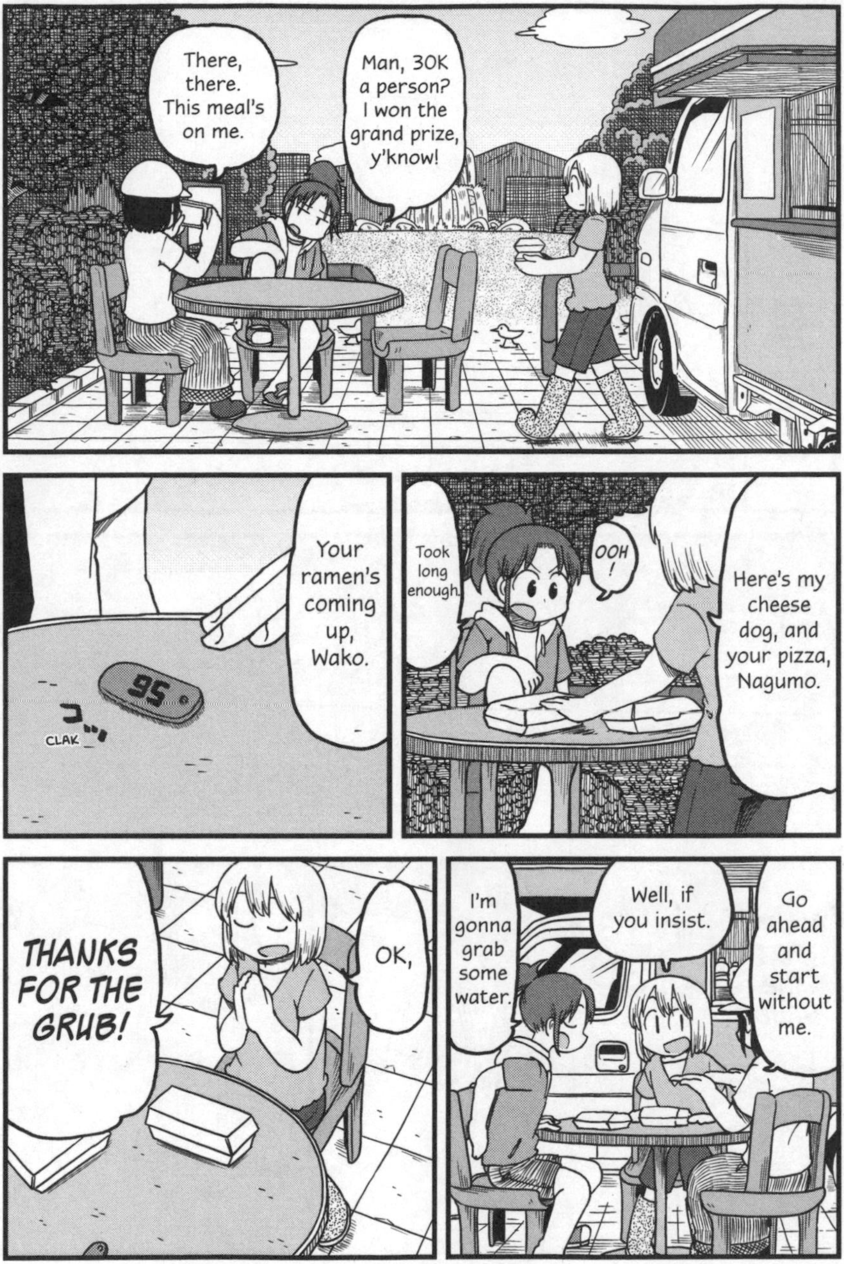

Man, 30K a person? I won the grand prize, y'know!
There, there. This meal's on me.
Here's my cheese dog, and your pizza, Nagumo.
OOH!
Took long enough.
Your ramen's coming up, Wako.
CLAK
Go ahead and start without me.
Well, if you insist.
I'm gonna grab some water.
OK,
THANKS FOR THE GRUB!

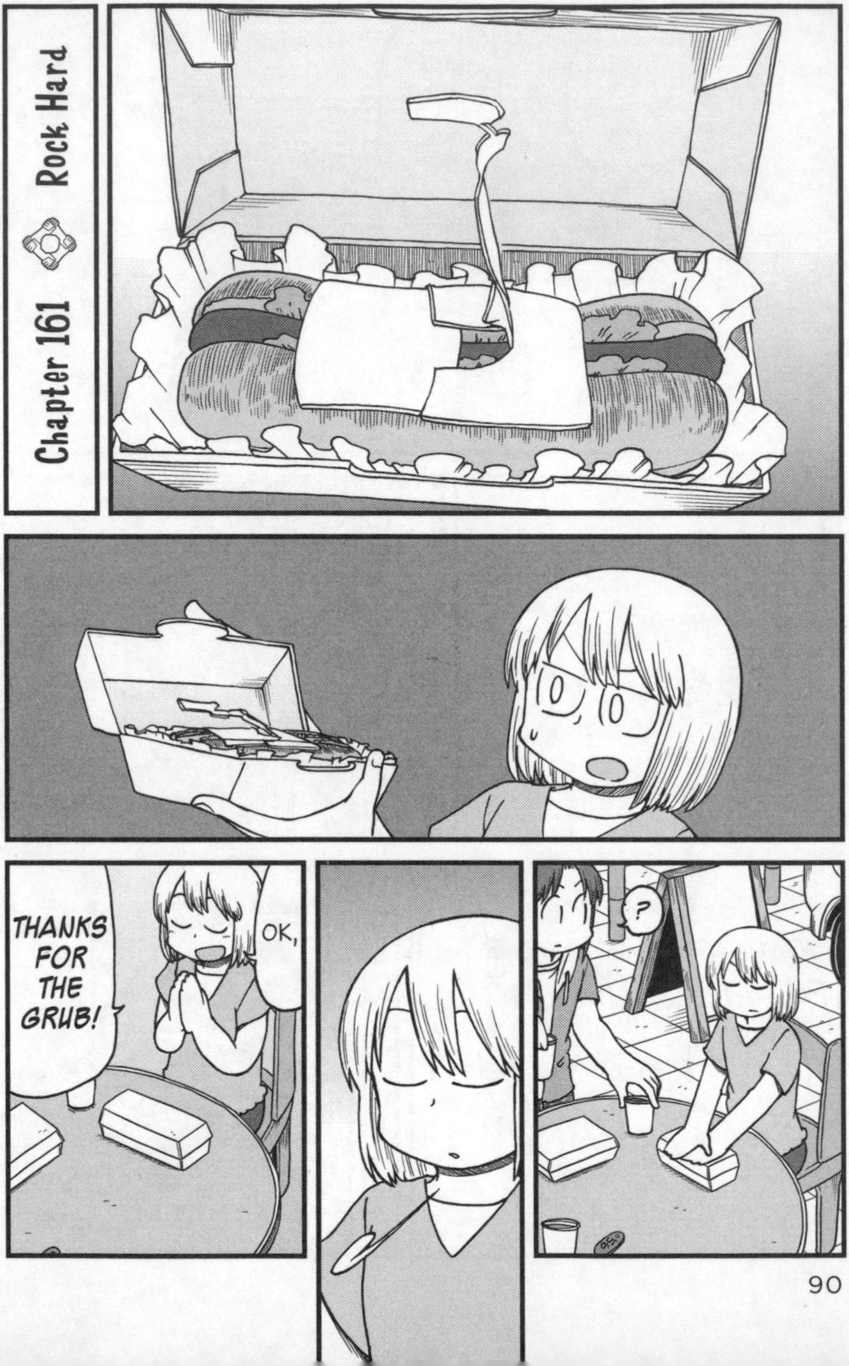
Chapter 161 Rock Hard
?
OK,
THANKS FOR THE GRUB!

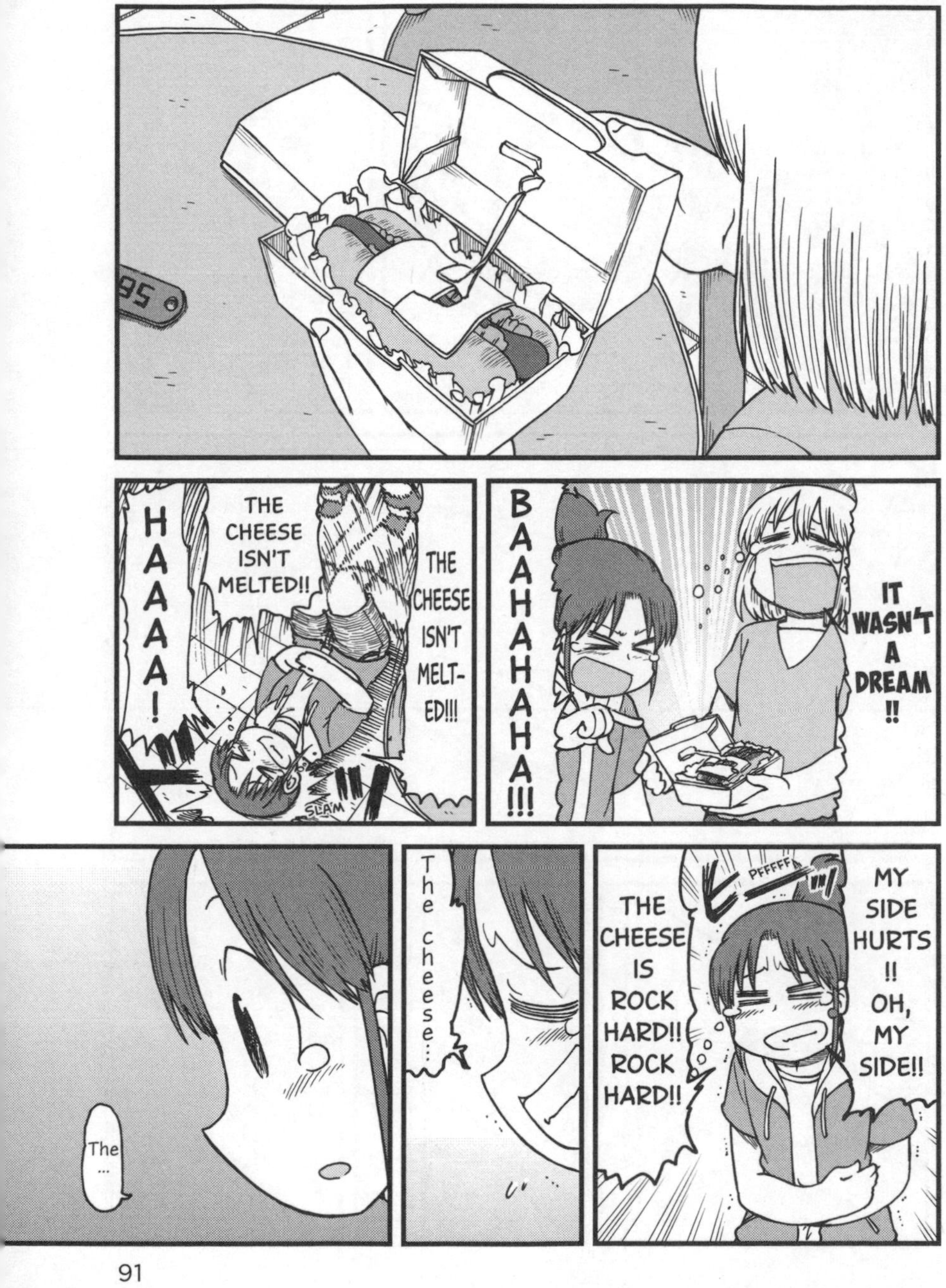
IT WASN'T A DREAM!!
BAAHAHAHA!!!
THE CHEESE ISN'T MELT-ED!!!
THE CHEESE ISN'T MELTED!!
HAAAAA!
SLAM
MY SIDE HURTS!! OH, MY SIDE!!
PFFFFF
THE CHEESE IS ROCK HARD!! ROCK HARD!!
The cheese...
The ...

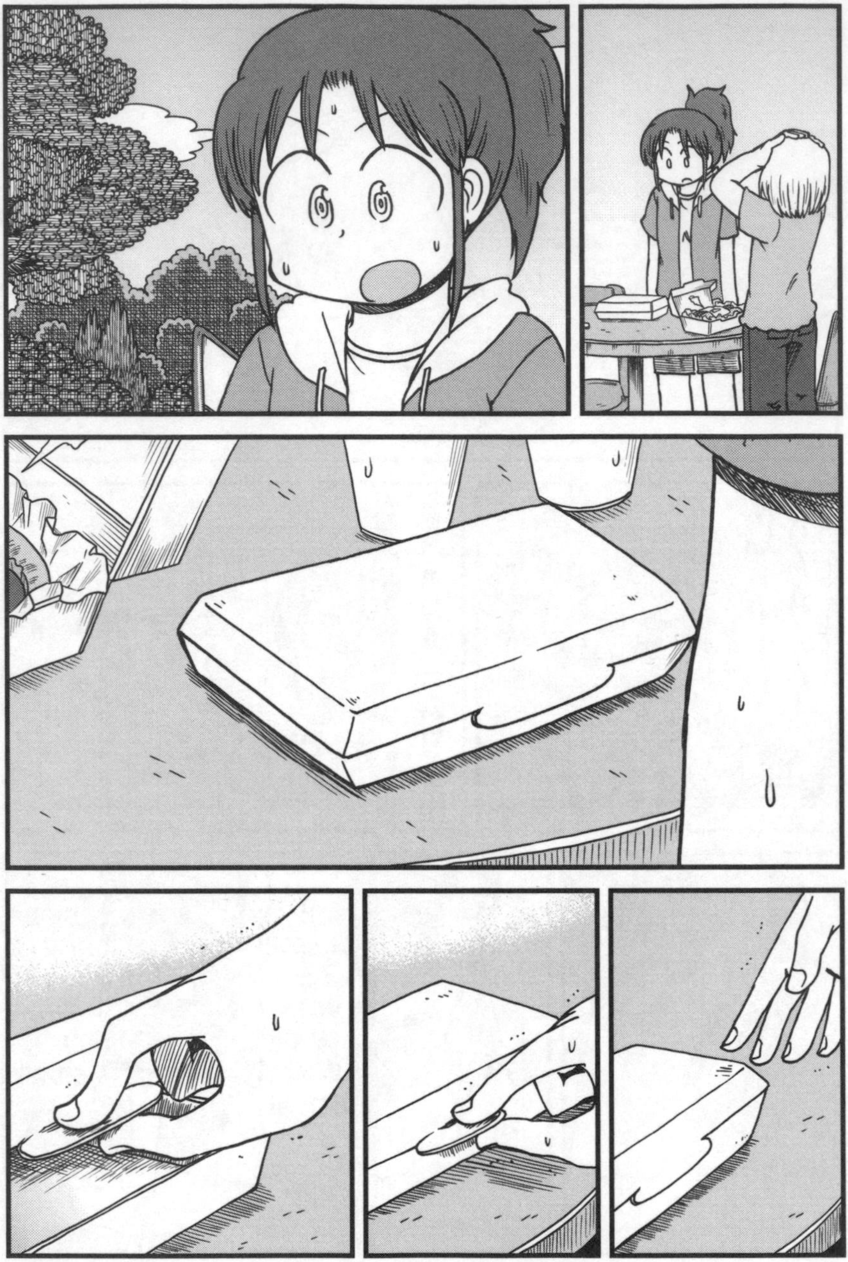

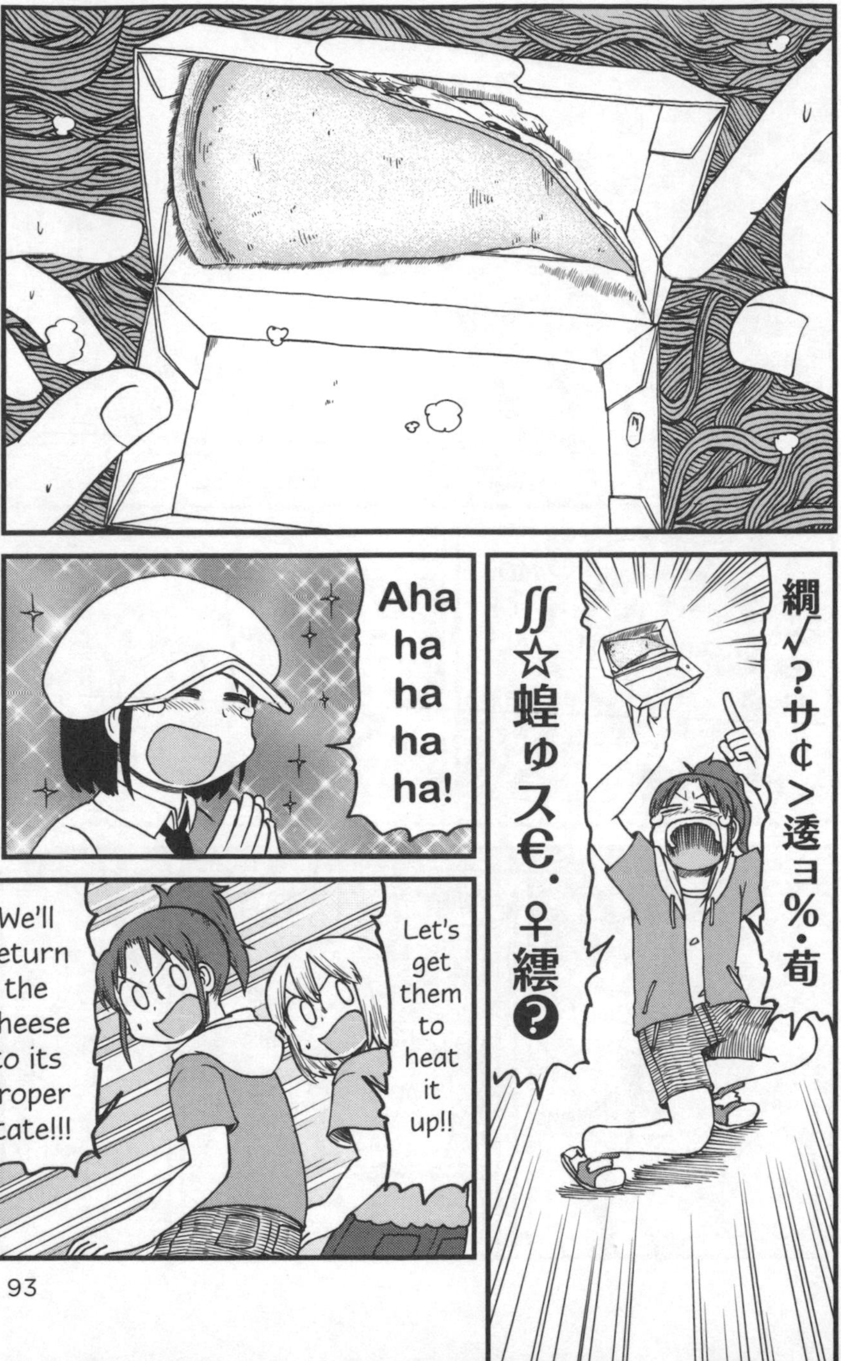

繝√?サ¢>透ョ%・荀
∬☆蝗ゅス€・♀縹❓
Aha ha ha ha ha!
Let's get them to heat it up!!
We'll return the cheese to its proper state!!!

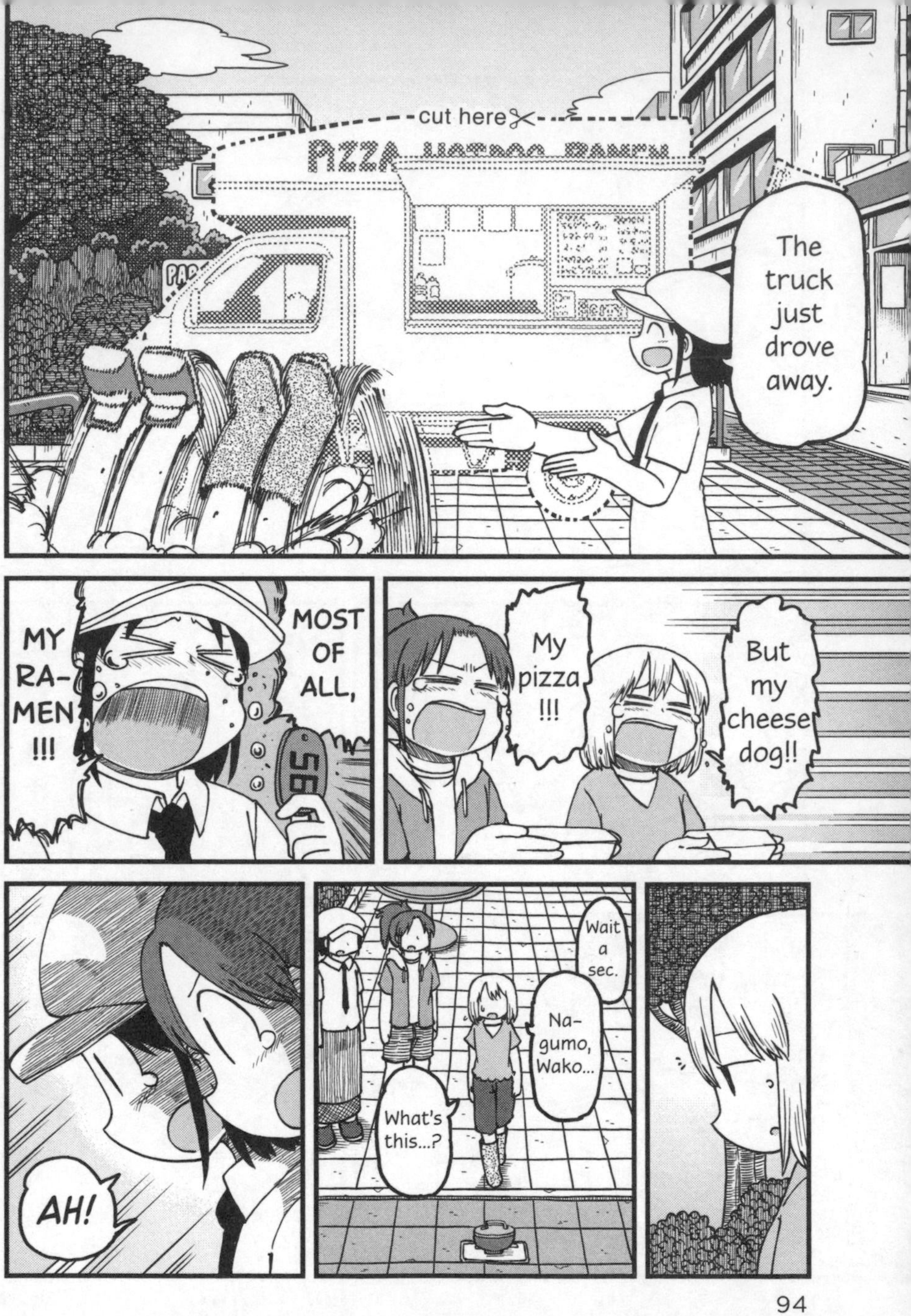
cut here
PIZZA
The truck just drove away.
But my cheese dog!!
My pizza!!!
MOST OF ALL,
MY RA-MEN!!!
Wait a sec.
Na-gumo, Wako...
What's this...?
AH!

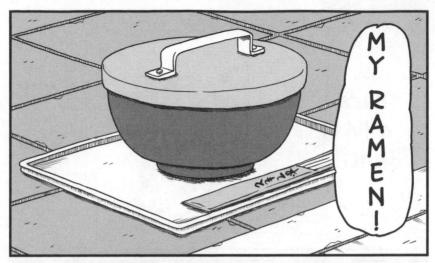

MY RAMEN!
Yaaaay!!!
They didn't forget mine!!!
I guess even that vile fiend
isn't completely devoid of humanity.
...
Huh?
What?
What is it?
Oh... I just ...

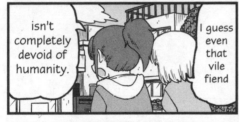

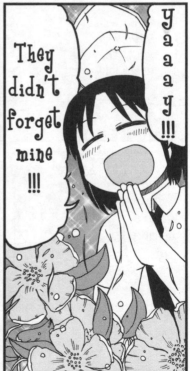

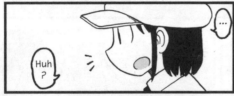

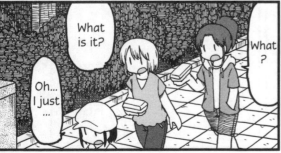

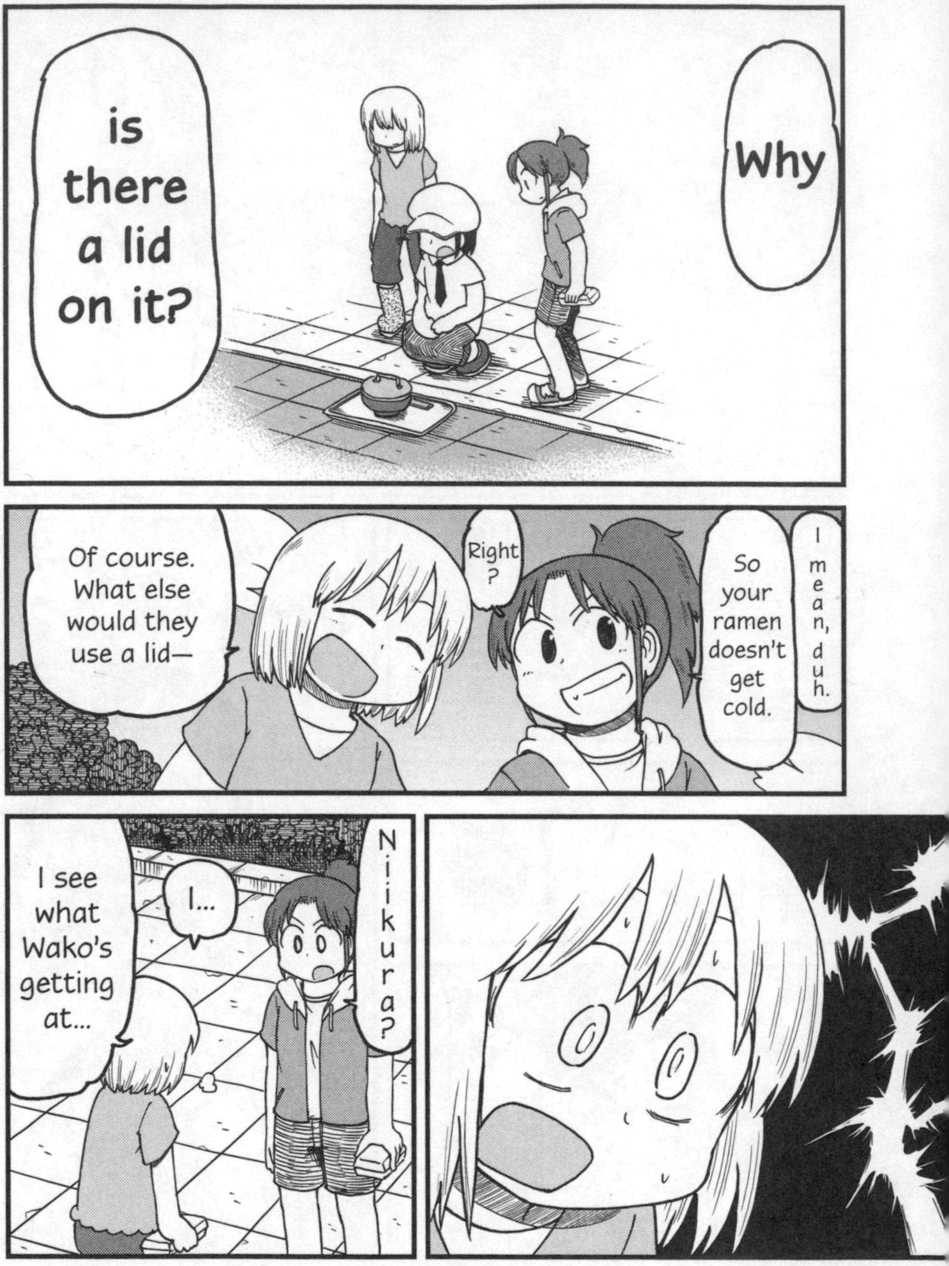
Why
is there a lid on it?
I mean, duh.
So your ramen doesn't get cold.
Right?
Of course. What else would they use a lid—
Niikura?
I...
I see what Wako's getting at...

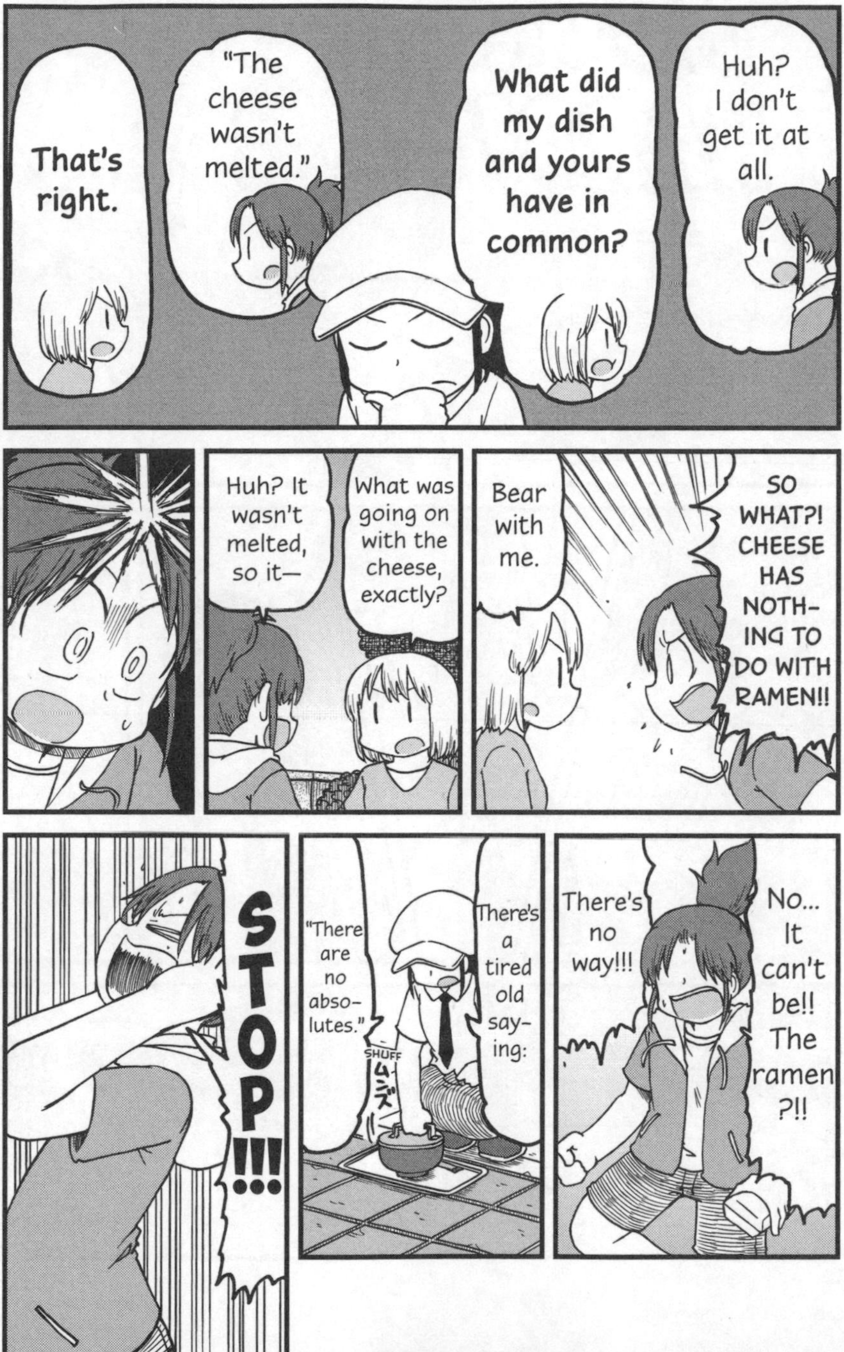
Huh? I don't get it at all.
What did my dish and yours have in common?
"The cheese wasn't melted."
That's right.
SO WHAT?! CHEESE HAS NOTH-ING TO DO WITH RAMEN!!
Bear with me.
What was going on with the cheese, exactly?
Huh? It wasn't melted, so it—
No... It can't be!! The ramen?!!
There's no way!!!
There's a tired old say-ing:
"There are no abso-lutes."
SHUFF
ムンズ
STOP!!!

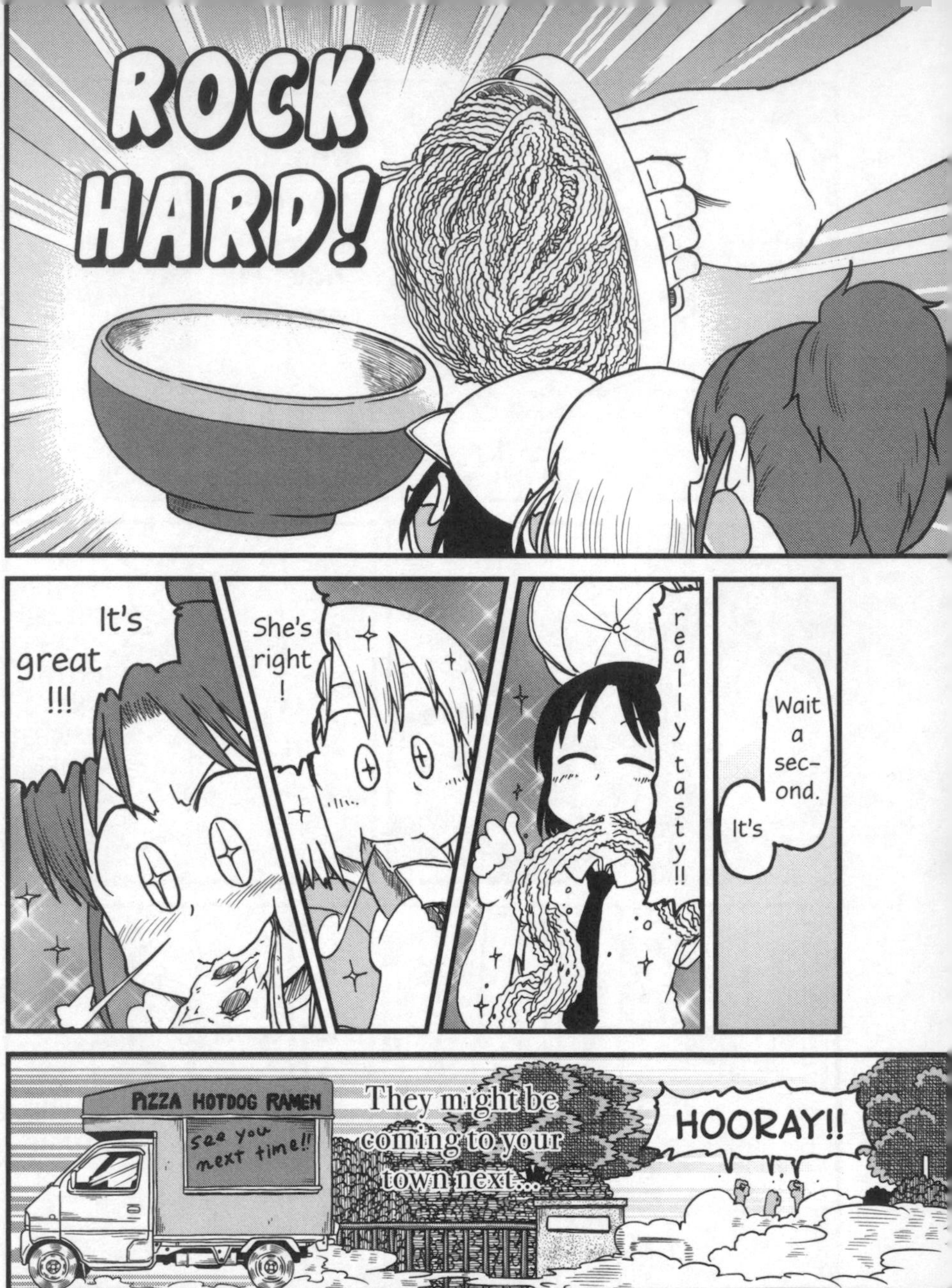
ROCK HARD!
Wait a sec-ond.
It's
really tasty!!
She's right!
It's great!!!
HOORAY!!
They might be coming to your town next...
PIZZA HOTDOG RAMEN
see you next time!!

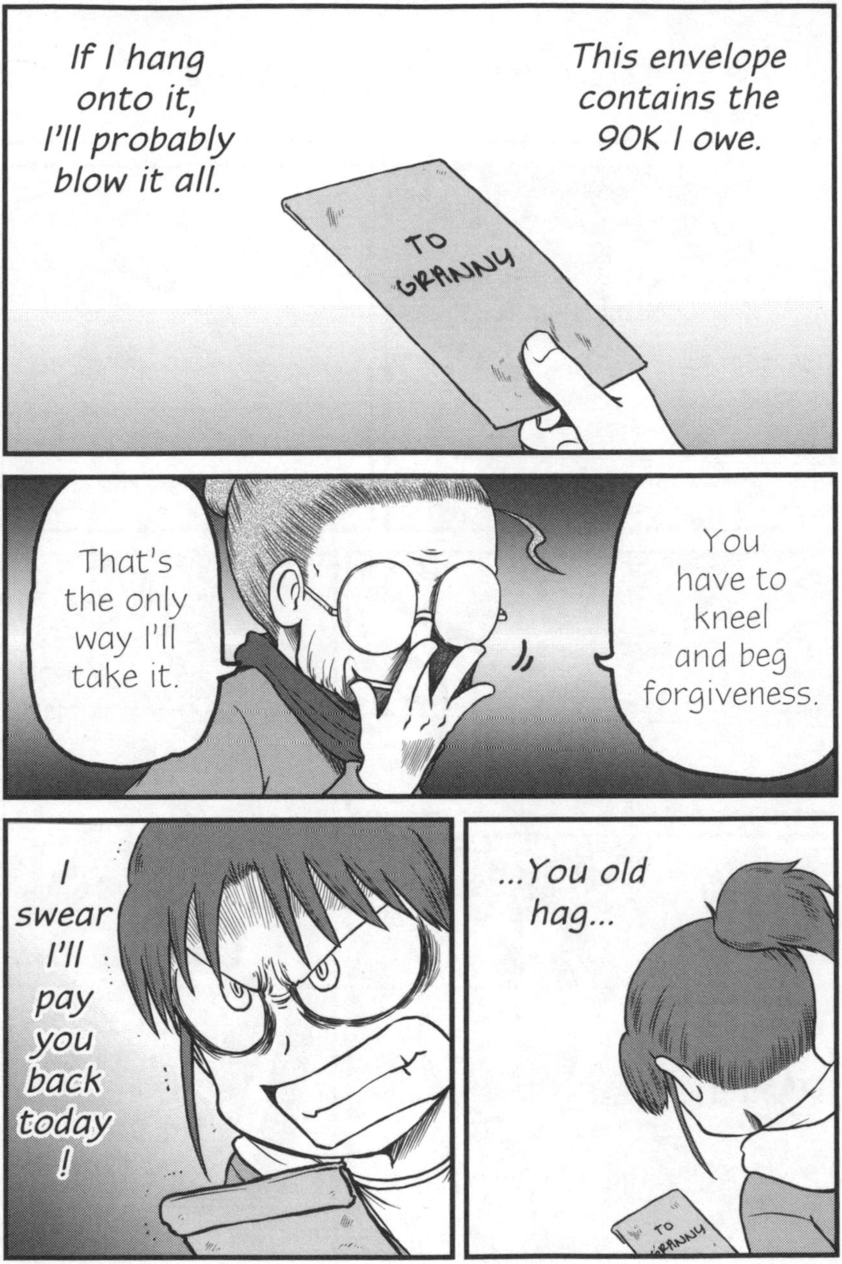
This envelope contains the 90K I owe.
If I hang onto it, I'll probably blow it all.
TO GRANNY
You have to kneel and beg forgiveness.
That's the only way I'll take it.
...You old hag...
TO GRANNY
I swear I'll pay you back today!

Chapter 162 ◈ Payback Plan

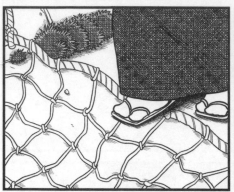

BAM

YOU FELL FOR IT!

OLD HAG !!!

FWIP

BWA HA HA

NOW LET ME PAY YOU BACK, DAMMIT!!!

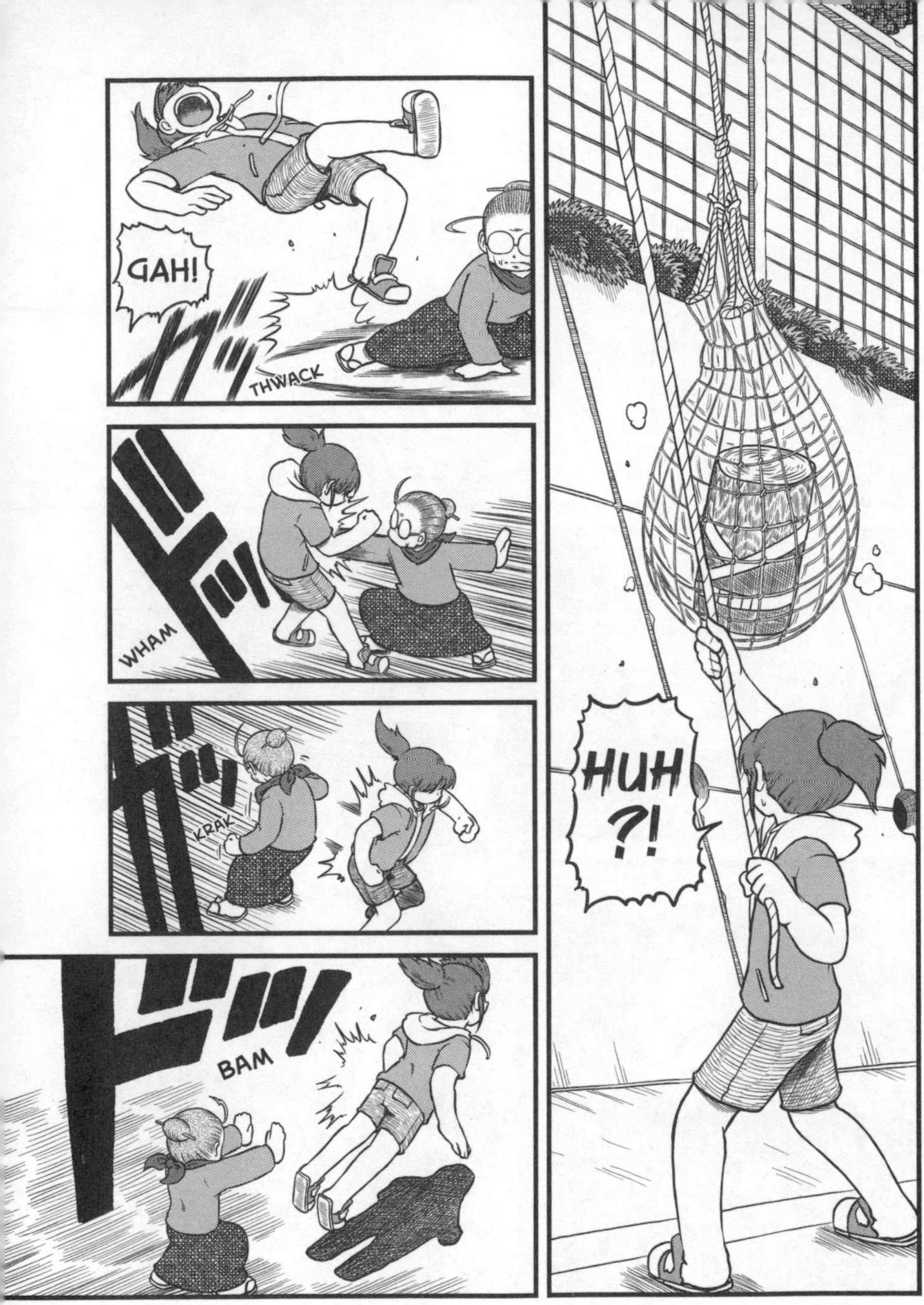
HUH ?!
GAH!
THWACK
WHAM
KRAK
BAM

!
YAMABUSHI
!
!
ド
THUD

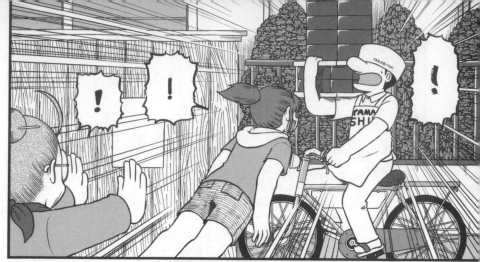

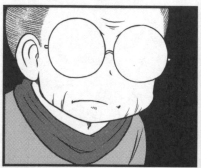

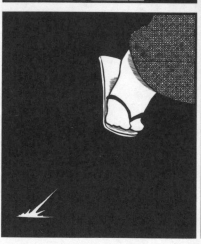

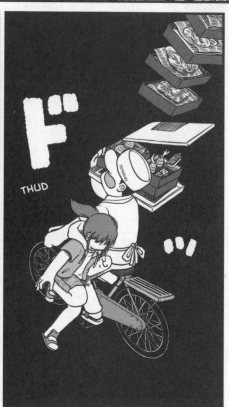

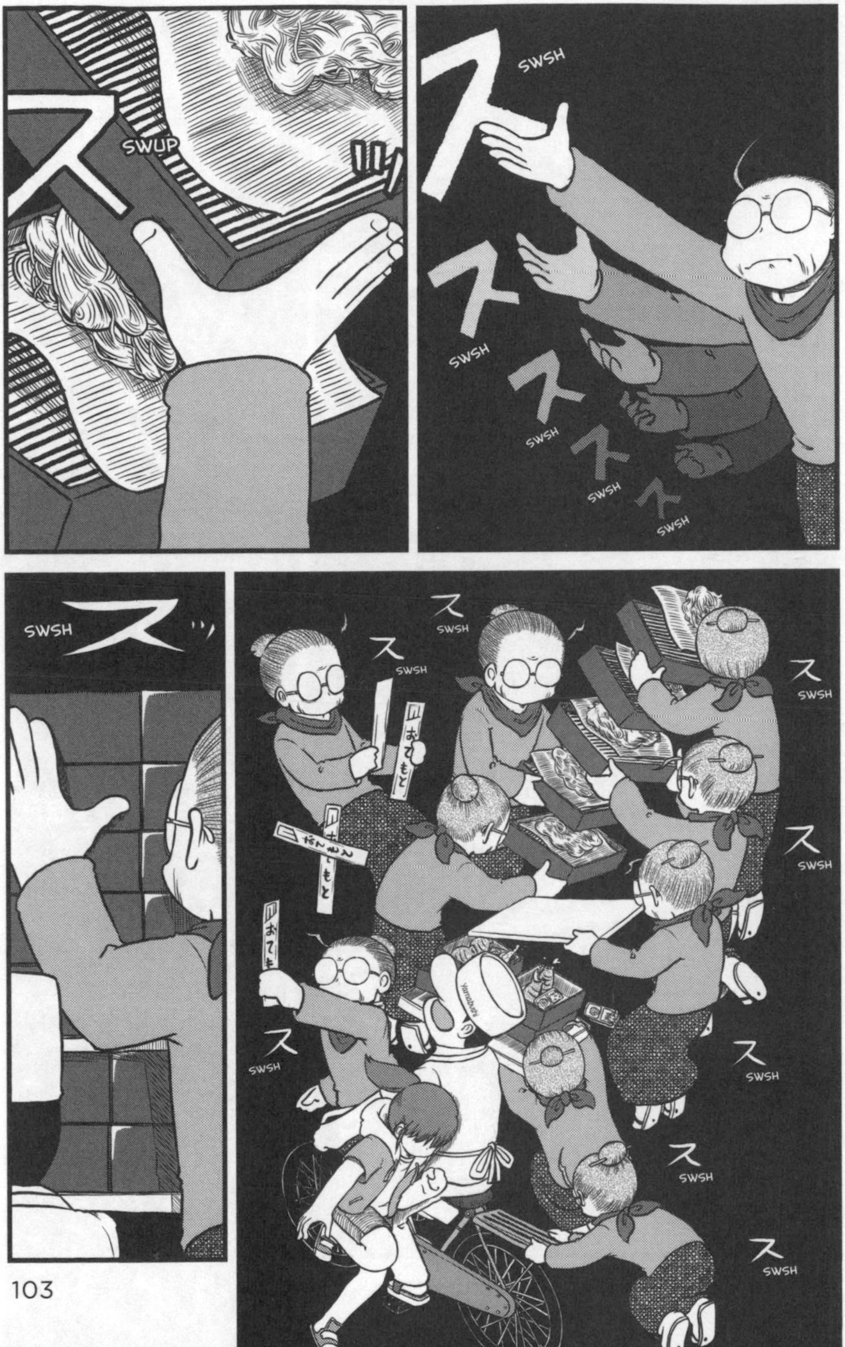

ス
SWSH
ス
SWSH
ス
SWSH
ス
SWSH
ス
SWSH
ス
SWUP
ス
SWSH
ス
SWSH
ス
SWSH
ス
SWSH
ス
SWSH
おてもと
ス
SWSH
ス
SWSH
ス
SWSH
SWSH
スッ

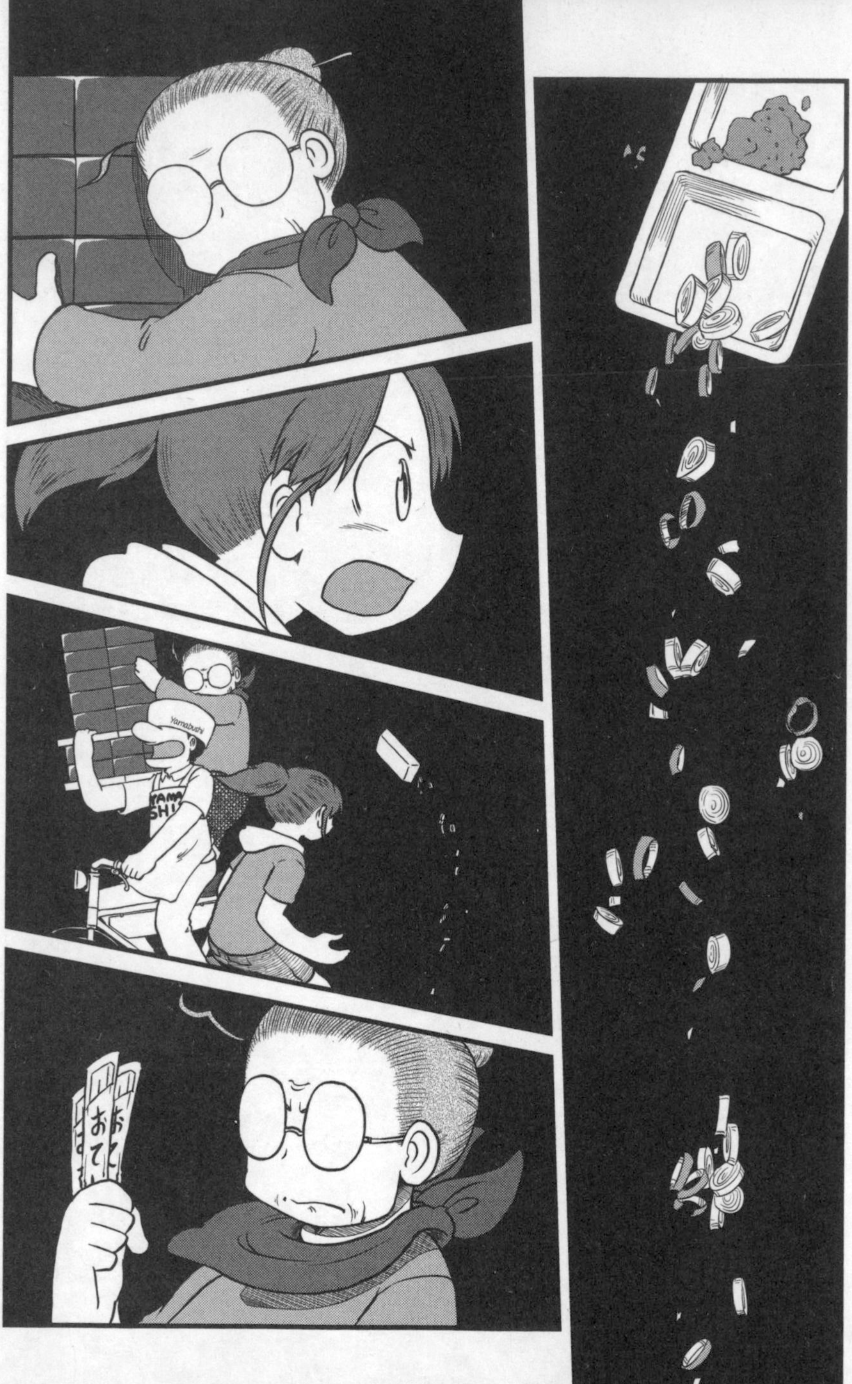
Yamabushi
おて

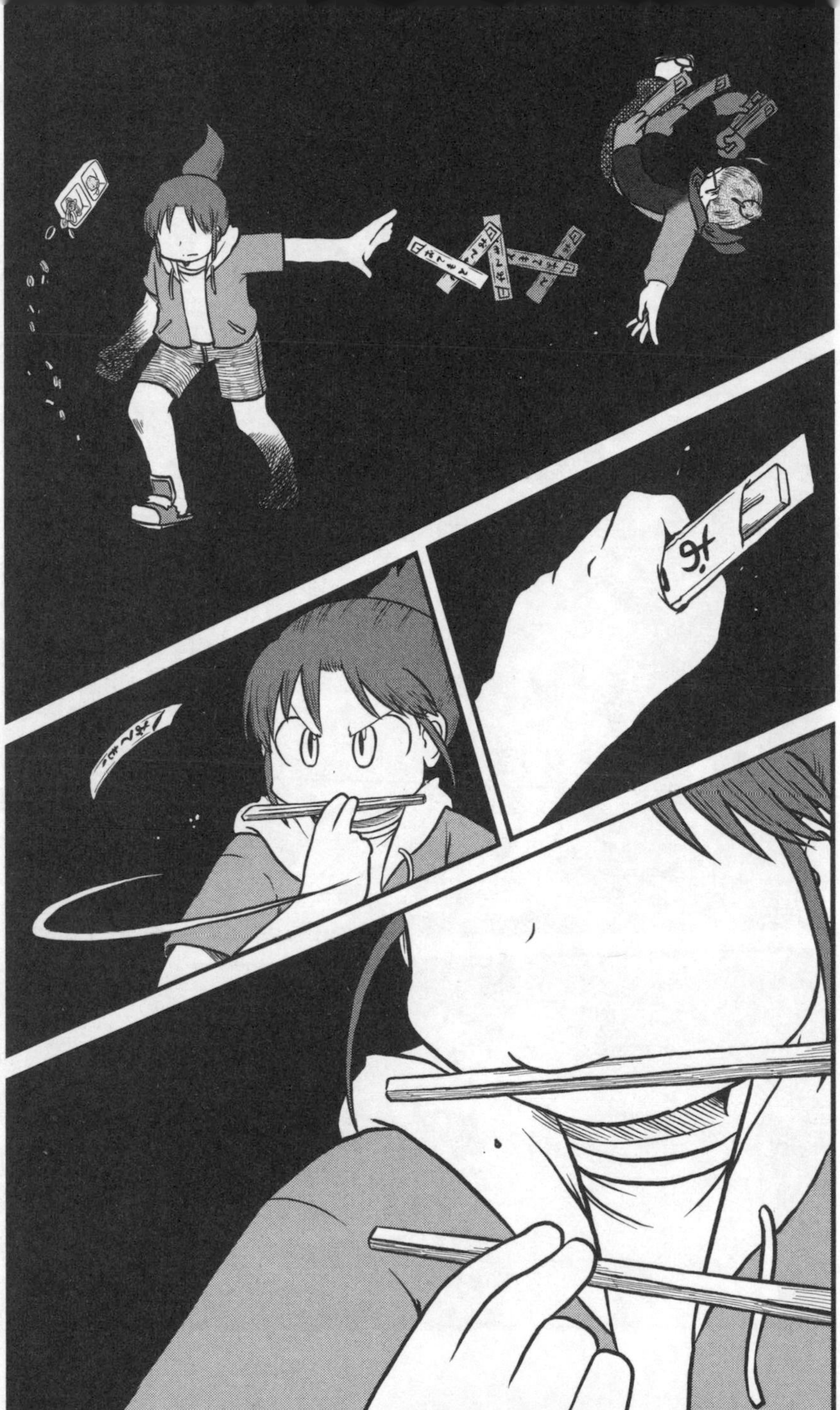

ス SWSH
ス SWSH
ス SWSH
パ WHP
パ WHP
パ WHP
ス SWSH
ス SWSH
ス SWSH
ス SWSH
ス SWSH
パ WHP
パ WHP
パ WHP
パ WHP
パ WHP
パ WHP
パ WHP
パ WHP
ス SWSH

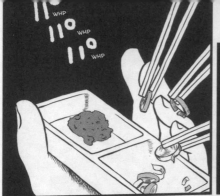

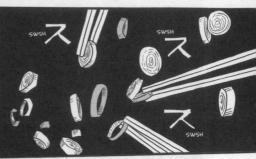

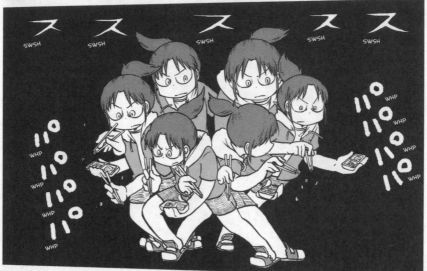

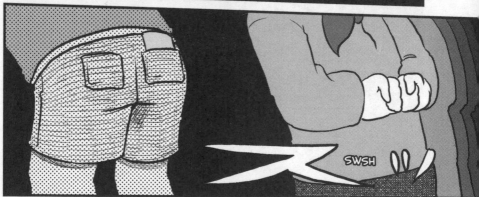

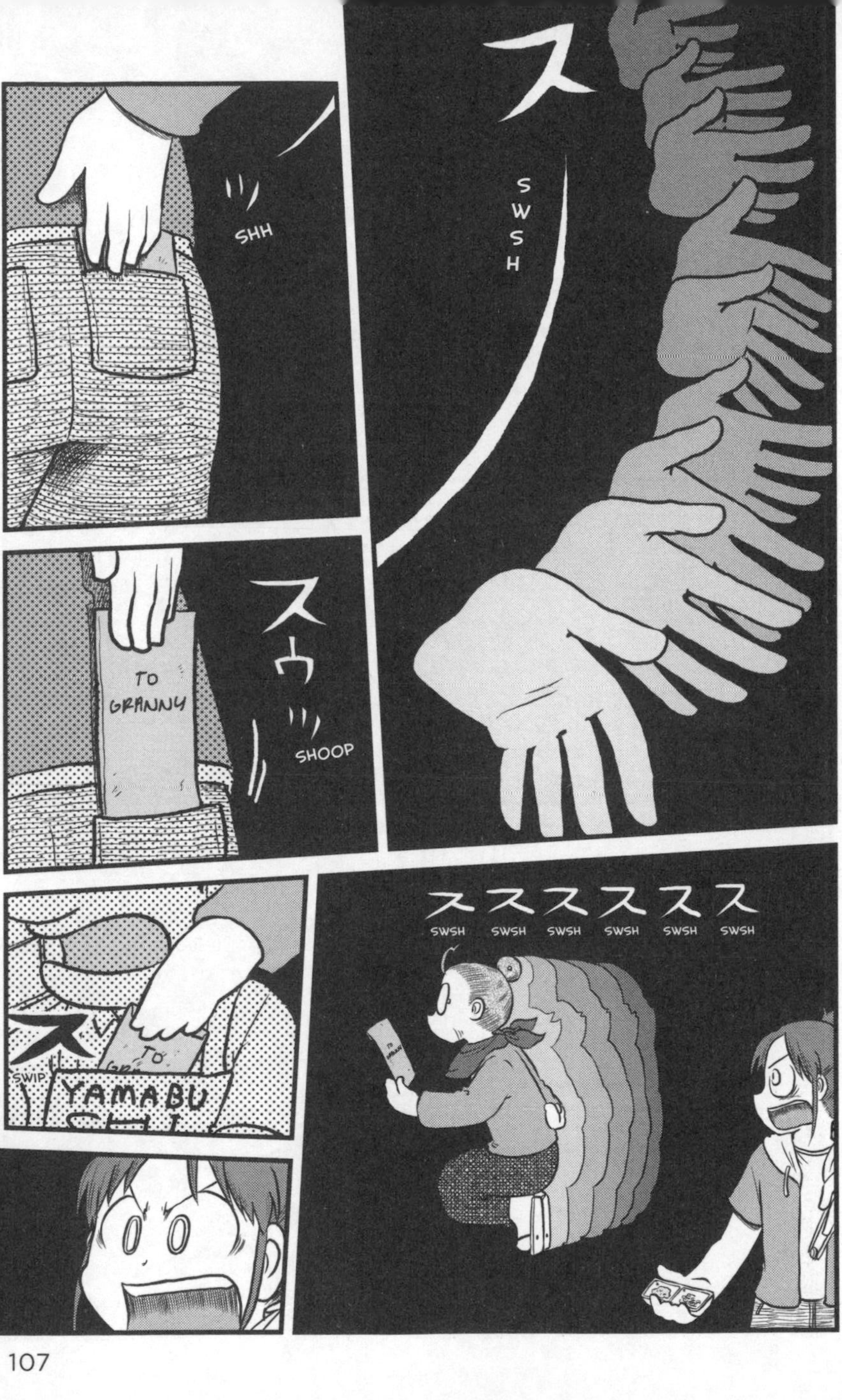
ス
SWSH
ッ
SHH
TO GRANNY
スウッ
SHOOP
スススススス
SWSH SWSH SWSH SWSH SWSH SWSH
ス
SWIP

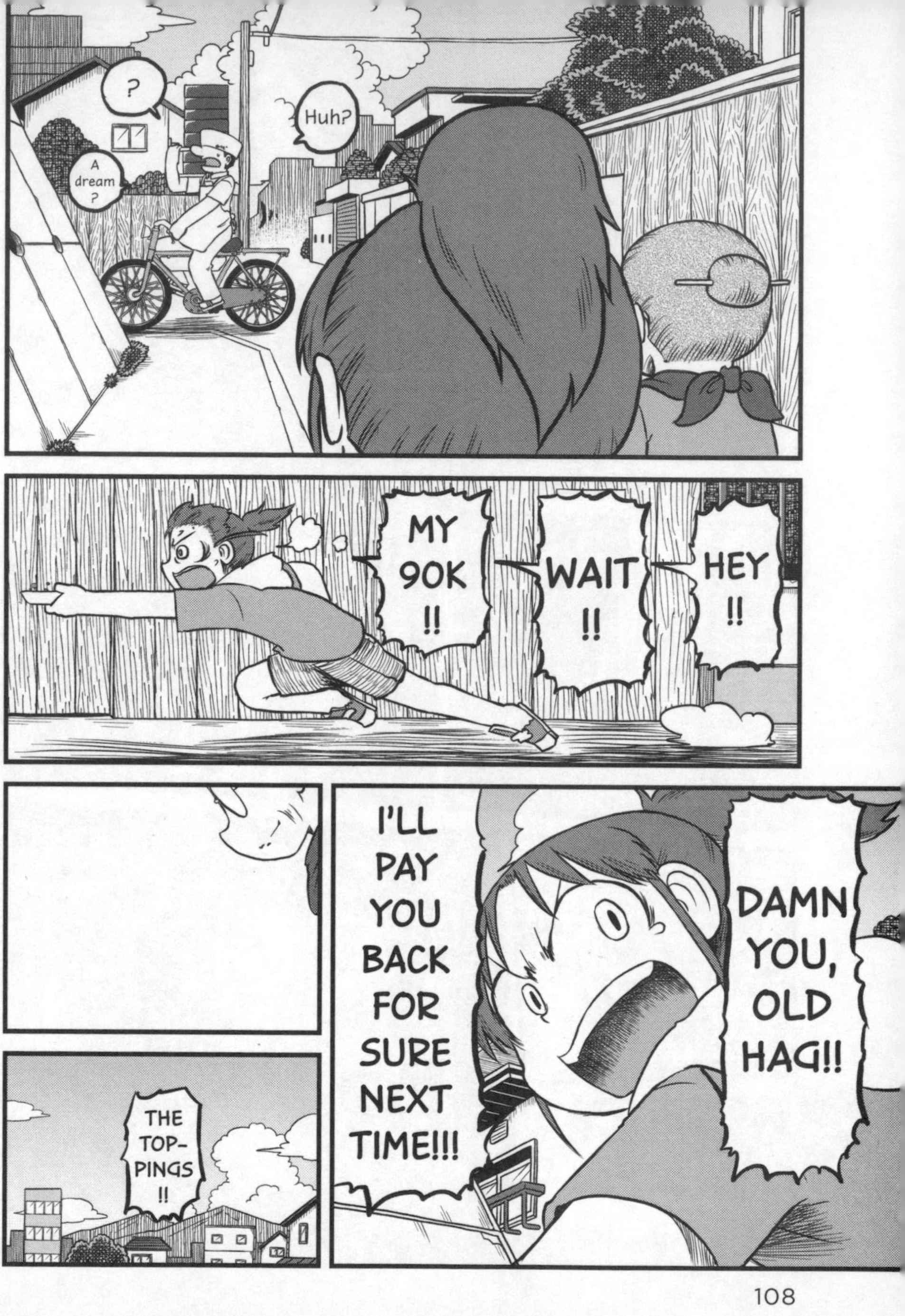
Huh?
?
A dream?
HEY!!
WAIT!!
MY 90K!!
DAMN YOU, OLD HAG!!
I'LL PAY YOU BACK FOR SURE NEXT TIME!!!
THE TOPPINGS!!

CITY

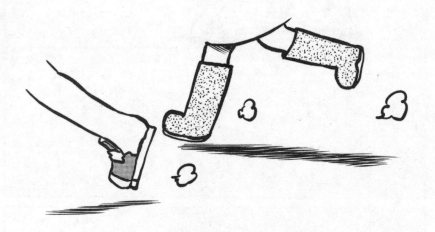

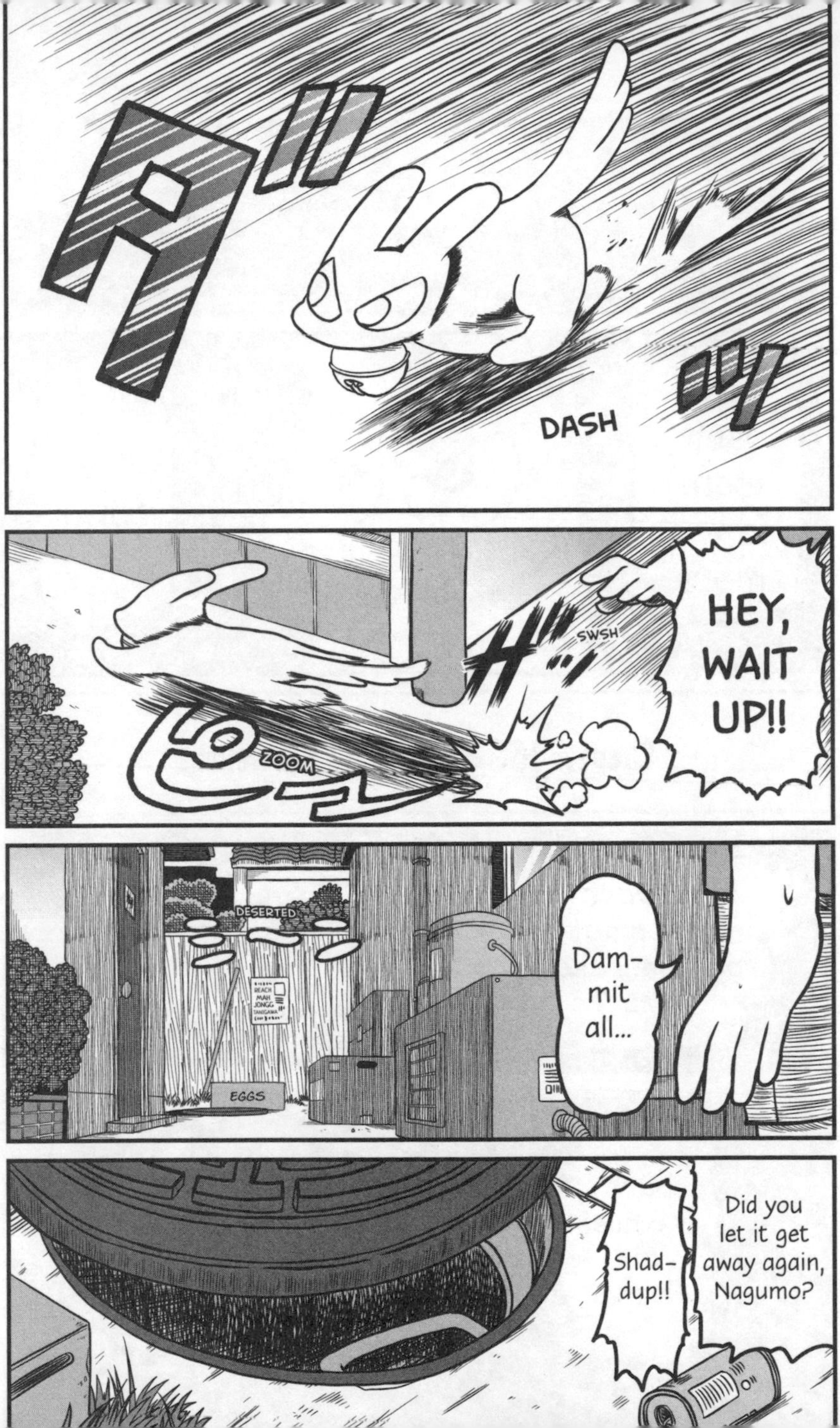
DASH
HEY, WAIT UP!!
SWSH
ZOOM
Dam-mit all...
DESERTED
REACH MAH JONGG TANIGAWA
EGGS
Did you let it get away again, Nagumo?
Shad-dup!!

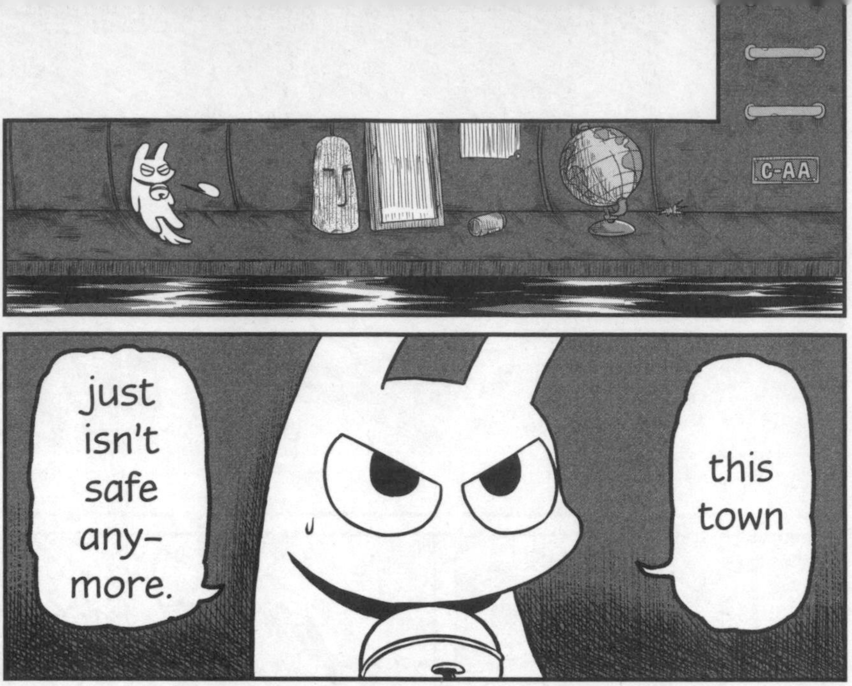
C-AA
this town
just isn't safe any-more.

Chapter 163 CITY Dwellers

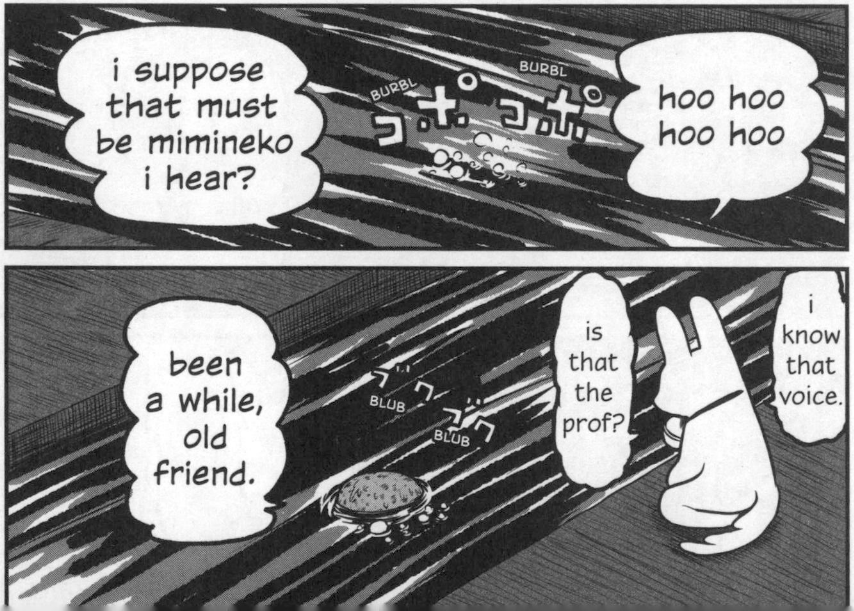
hoo hoo hoo hoo
BURBL
BURBL
i suppose that must be mimineko i hear?
i know that voice.
is that the prof?
BLUB
BLUB
been a while, old friend.

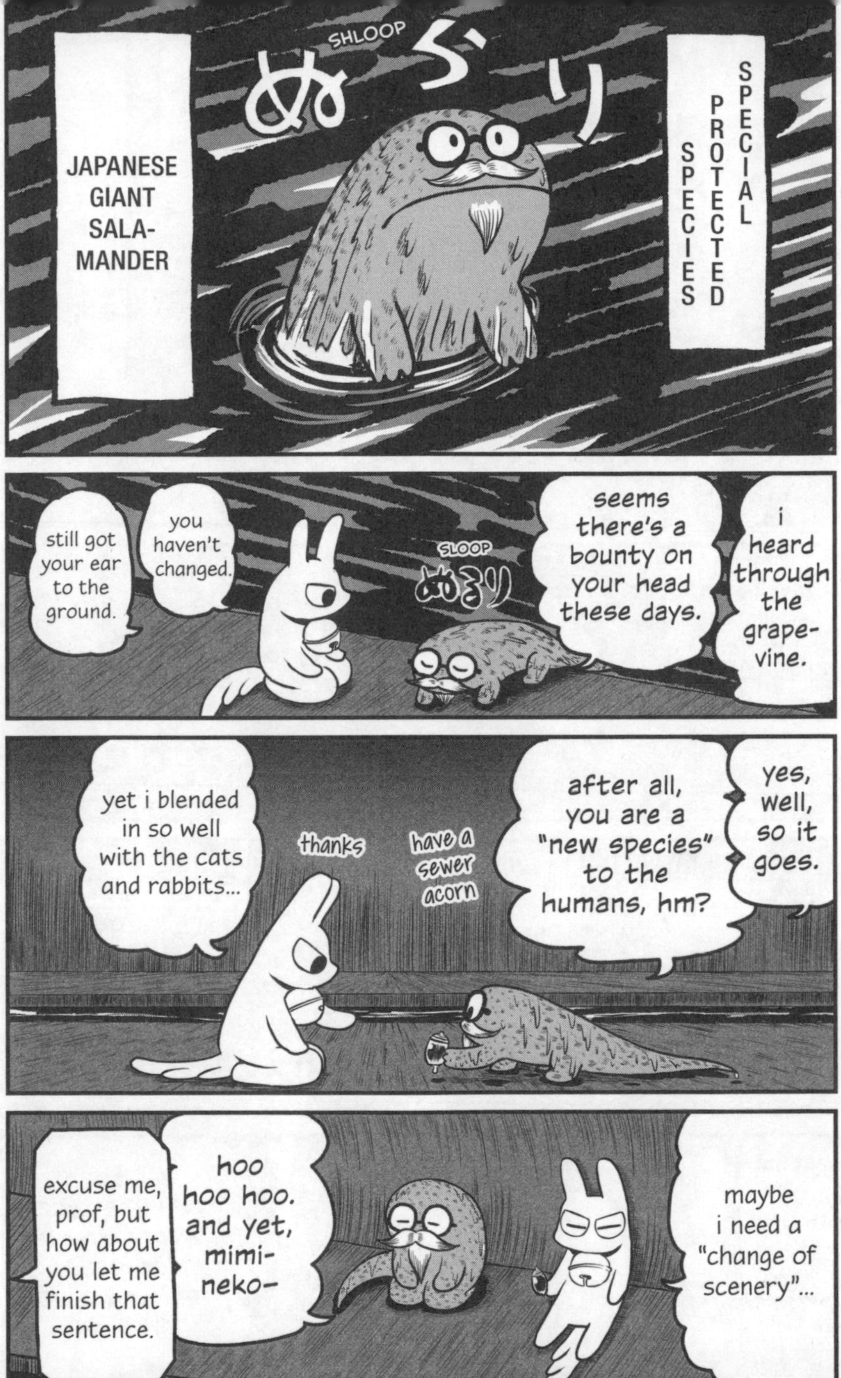
SPECIAL PROTECTED SPECIES
ぬらり
SHLOOP
JAPANESE GIANT SALA-MANDER
i heard through the grape-vine.
seems there's a bounty on your head these days.
ぬるり
SLOOP
you haven't changed.
still got your ear to the ground.
yes, well, so it goes.
after all, you are a "new species" to the humans, hm?
have a sewer acorn
thanks
yet i blended in so well with the cats and rabbits...
maybe i need a "change of scenery"...
hoo hoo hoo. and yet, mimi-neko-
excuse me, prof, but how about you let me finish that sentence.

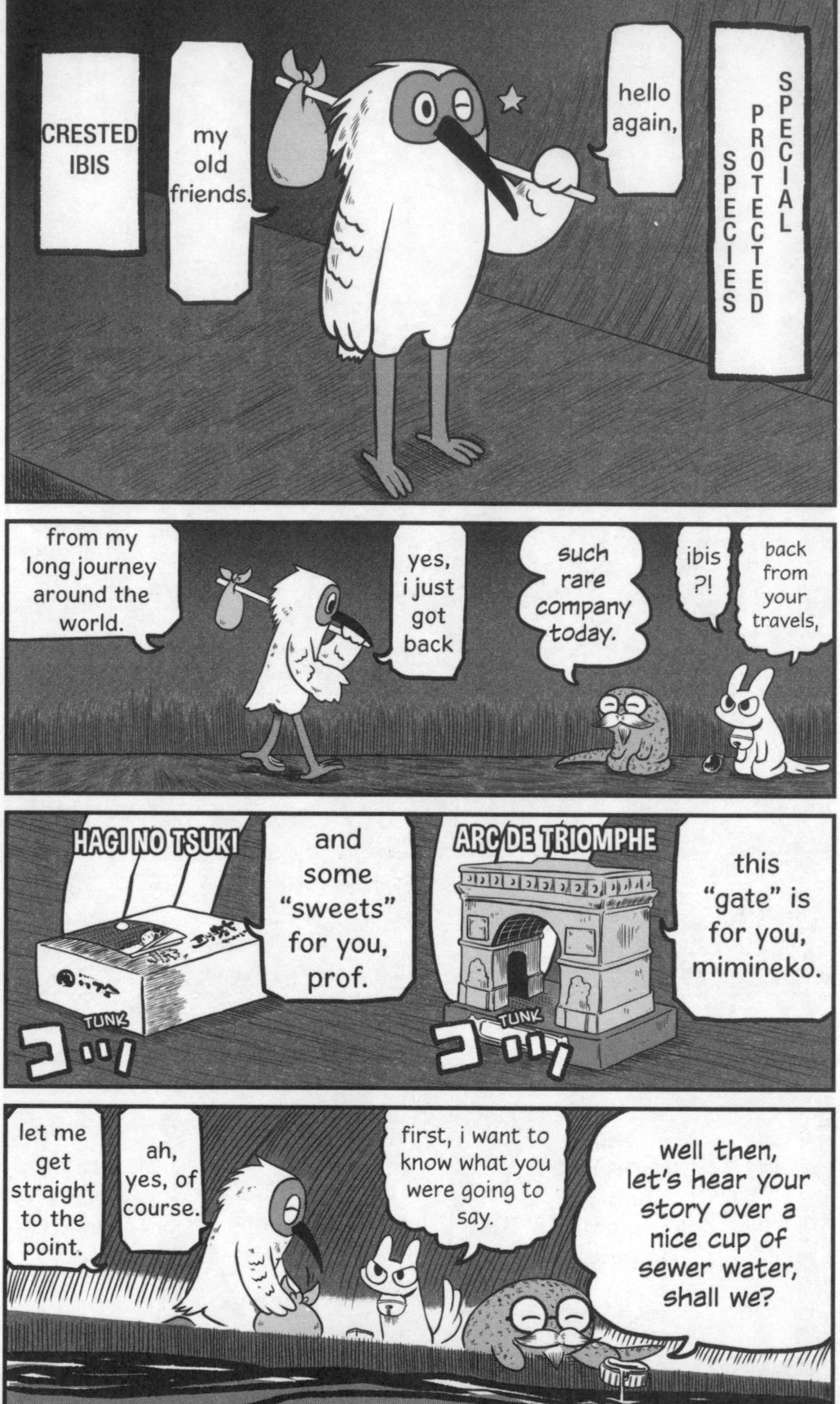
SPECIAL PROTECTED SPECIES
hello again,
my old friends.
CRESTED IBIS
back from your travels,
ibis ?!
such rare company today.
yes, i just got back
from my long journey around the world.
this "gate" is for you, mimineko.
ARC DE TRIOMPHE
TUNK
and some "sweets" for you, prof.
HAGI NO TSUKI
TUNK
well then, let's hear your story over a nice cup of sewer water, shall we?
first, i want to know what you were going to say.
ah, yes, of course.
let me get straight to the point.

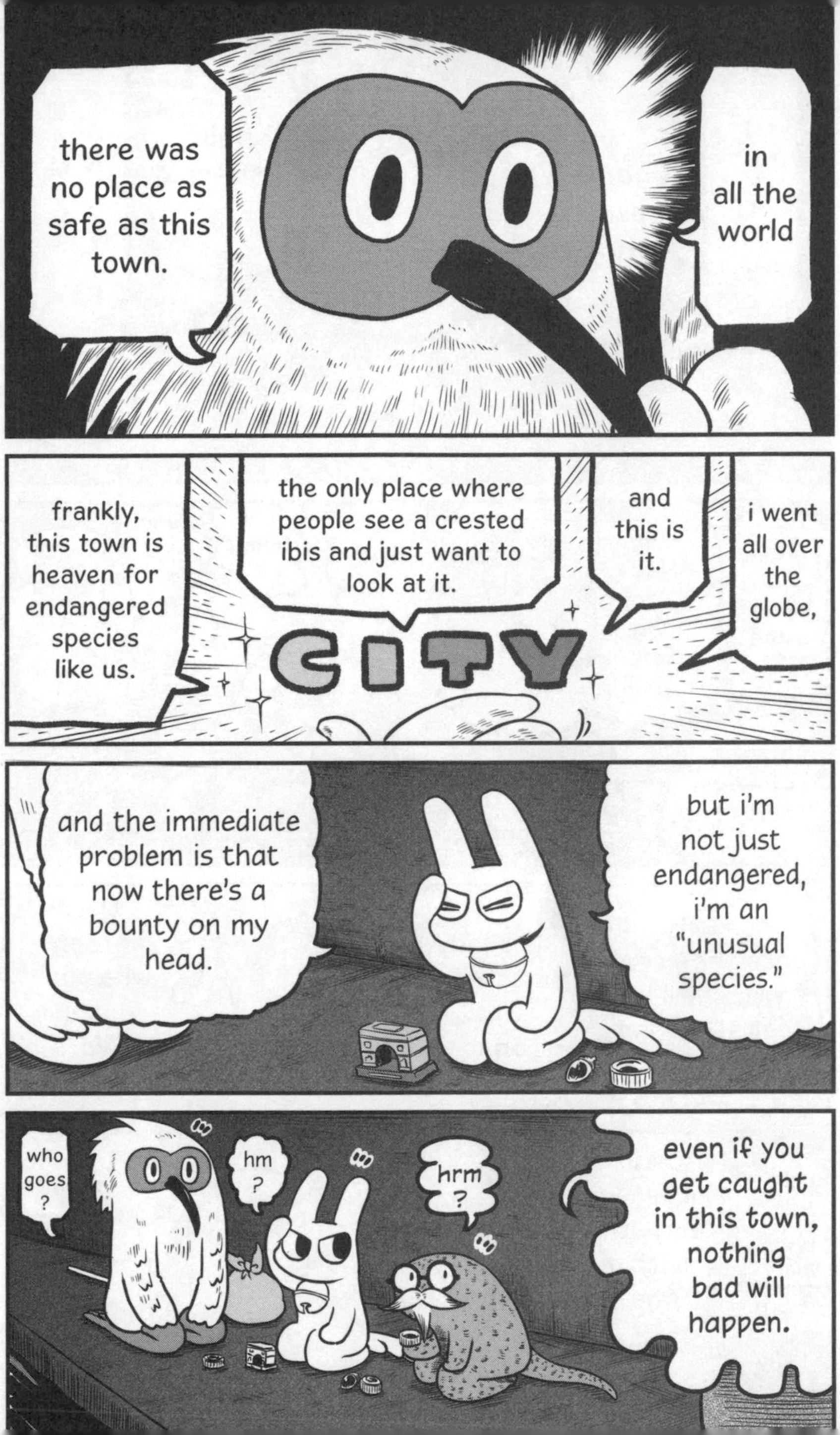
in all the world
there was no place as safe as this town.
i went all over the globe,
and this is it.
the only place where people see a crested ibis and just want to look at it.
frankly, this town is heaven for endangered species like us.
CITY
but i'm not just endangered, i'm an "unusual species."
and the immediate problem is that now there's a bounty on my head.
even if you get caught in this town, nothing bad will happen.
hrm ?
hm ?
who goes ?

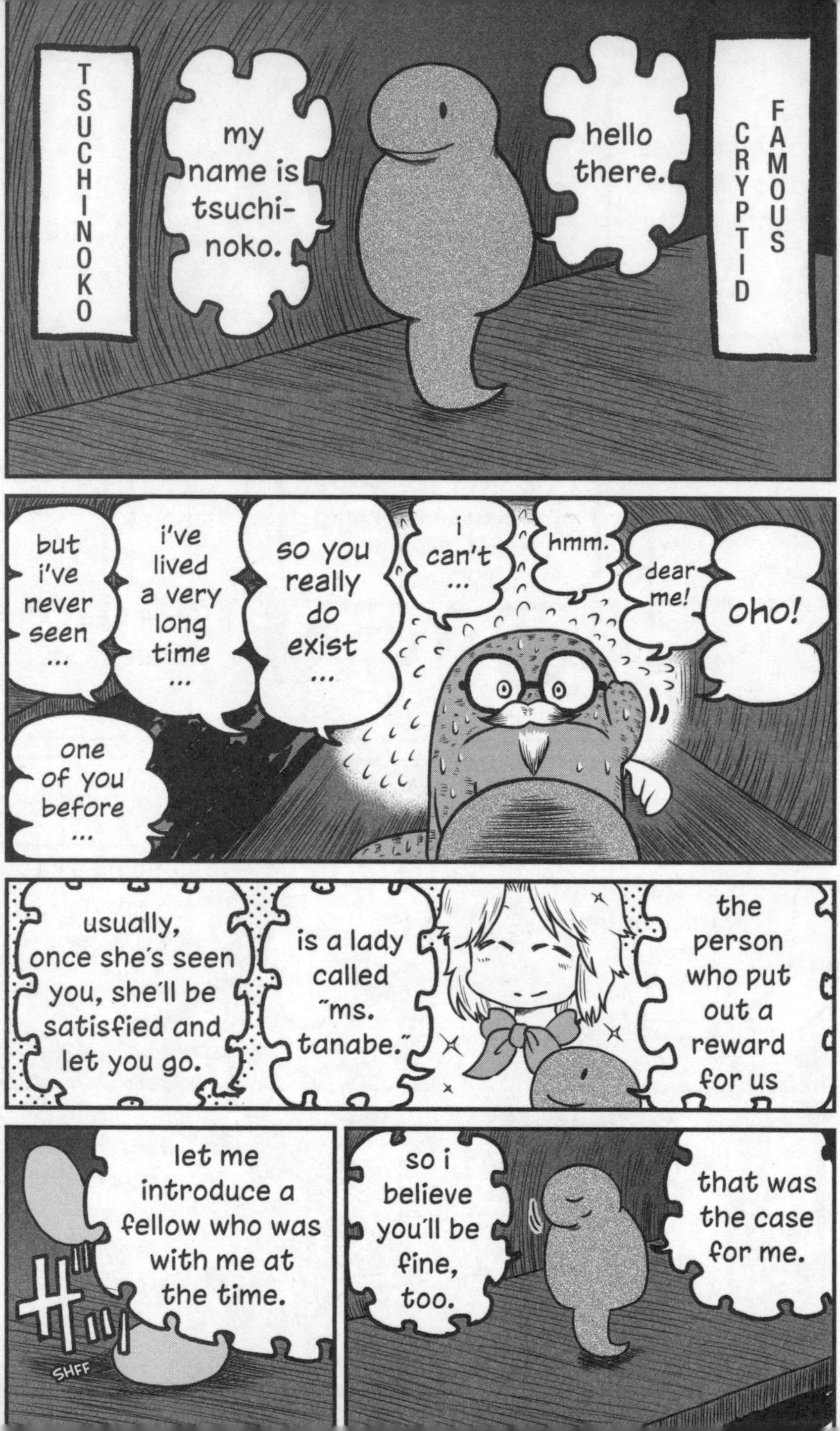
FAMOUS CRYPTID
hello there.
my name is tsuchi-noko.
TSUCHINOKO
oho!
dear me!
hmm.
i can't ...
so you really do exist ...
i've lived a very long time ...
but i've never seen ...
one of you before ...
the person who put out a reward for us
is a lady called "ms. tanabe."
usually, once she's seen you, she'll be satisfied and let you go.
that was the case for me.
so i believe you'll be fine, too.
let me introduce a fellow who was with me at the time.
SHFF

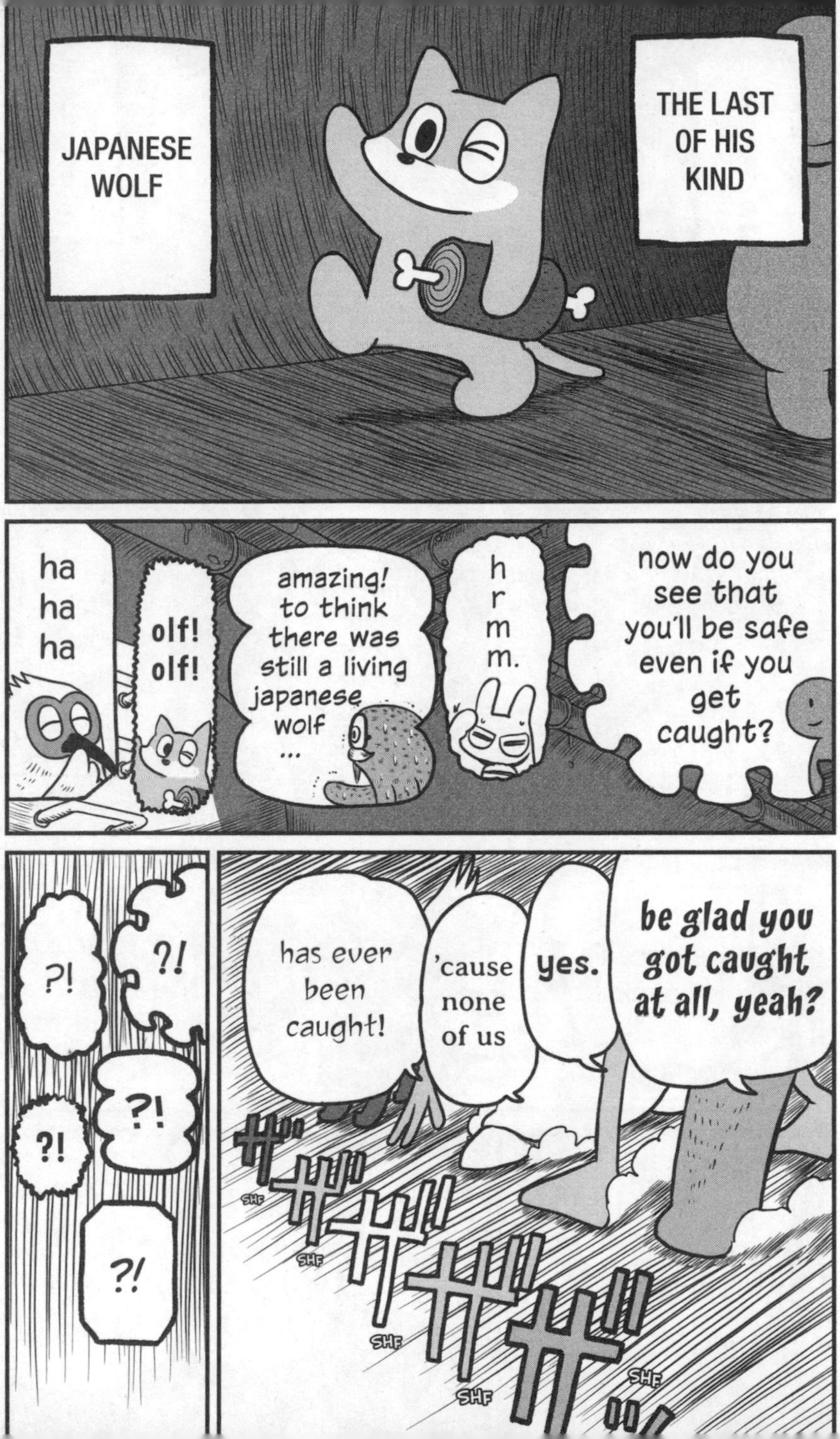
THE LAST OF HIS KIND
JAPANESE WOLF
now do you see that you'll be safe even if you get caught?
hrmm.
amazing! to think there was still a living japanese wolf ...
olf! olf!
ha ha ha
be glad you got caught at all, yeah?
yes.
'cause none of us
has ever been caught!
SHF
SHF
SHF
SHF
SHF
?!
?!
?!
?!
?!

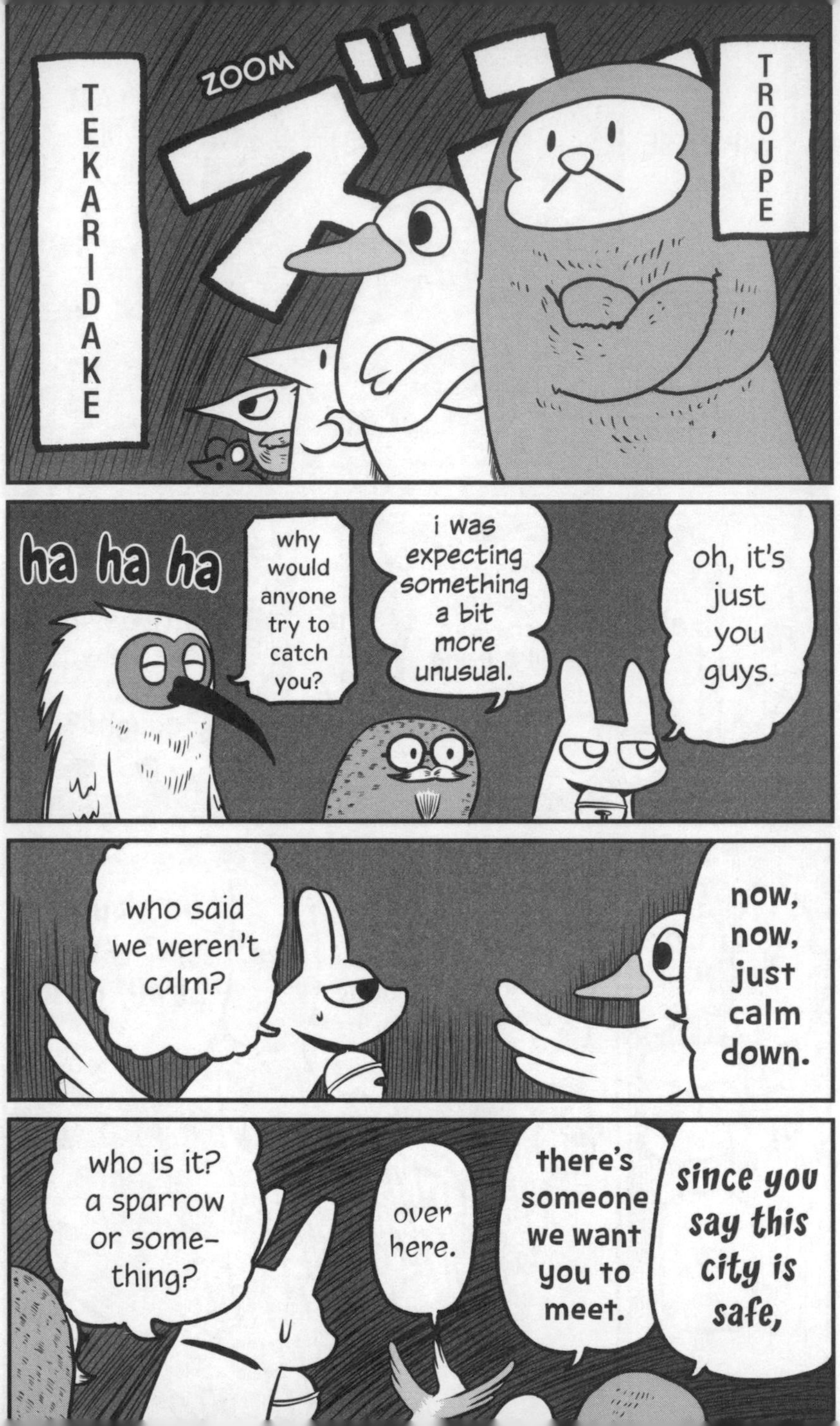
TROUPE
ZOOM
TEKARIDAKE
oh, it's just you guys.
i was expecting something a bit more unusual.
why would anyone try to catch you?
ha ha ha
now, now, just calm down.
who said we weren't calm?
since you say this city is safe,
there's someone we want you to meet.
over here.
who is it? a sparrow or some-thing?

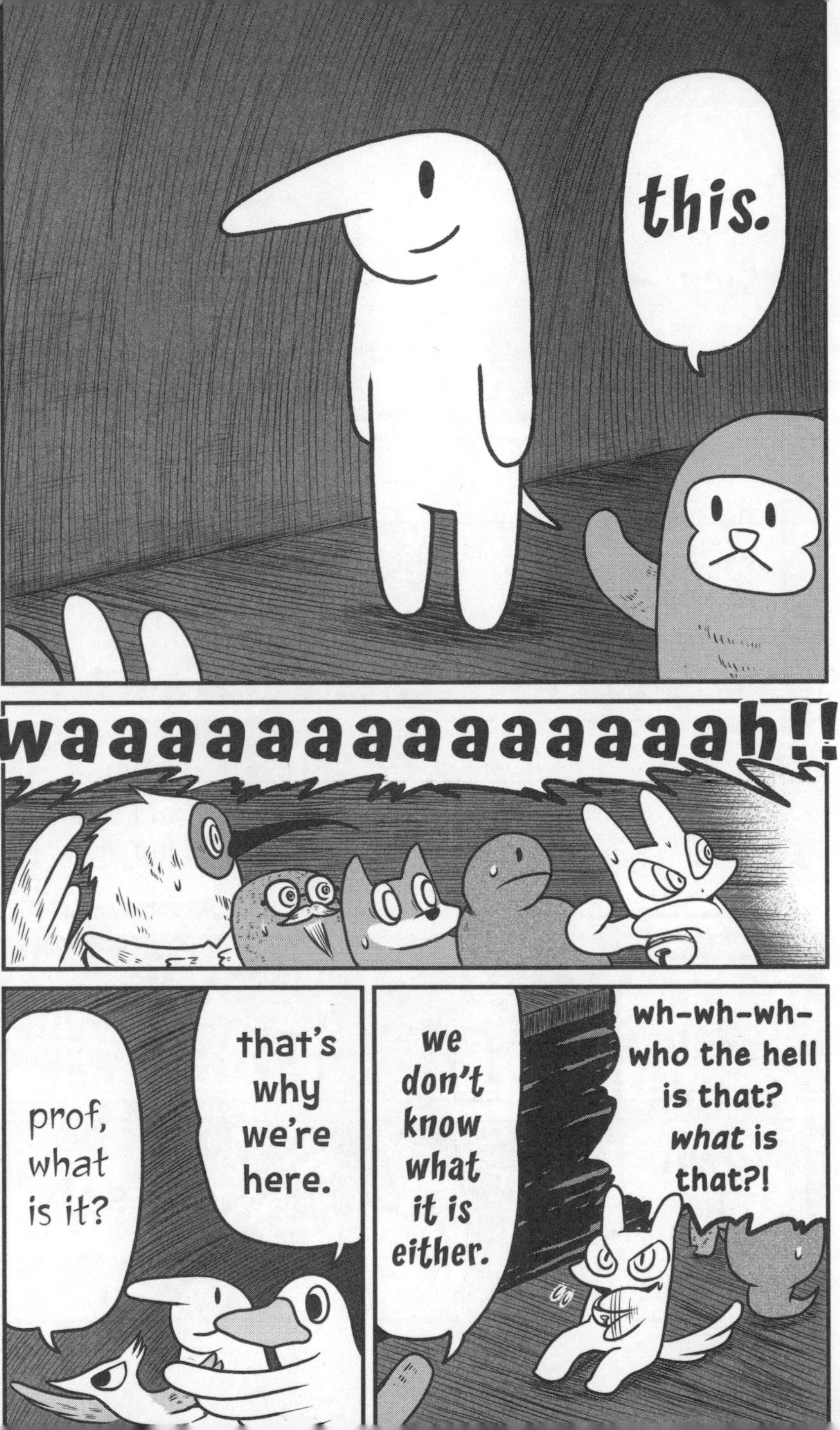
this.
waaaaaaaaaaaaaaah!!
wh-wh-wh- who the hell is that? *what* is that?!
we don't know what it is either.
that's why we're here.
prof, what is it?

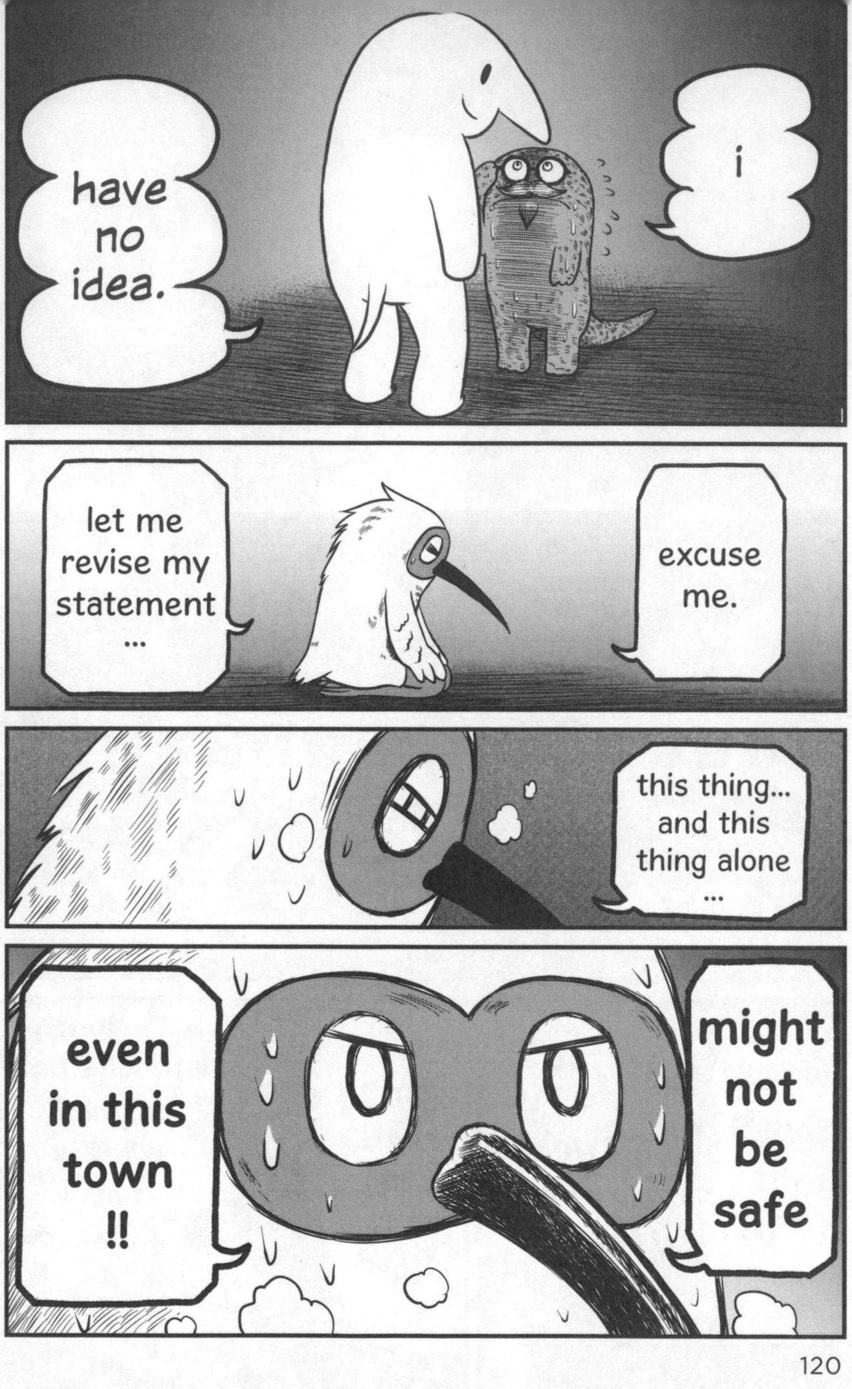
i
have no idea.
excuse me.
let me revise my statement ...
this thing... and this thing alone ...
might not be safe
even in this town !!

TO
GRANNY

CITY

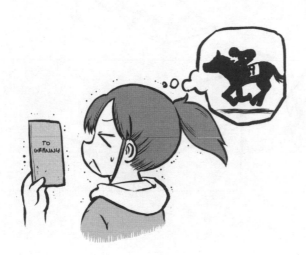

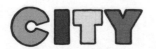

CITY

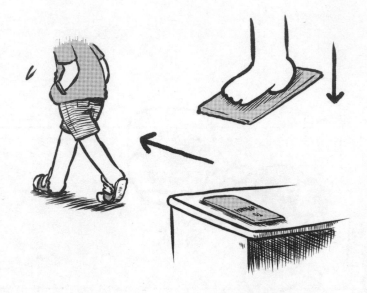

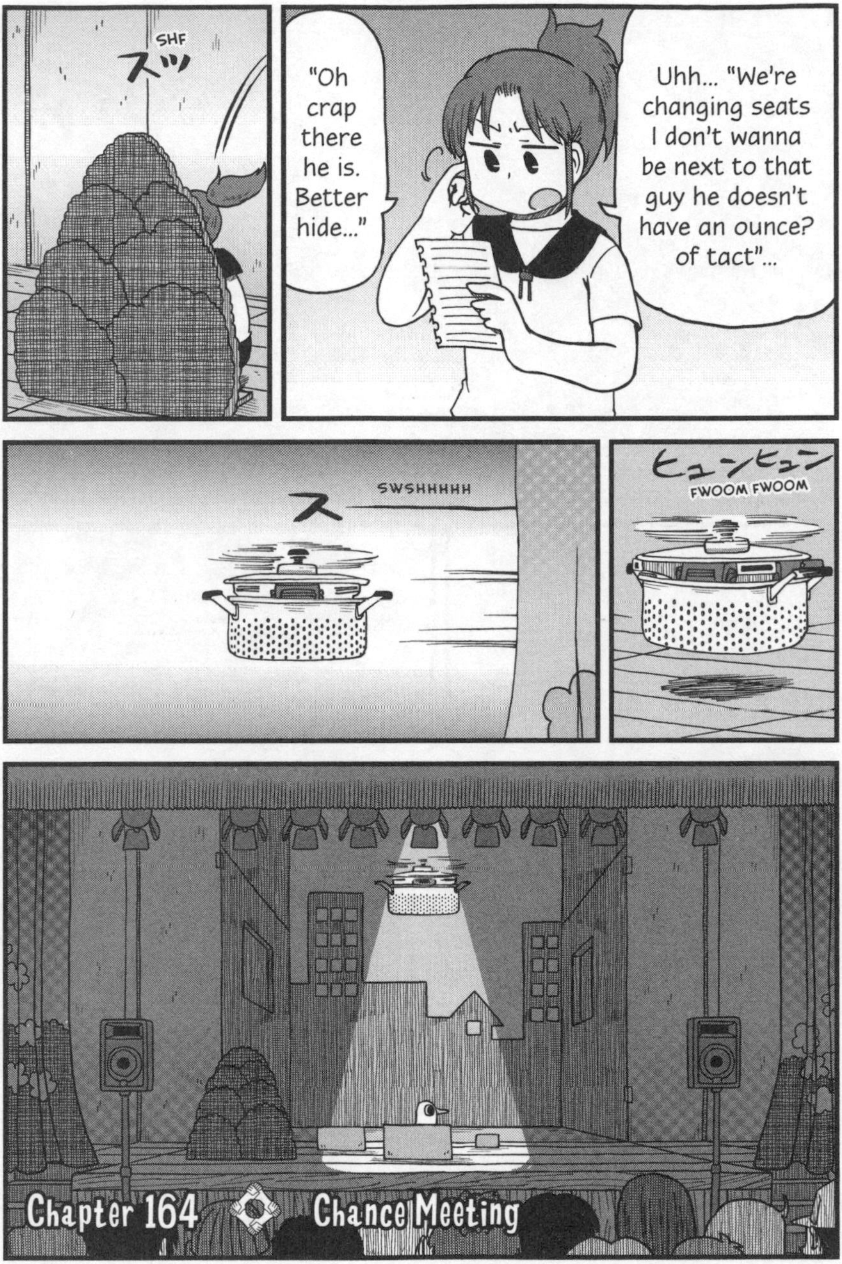
Uhh... "We're changing seats I don't wanna be next to that guy he doesn't have an ounce? of tact"...
"Oh crap there he is. Better hide..."
スッ
SHF
ヒュンヒュン
FWOOM FWOOM
ス
SWSHHHHH
Chapter 164
Chance Meeting

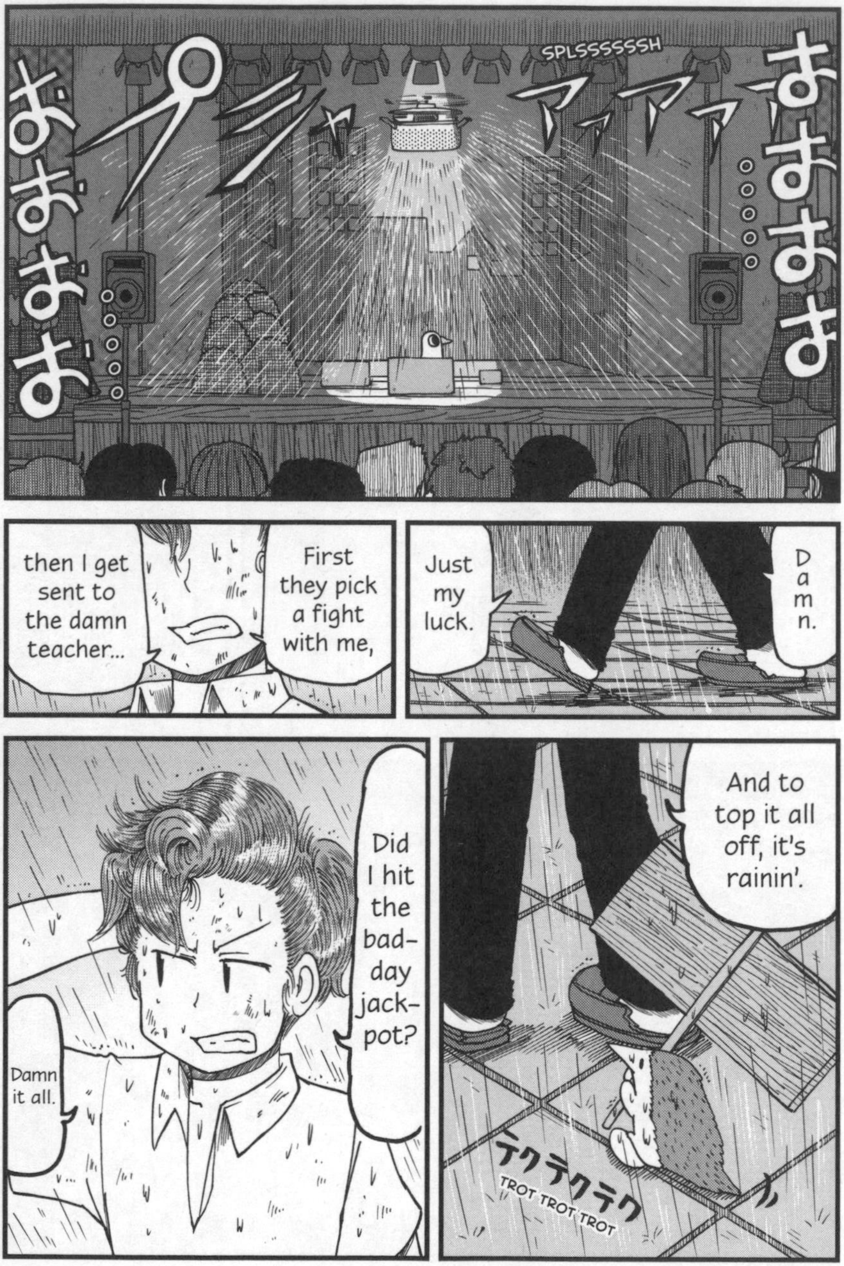
おおおお……
パシャァァアァァ
SPLSSSSSSH
おおおお……
Damn.
Just my luck.
First they pick a fight with me,
then I get sent to the damn teacher...
And to top it all off, it's rainin'.
テクテクテク
TROT TROT TROT
Did I hit the bad-day jackpot?
Damn it all.

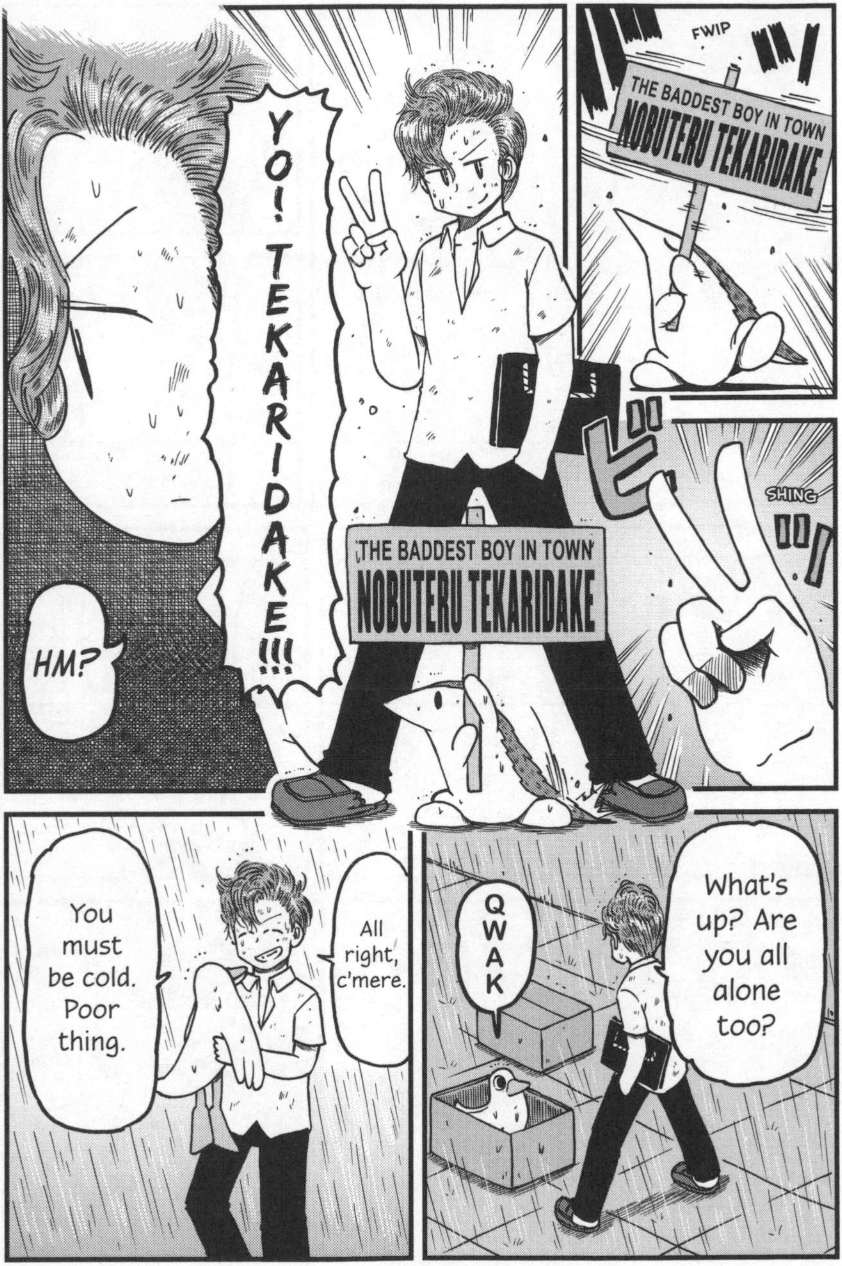
FWIP
THE BADDEST BOY IN TOWN
NOBUTERU TEKARIDAKE
SHING
YO! TEKARIDAKE!!!
THE BADDEST BOY IN TOWN
NOBUTERU TEKARIDAKE
HM?
What's up? Are you all alone too?
QWAK
All right, c'mere.
You must be cold. Poor thing.

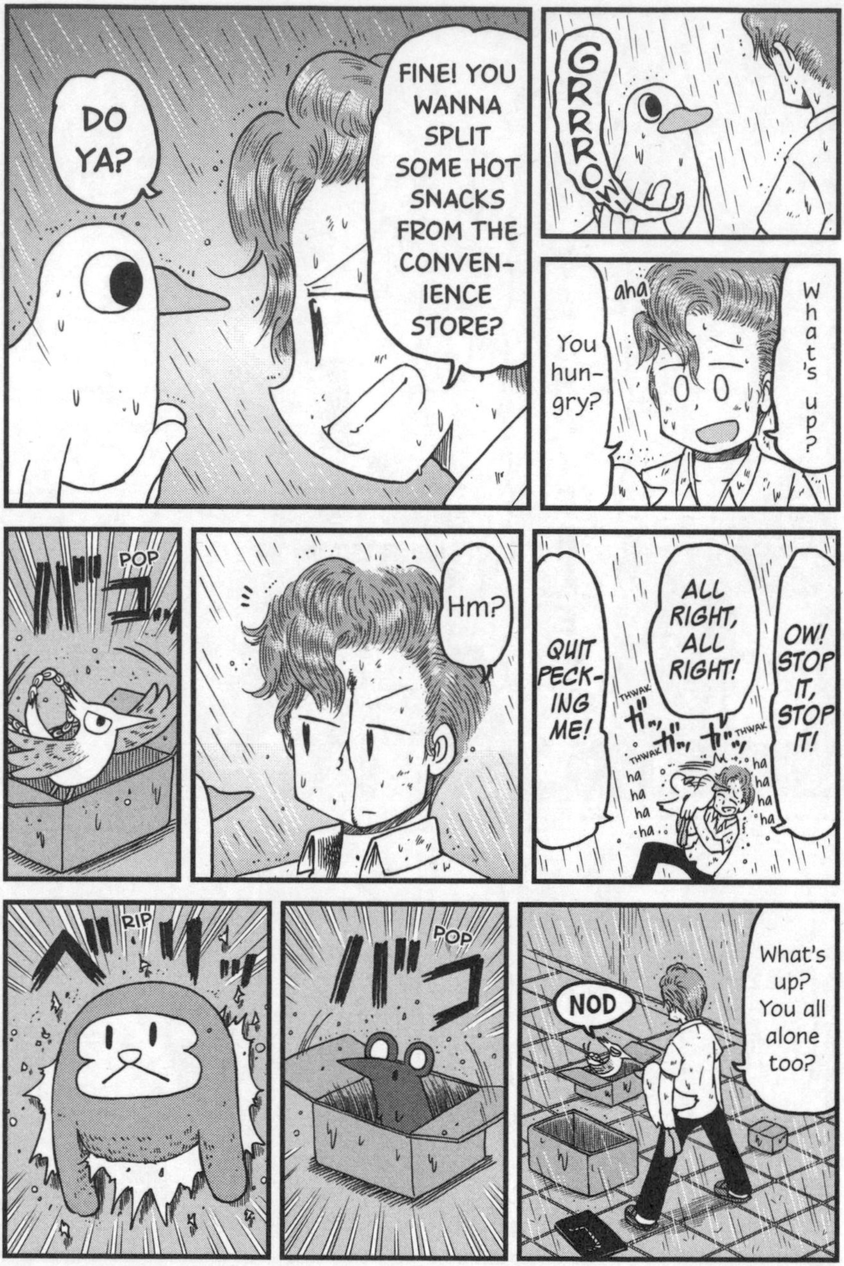
GRRROW
What's up?
You hungry?
aha
FINE! YOU WANNA SPLIT SOME HOT SNACKS FROM THE CONVENIENCE STORE?
DO YA?
OW! STOP IT, STOP IT!
ALL RIGHT, ALL RIGHT!
QUIT PECKING ME!
THWAK
THWAK
THWAK
ha ha ha ha
ha ha ha ha
Hm?
POP
What's up? You all alone too?
NOD
POP
RIP

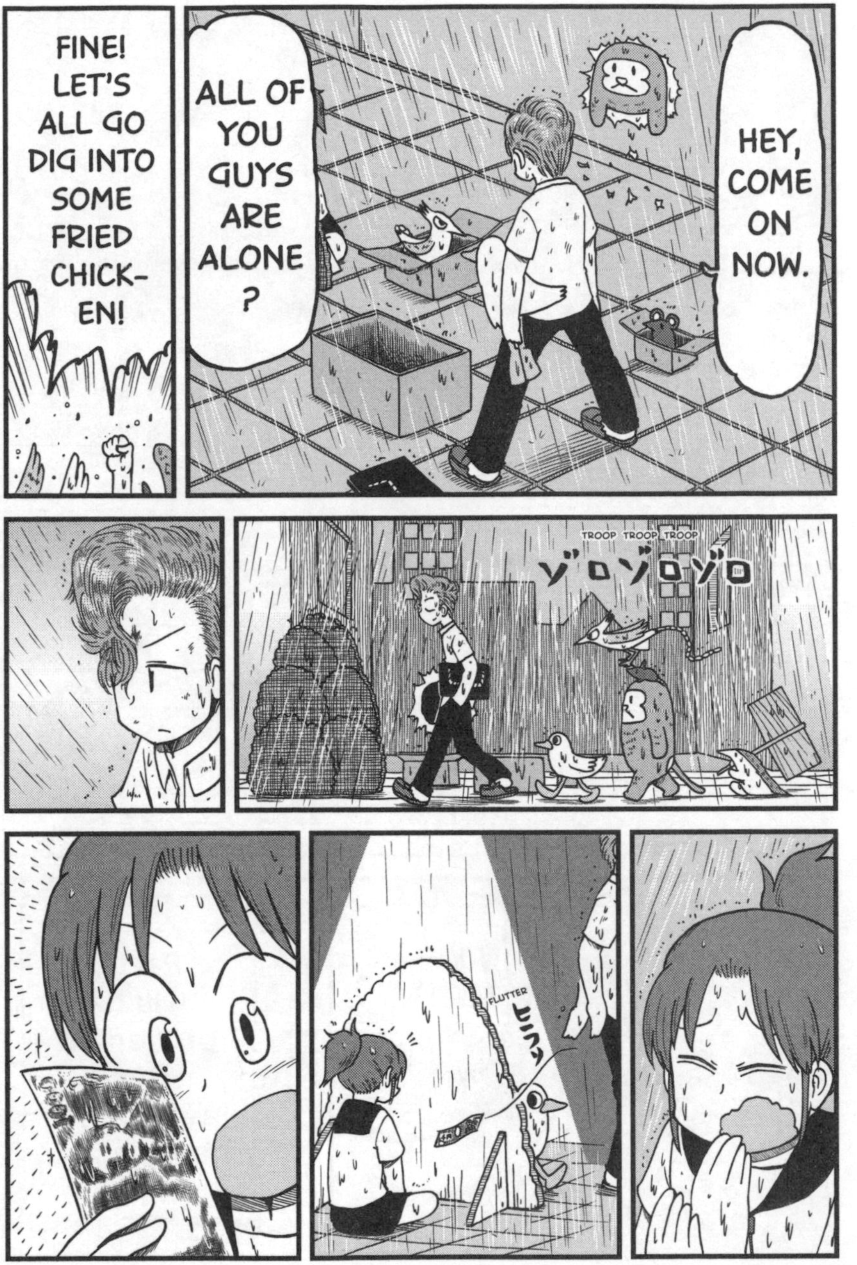
HEY, COME ON NOW.
ALL OF YOU GUYS ARE ALONE?
FINE! LET'S ALL GO DIG INTO SOME FRIED CHICK-EN!
TROOP TROOP TROOP
ゾロゾロゾロ
FLUTTER
ヒラッ

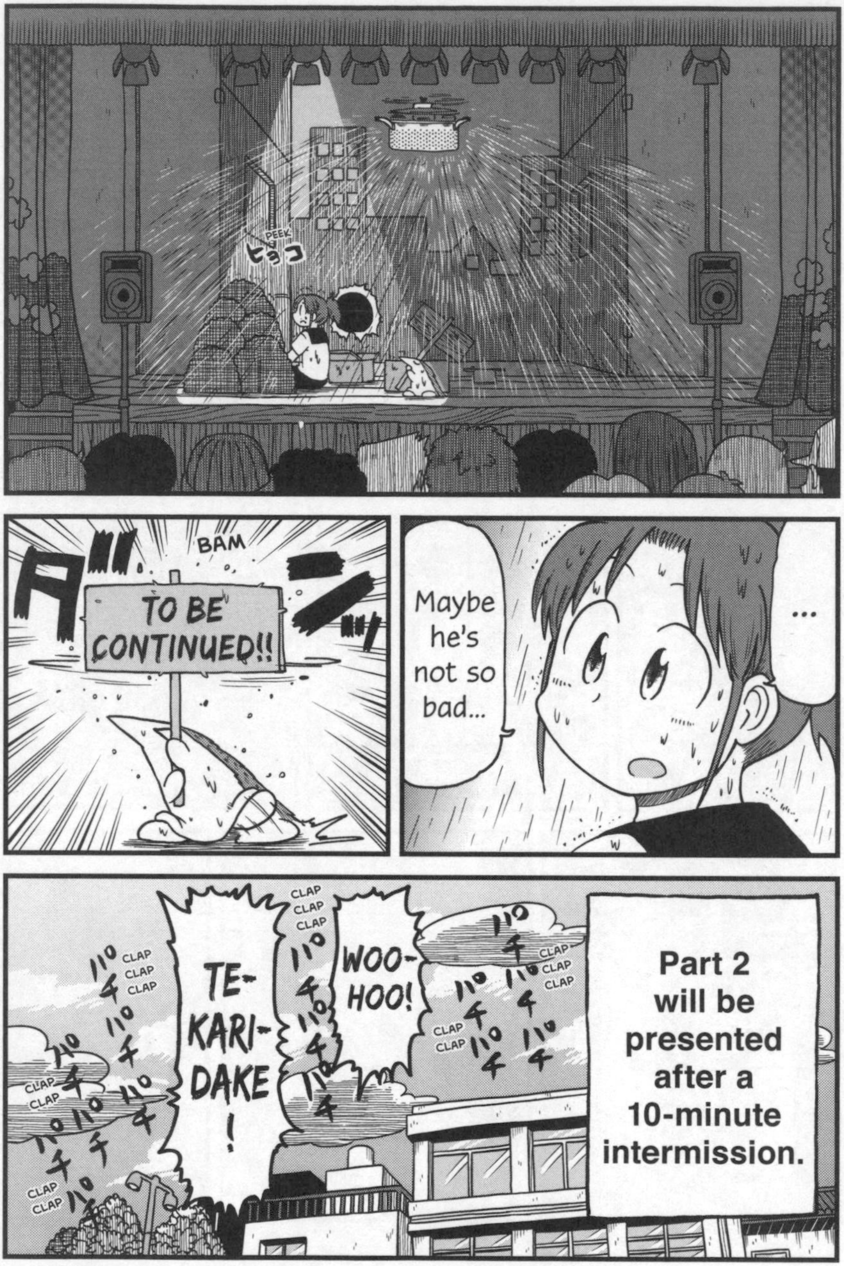
PEEK
ヒョコ
...
Maybe he's not so bad...
BAM
TO BE CONTINUED!!
Part 2 will be presented after a 10-minute intermission.
CLAP CLAP CLAP
CLAP CLAP
WOO-HOO!
CLAP CLAP CLAP
TE-KARI-DAKE!
CLAP CLAP CLAP
CLAP CLAP
CLAP CLAP

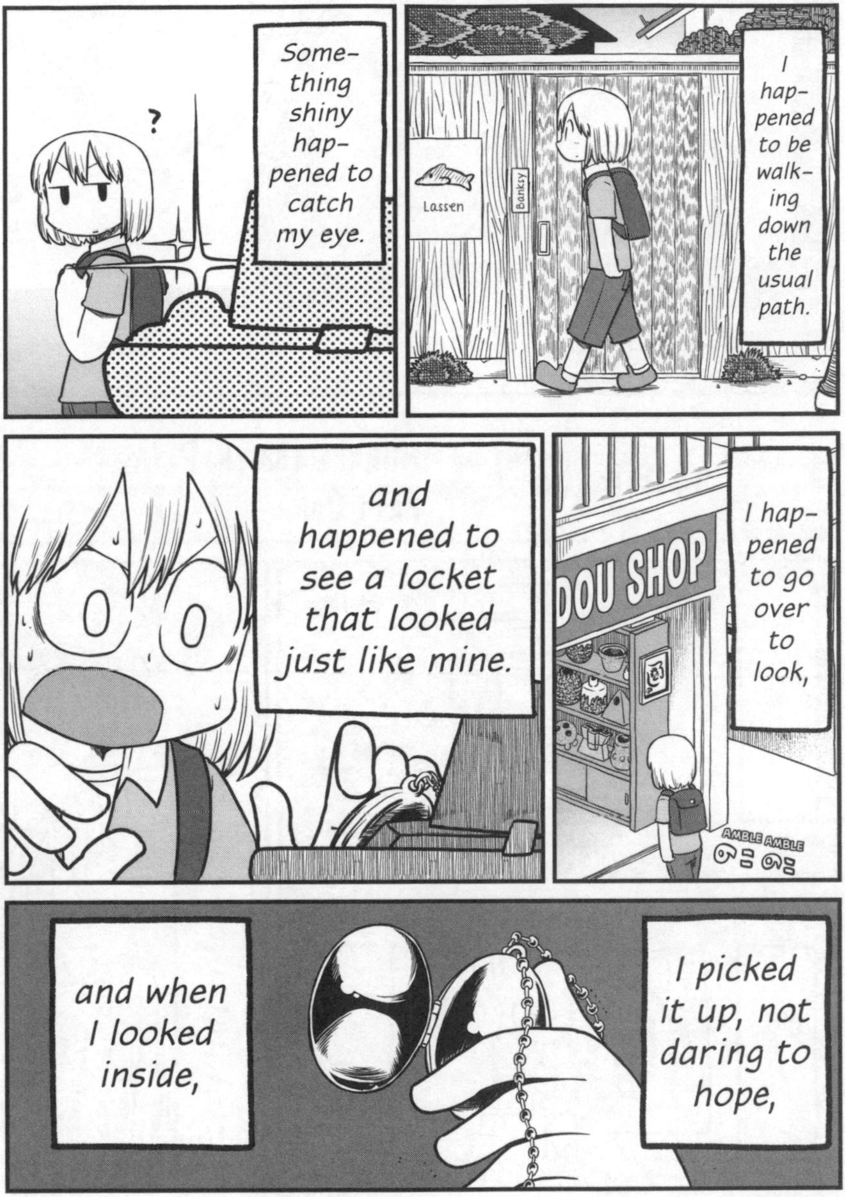
I happened to be walking down the usual path.
Lassen
Banksy
Something shiny happened to catch my eye.
?
I happened to go over to look,
DOU SHOP
AMBLE AMBLE
and happened to see a locket that looked just like mine.
I picked it up, not daring to hope,
and when I looked inside,

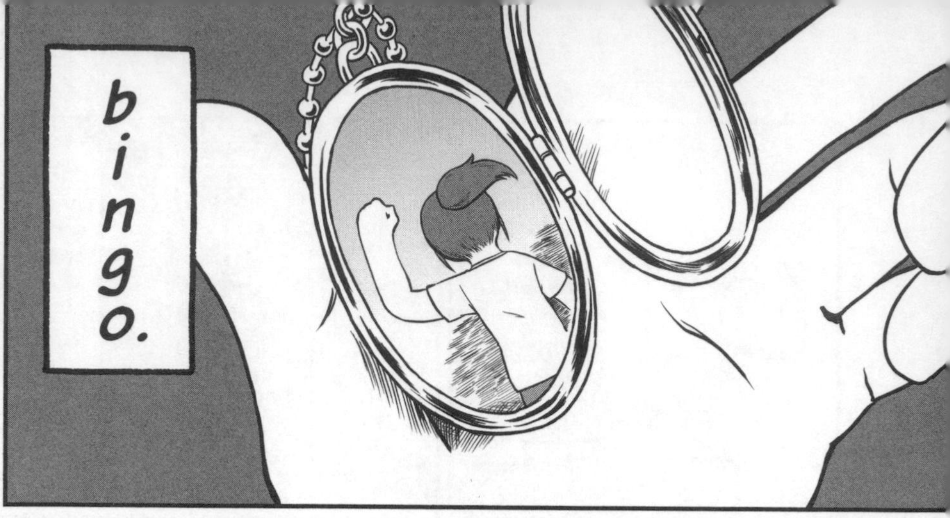
bingo.

Chapter 165 Niikura and the Path Part One

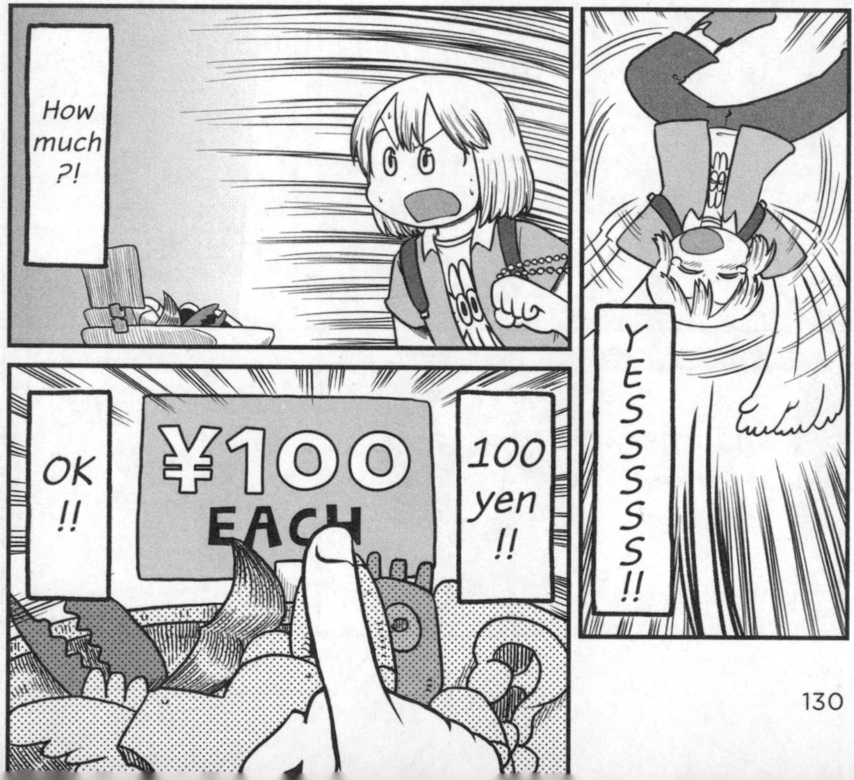
YESSSSSS!!
How much?!
100 yen!!
¥100
EACH
OK!!

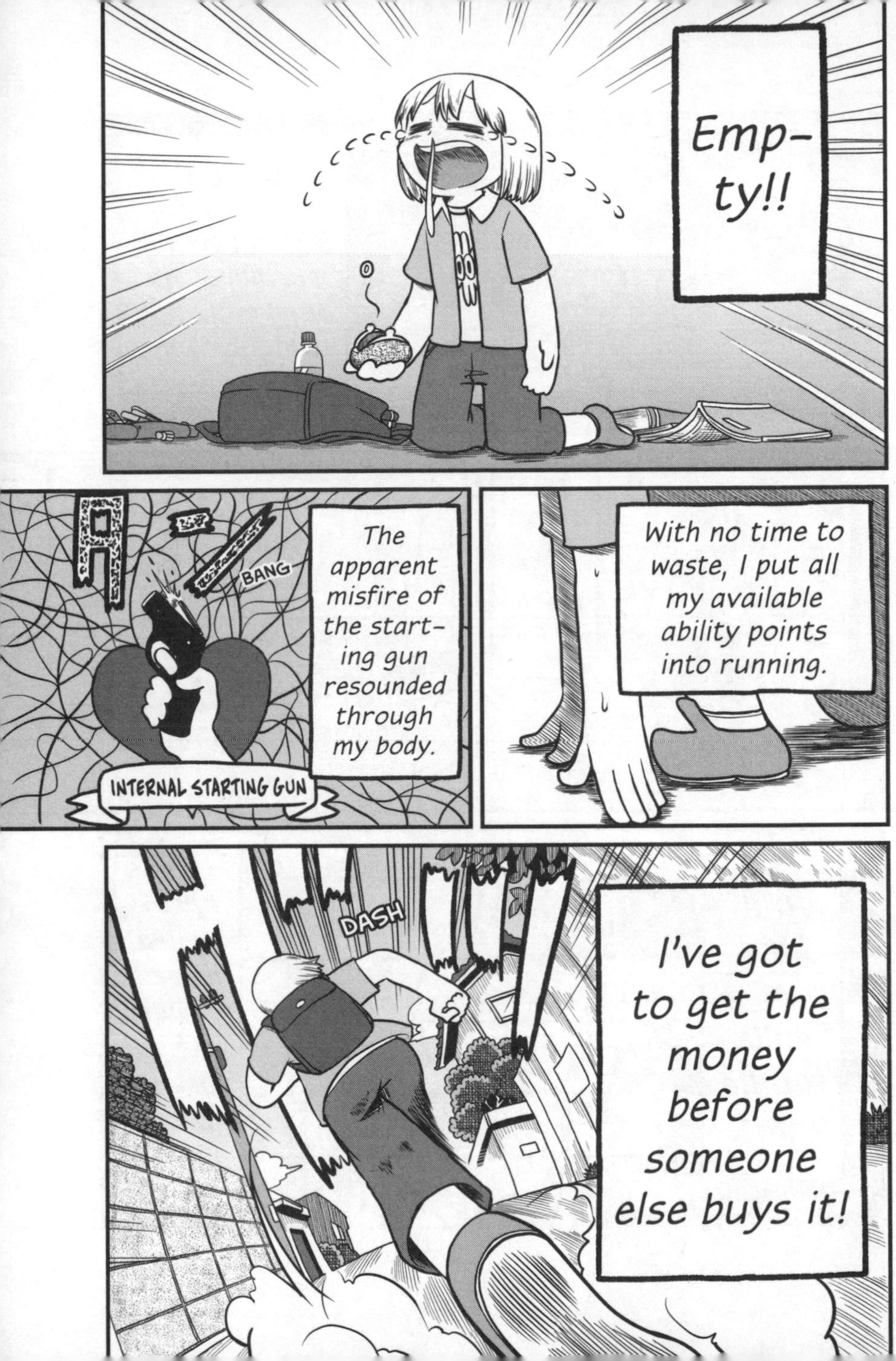
Emp-
ty!!
With no time to waste, I put all my available ability points into running.
The apparent misfire of the start-ing gun resounded through my body.
BANG
INTERNAL STARTING GUN
DASH
I've got to get the money before someone else buys it!

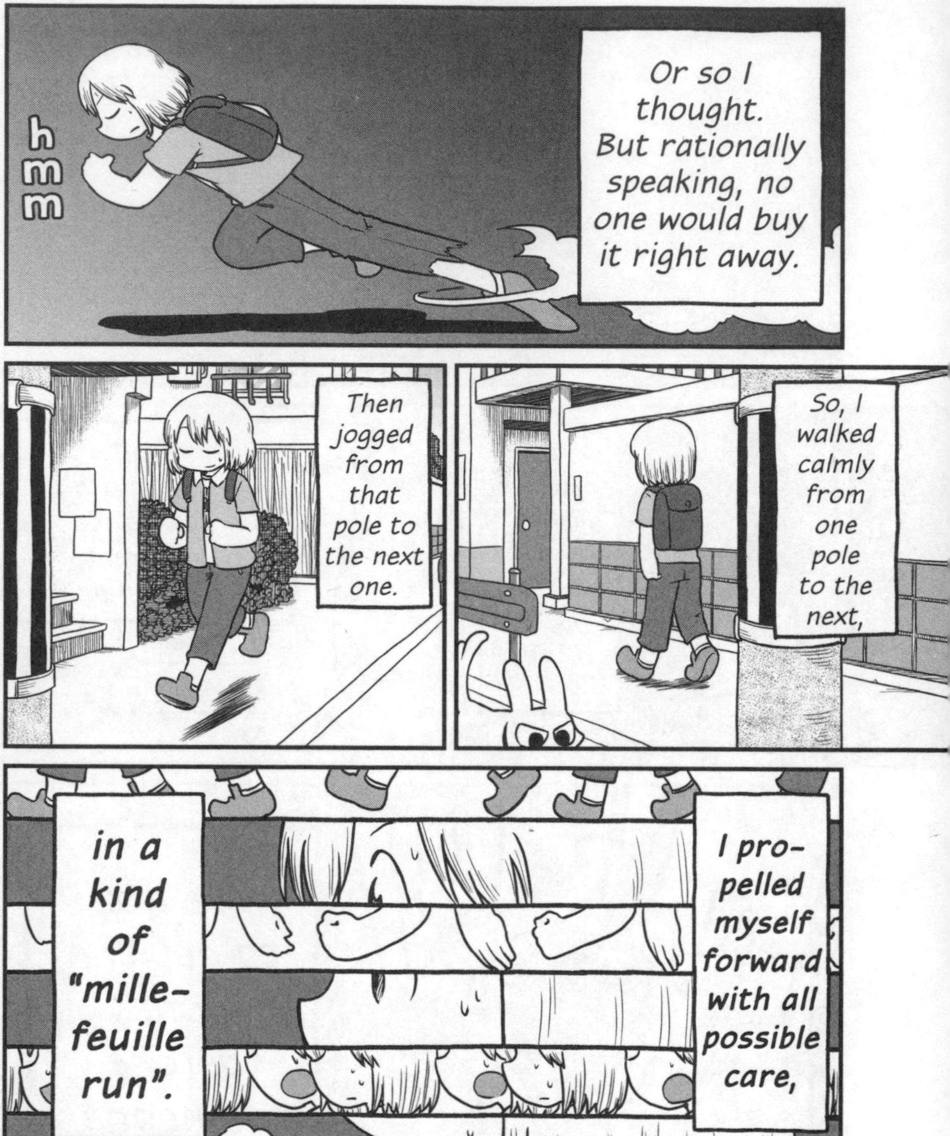
Or so I thought. But rationally speaking, no one would buy it right away.
hmm
So, I walked calmly from one pole to the next,
Then jogged from that pole to the next one.
I pro-pelled myself forward with all possible care,
in a kind of "mille-feuille run".

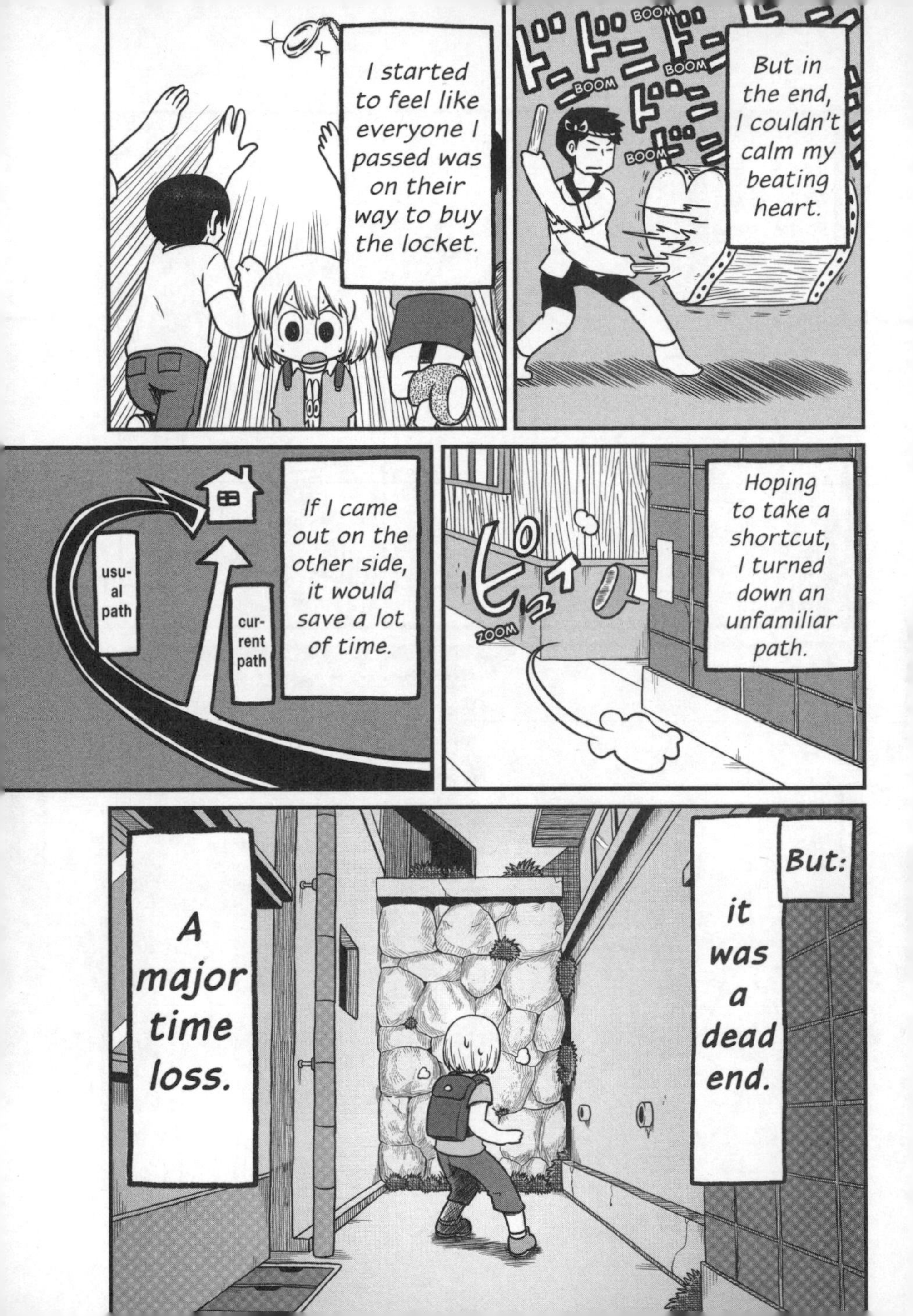
BOOM
BOOM
BOOM
BOOM
But in the end, I couldn't calm my beating heart.
I started to feel like everyone I passed was on their way to buy the locket.
Hoping to take a shortcut, I turned down an unfamiliar path.
ZOOM
If I came out on the other side, it would save a lot of time.
usu-al path
cur-rent path
But:
it was a dead end.
A major time loss.

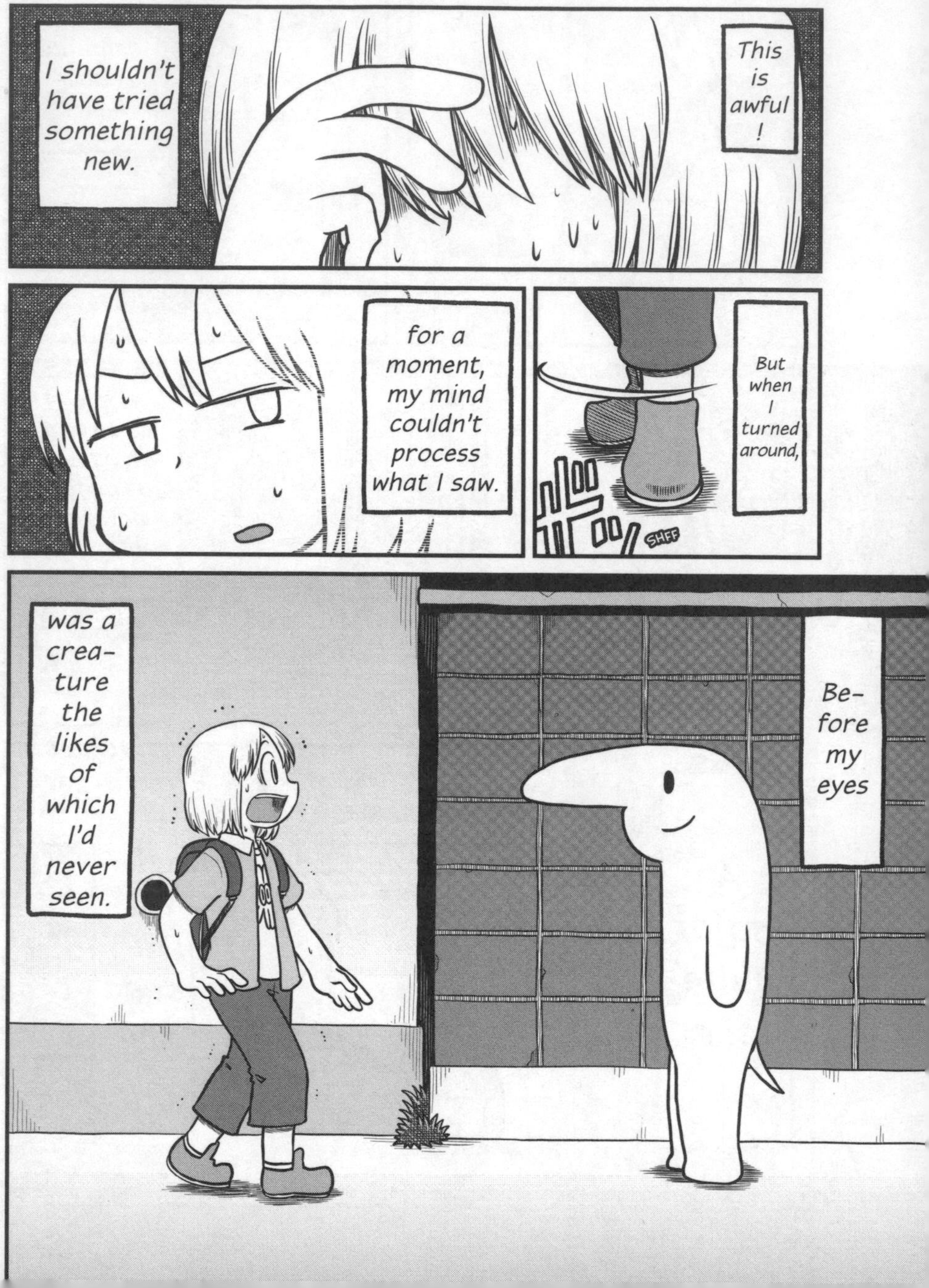
This is awful!
I shouldn't have tried something new.
But when I turned around,
SHFF
for a moment, my mind couldn't process what I saw.
Be-fore my eyes
was a crea-ture the likes of which I'd never seen.

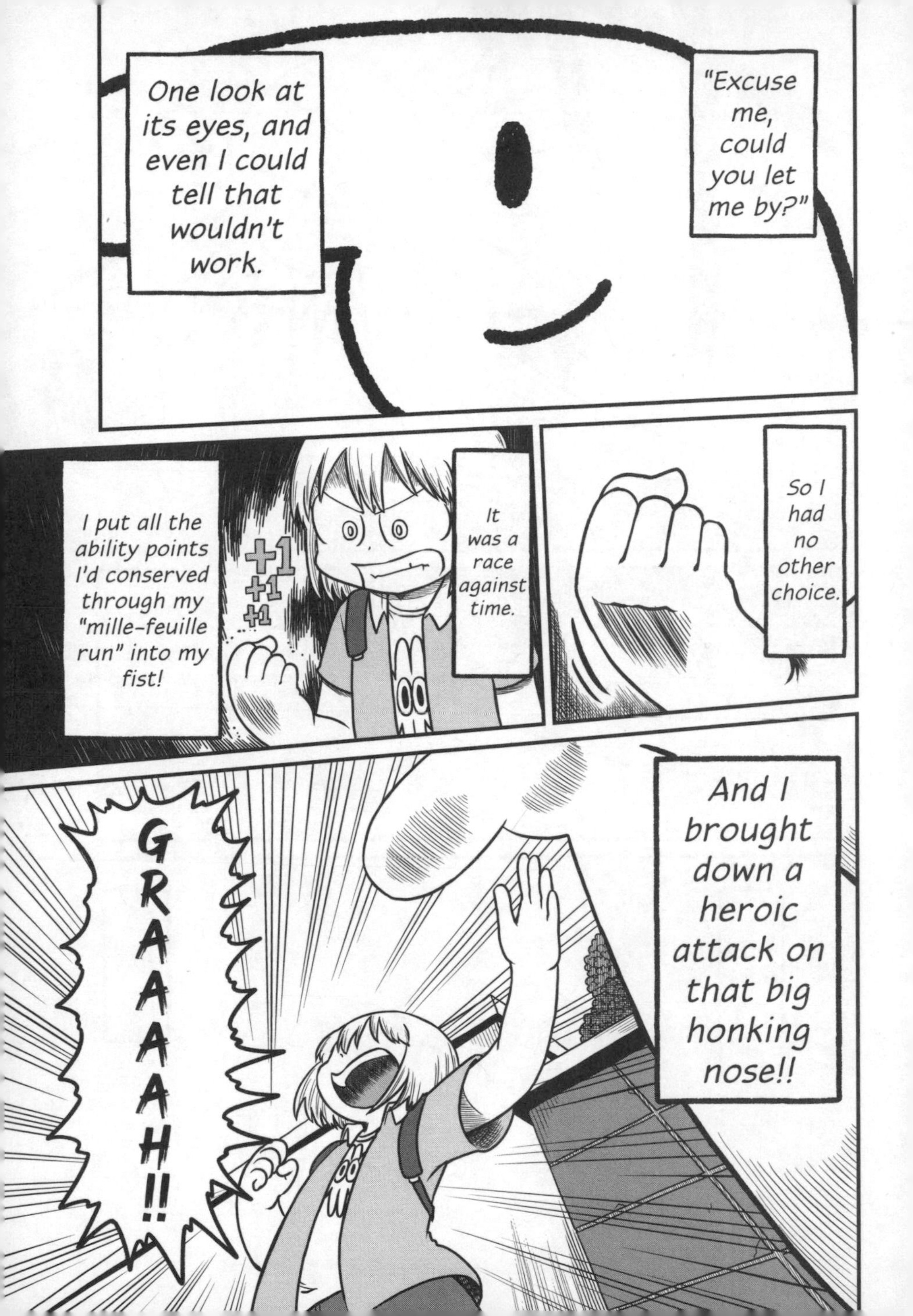
"Excuse me, could you let me by?"
One look at its eyes, and even I could tell that wouldn't work.
So I had no other choice.
It was a race against time.
I put all the ability points I'd conserved through my "mille-feuille run" into my fist!
+1 +1 +1
And I brought down a heroic attack on that big honking nose!!
GRAAAAAH!!

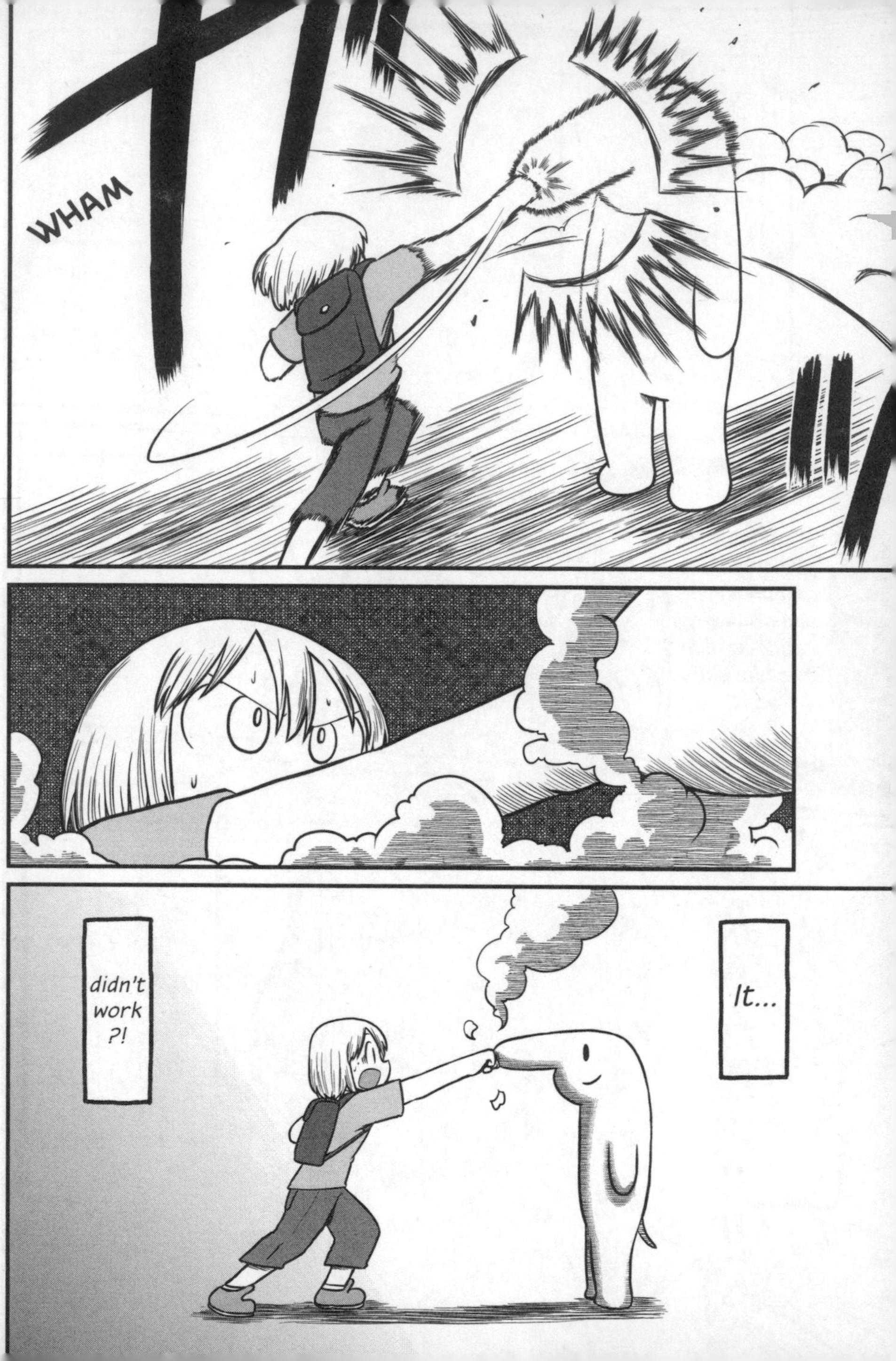
WHAM
It...
didn't work ?!

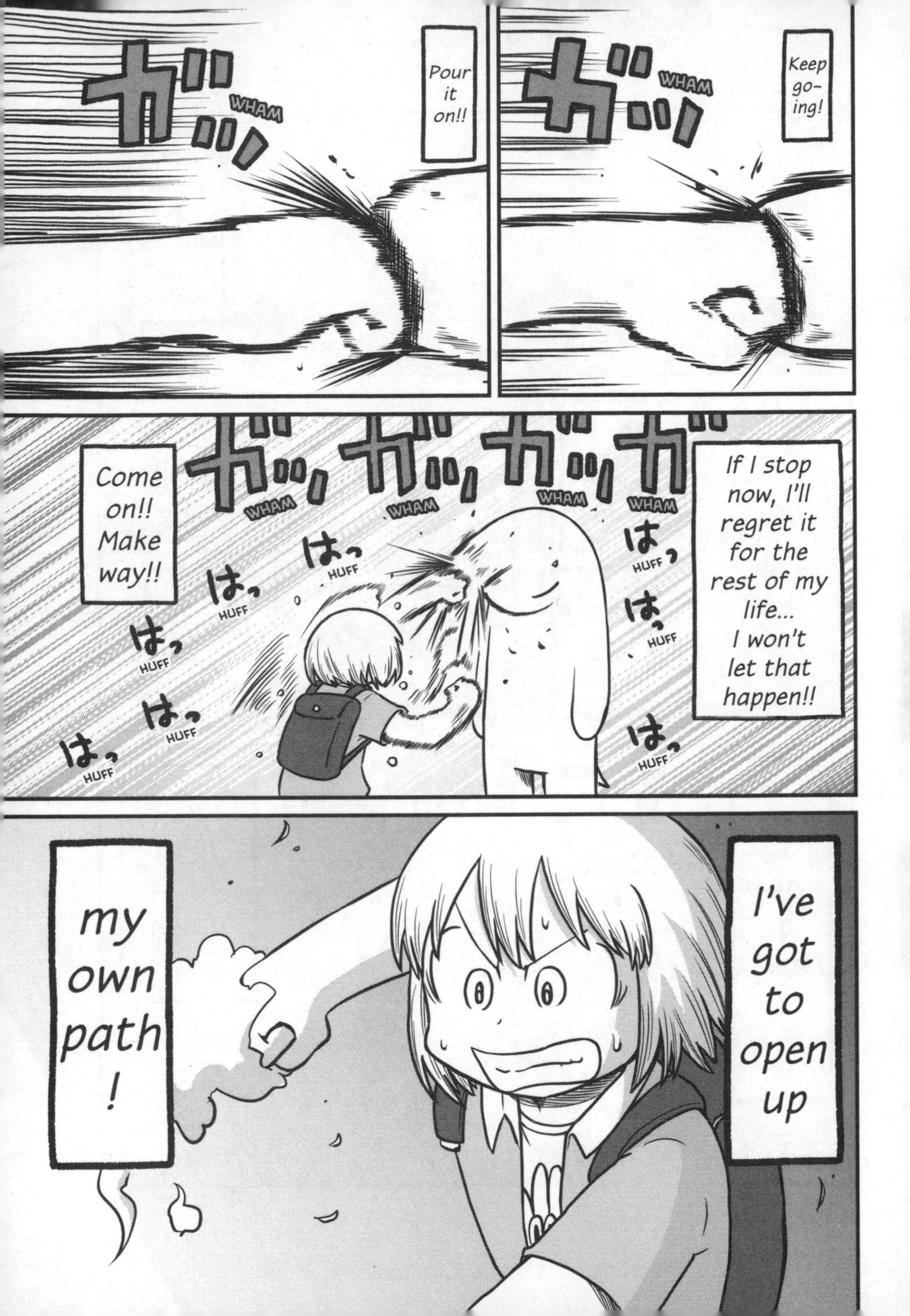
Keep go-ing!
ガッ
WHAM
Pour it on!!
ガッ
WHAM
If I stop now, I'll regret it for the rest of my life... I won't let that happen!!
ガッ ガッ ガッ ガッ
WHAM WHAM WHAM WHAM
はっ HUFF
はっ HUFF
はっ HUFF
はっ HUFF
はっ HUFF
はっ HUFF
はっ HUFF
はっ HUFF
Come on!! Make way!!
I've got to open up
my own path!

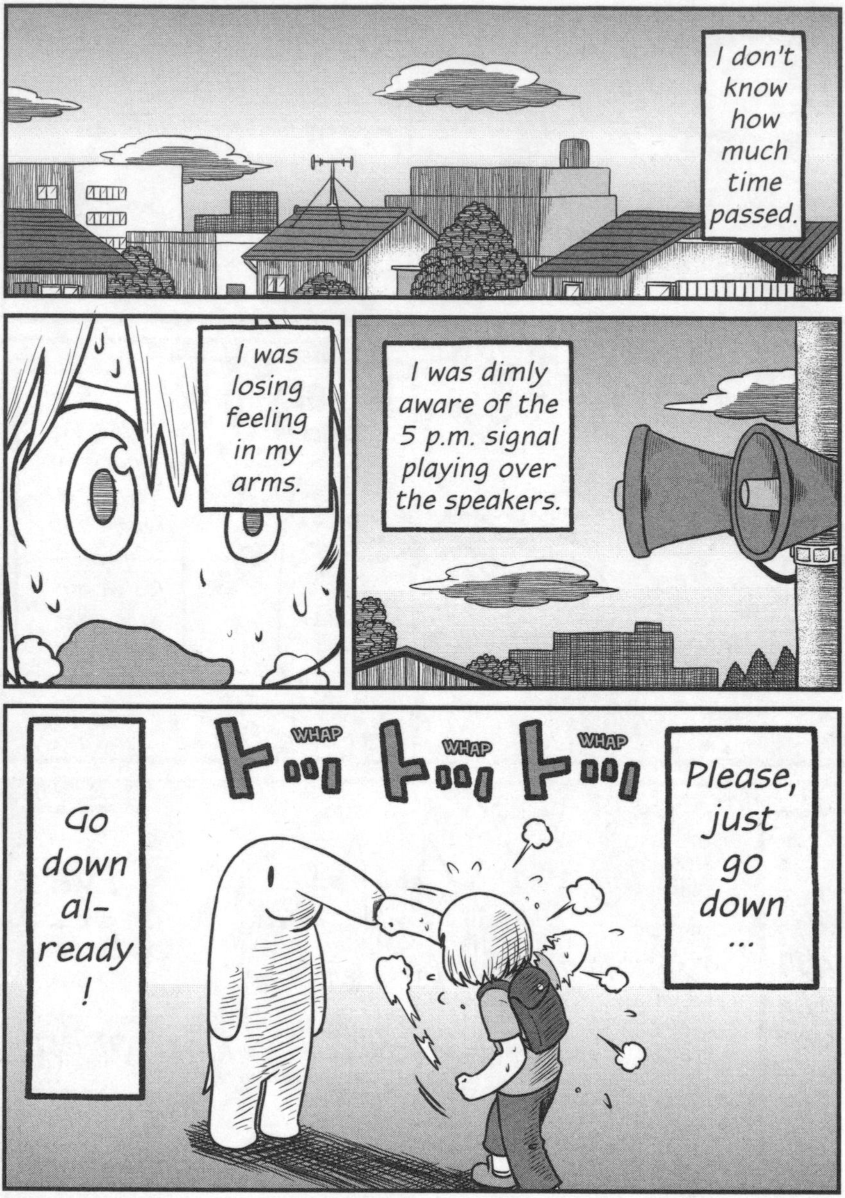
I don't know how much time passed.
I was dimly aware of the 5 p.m. signal playing over the speakers.
I was losing feeling in my arms.
Please, just go down ...
WHAP
WHAP
WHAP
Go down al-ready!

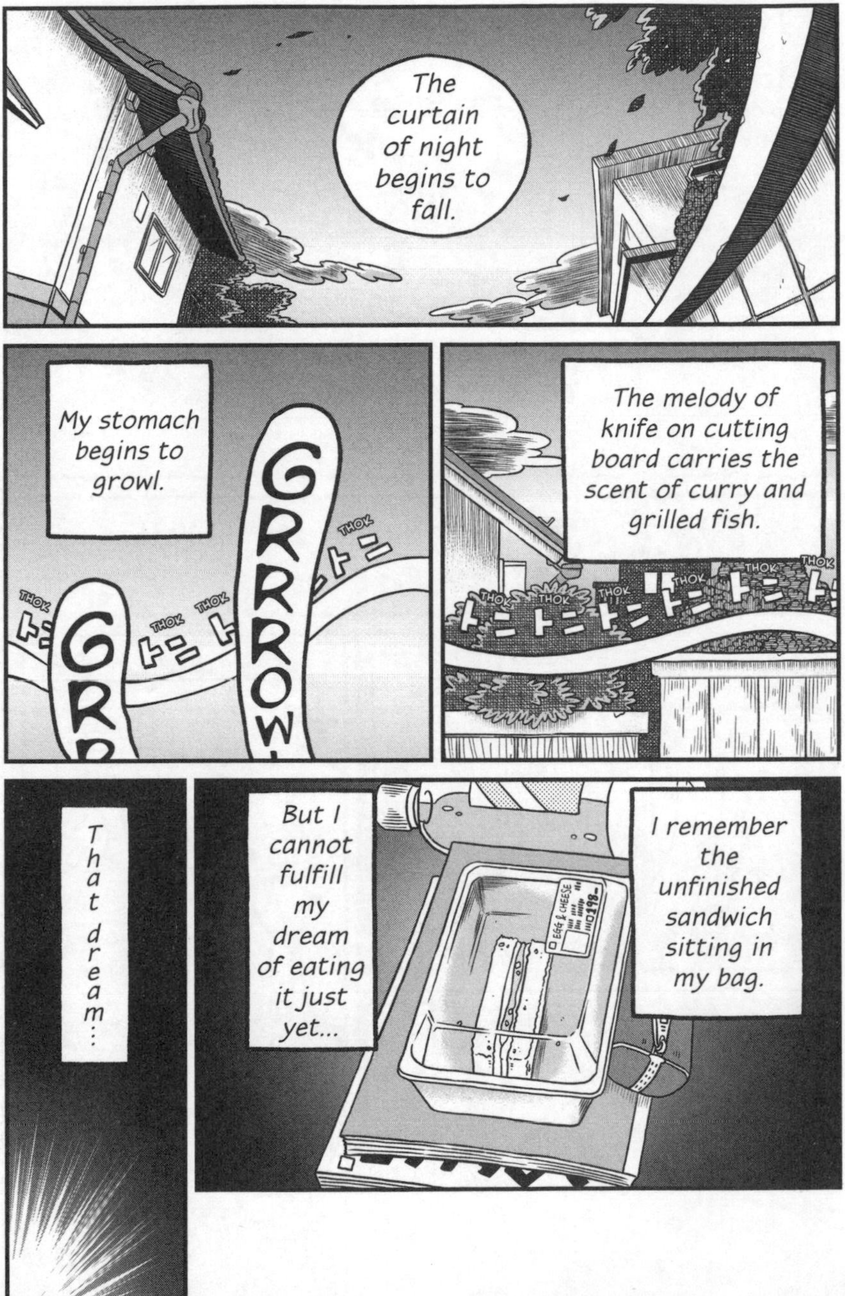

The curtain of night begins to fall.
The melody of knife on cutting board carries the scent of curry and grilled fish.
THOK THOK THOK THOK THOK
My stomach begins to growl.
GRRROW
THOK THOK THOK THOK
GRR
I remember the unfinished sandwich sitting in my bag.
But I cannot fulfill my dream of eating it just yet...
EGG & CHEESE
That dream...

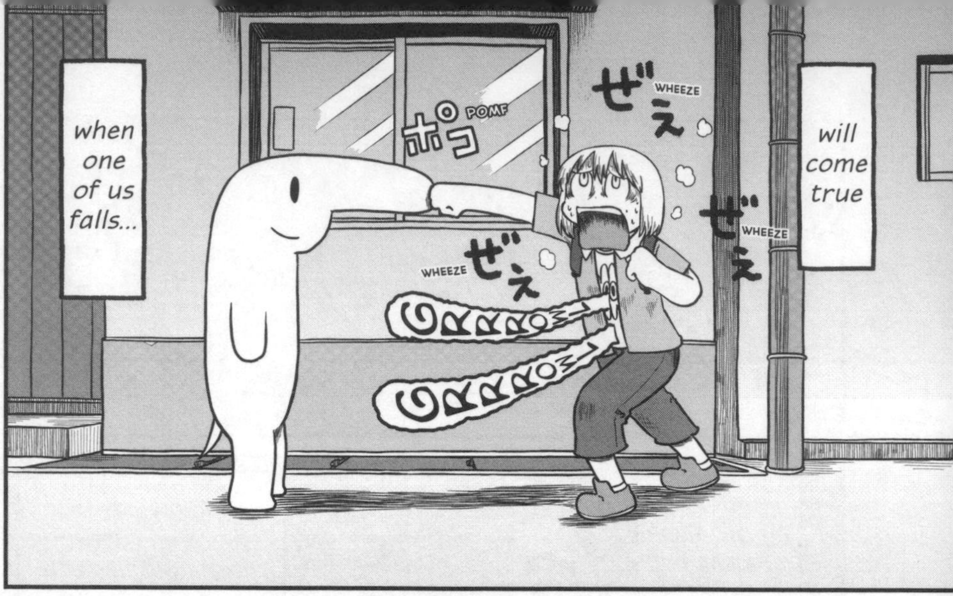
will come true
ぜぇ WHEEZE
ぜぇ WHEEZE
ポコ POMF
ぜぇ WHEEZE
GRRROWL
GRRROWL
when one of us falls...

Chapter 166 Niikura and the Path Part Two

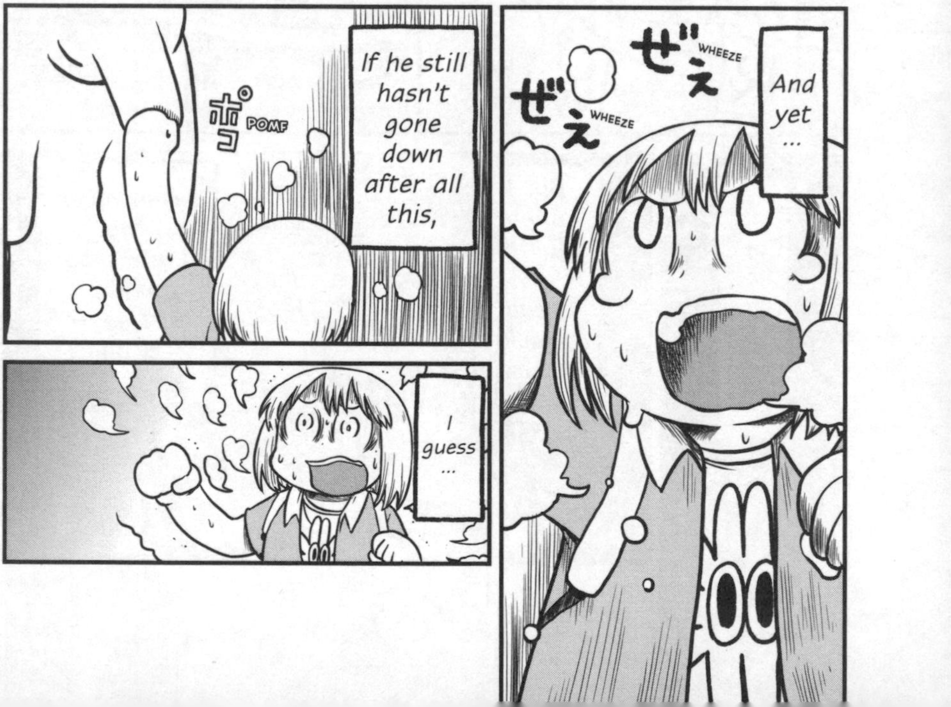
ぜぇ WHEEZE
ぜぇ WHEEZE
And yet ...
If he still hasn't gone down after all this,
ポコ POMF
I guess ...

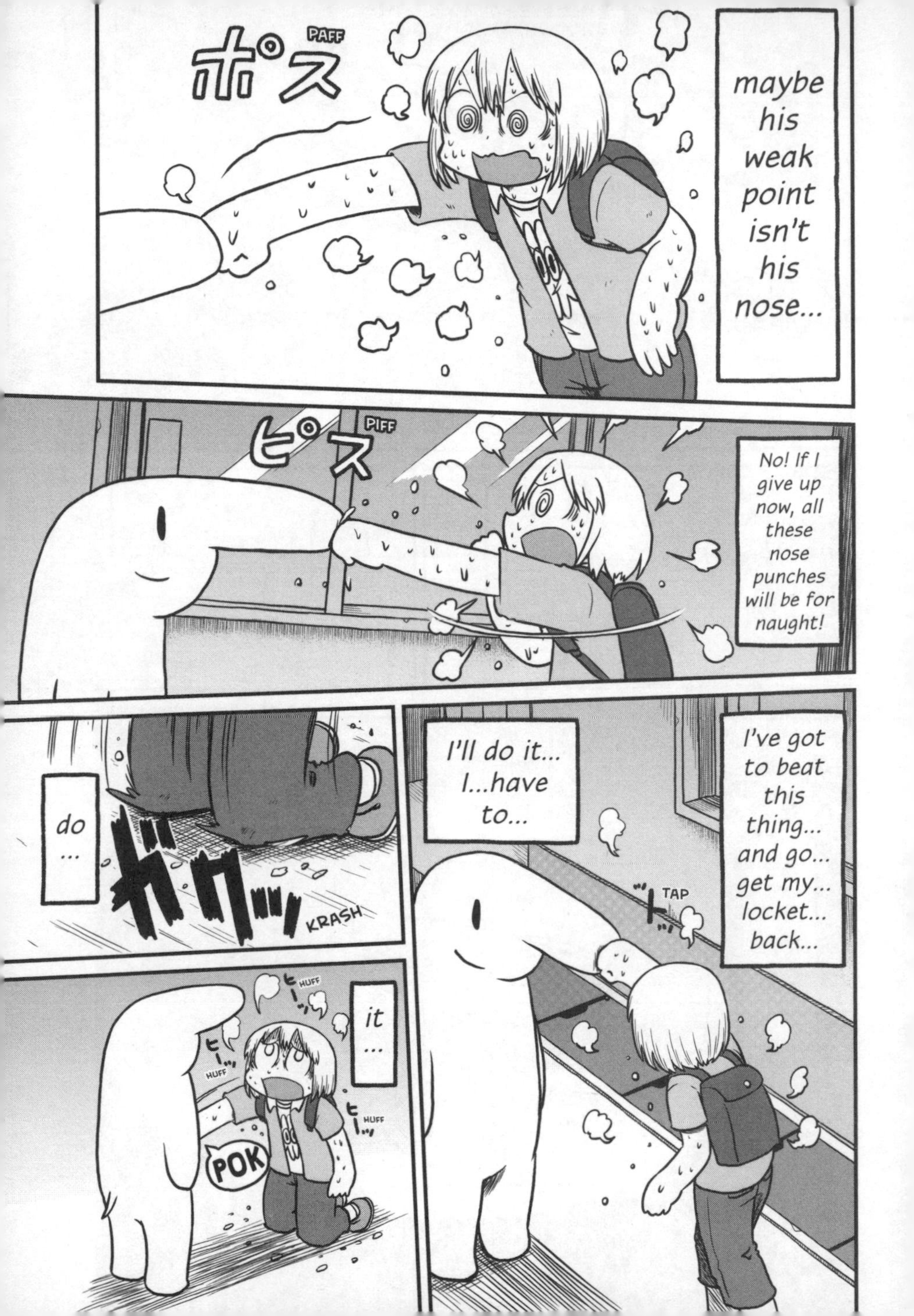
maybe his weak point isn't his nose...
ポス
PAFF
No! If I give up now, all these nose punches will be for naught!
ピス
PIFF
I've got to beat this thing... and go... get my... locket... back...
I'll do it... I...have to...
TAP
do ...
ガク
KRASH
it ...
ヒーッ
HUFF
ヒーッ
HUFF
ヒーッ
HUFF
POK

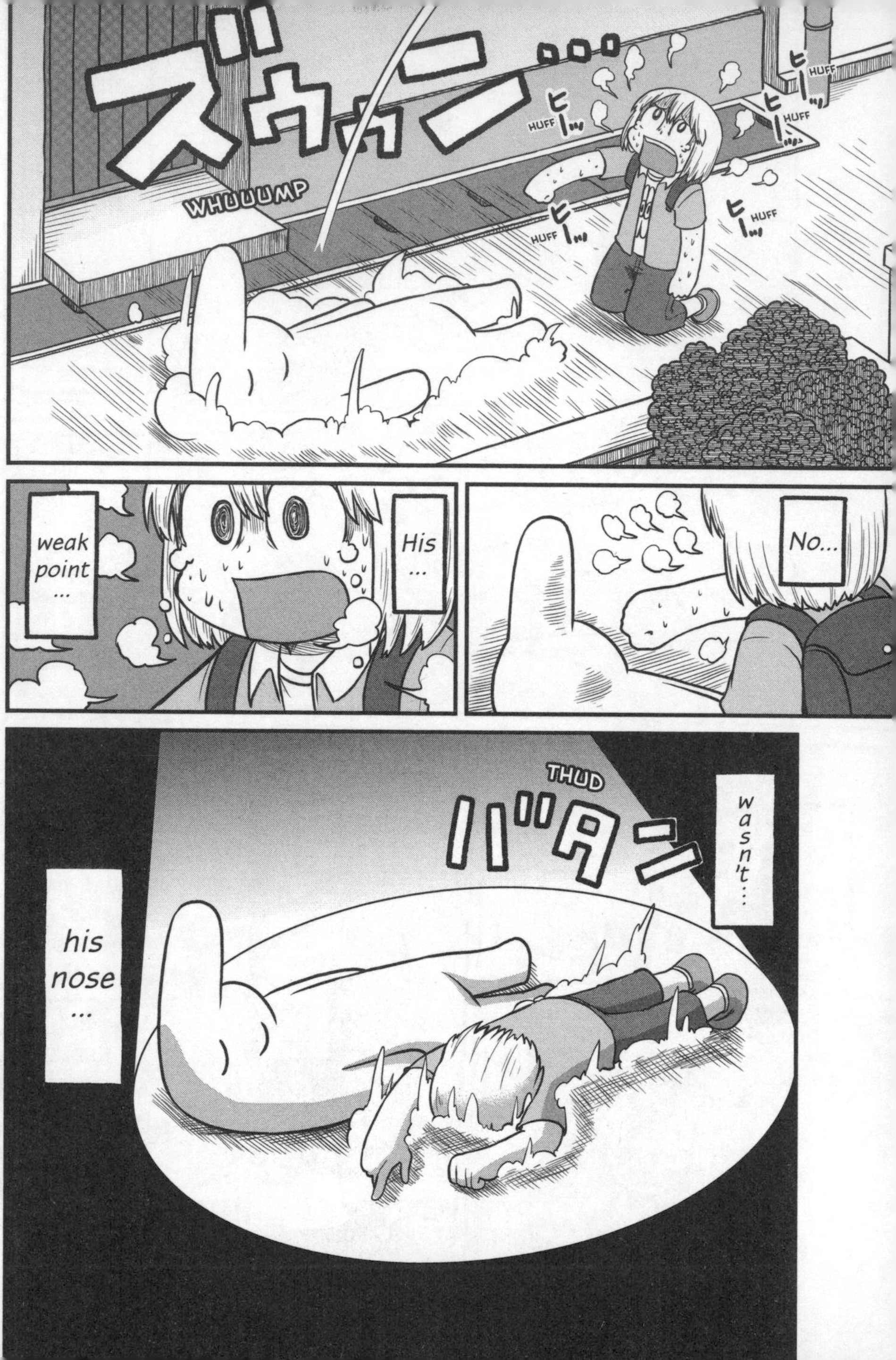

ズゥゥン…
WHUUUMP
ヒー… HUFF
ヒー… HUFF
ヒー… HUFF
ヒー… HUFF
ヒー… HUFF
No...
His ...
weak point ...
THUD
バタン
wasn't...
his nose ...

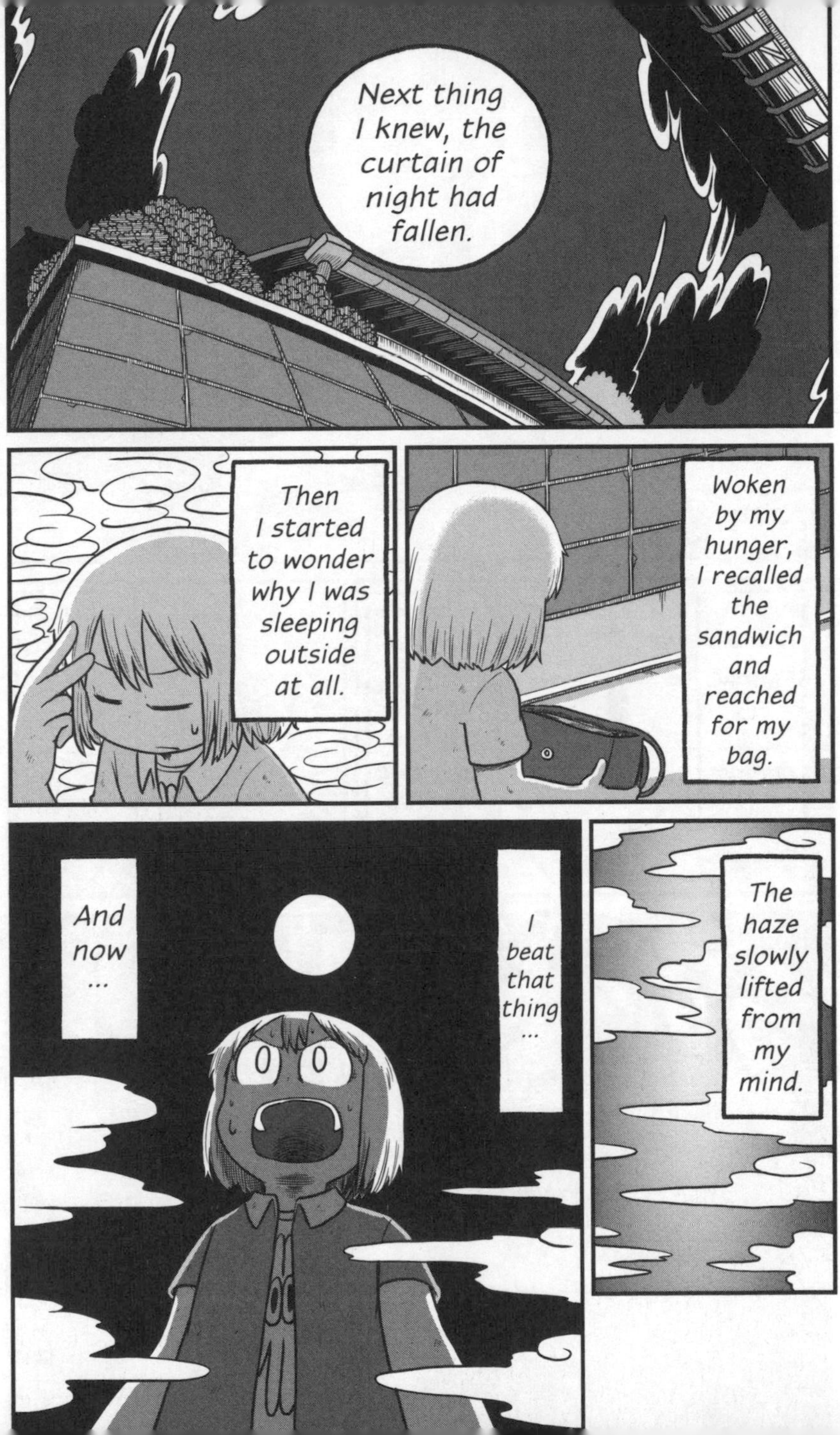
Next thing I knew, the curtain of night had fallen.
Woken by my hunger, I recalled the sandwich and reached for my bag.
Then I started to wonder why I was sleeping outside at all.
The haze slowly lifted from my mind.
I beat that thing ...
And now ...

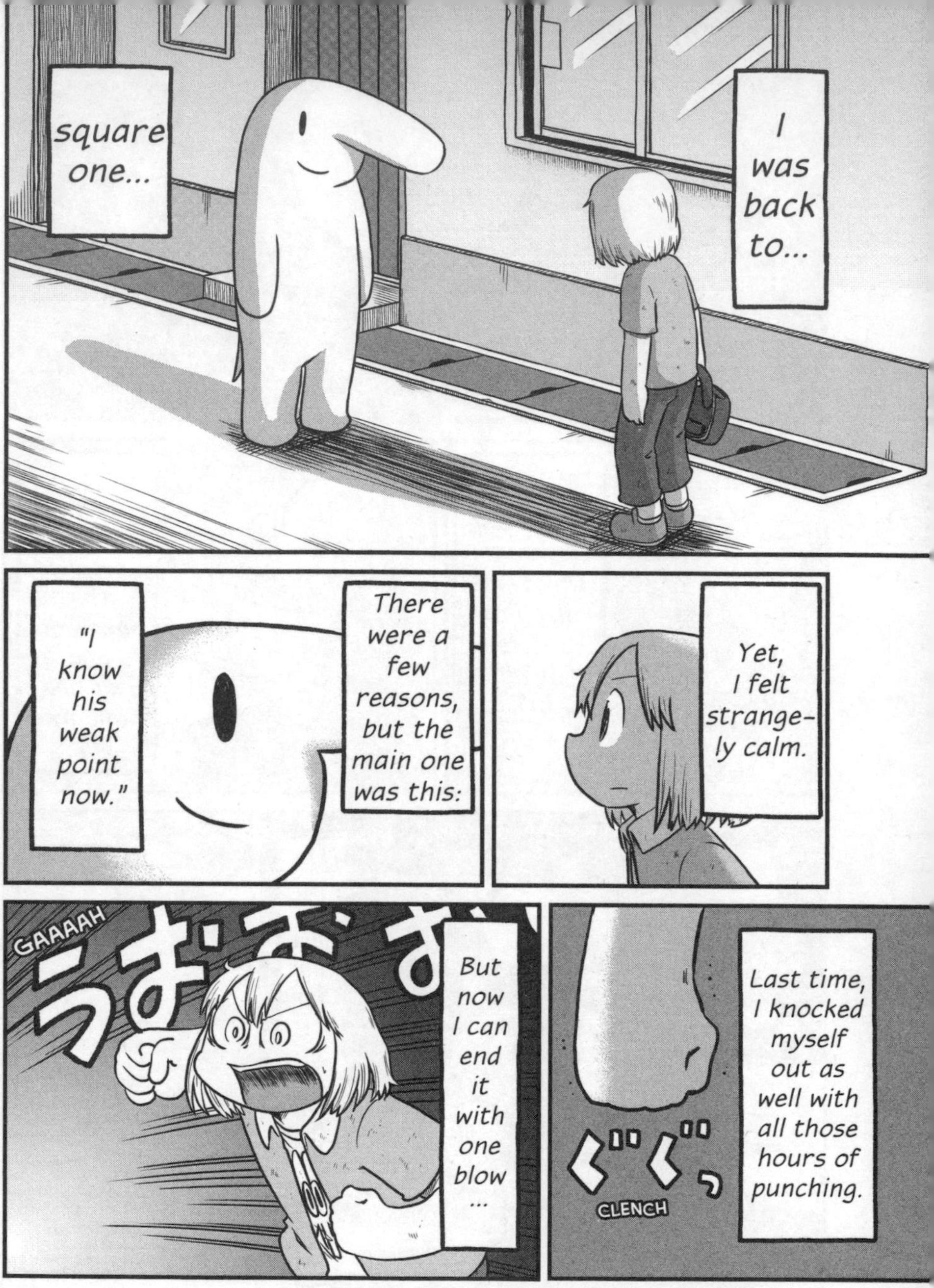
I was back to...
square one...
Yet, I felt strange-ly calm.
There were a few reasons, but the main one was this:
"I know his weak point now."
Last time, I knocked myself out as well with all those hours of punching.
ぐぐっ
CLENCH
But now I can end it with one blow...
うおおお
GAAAAH

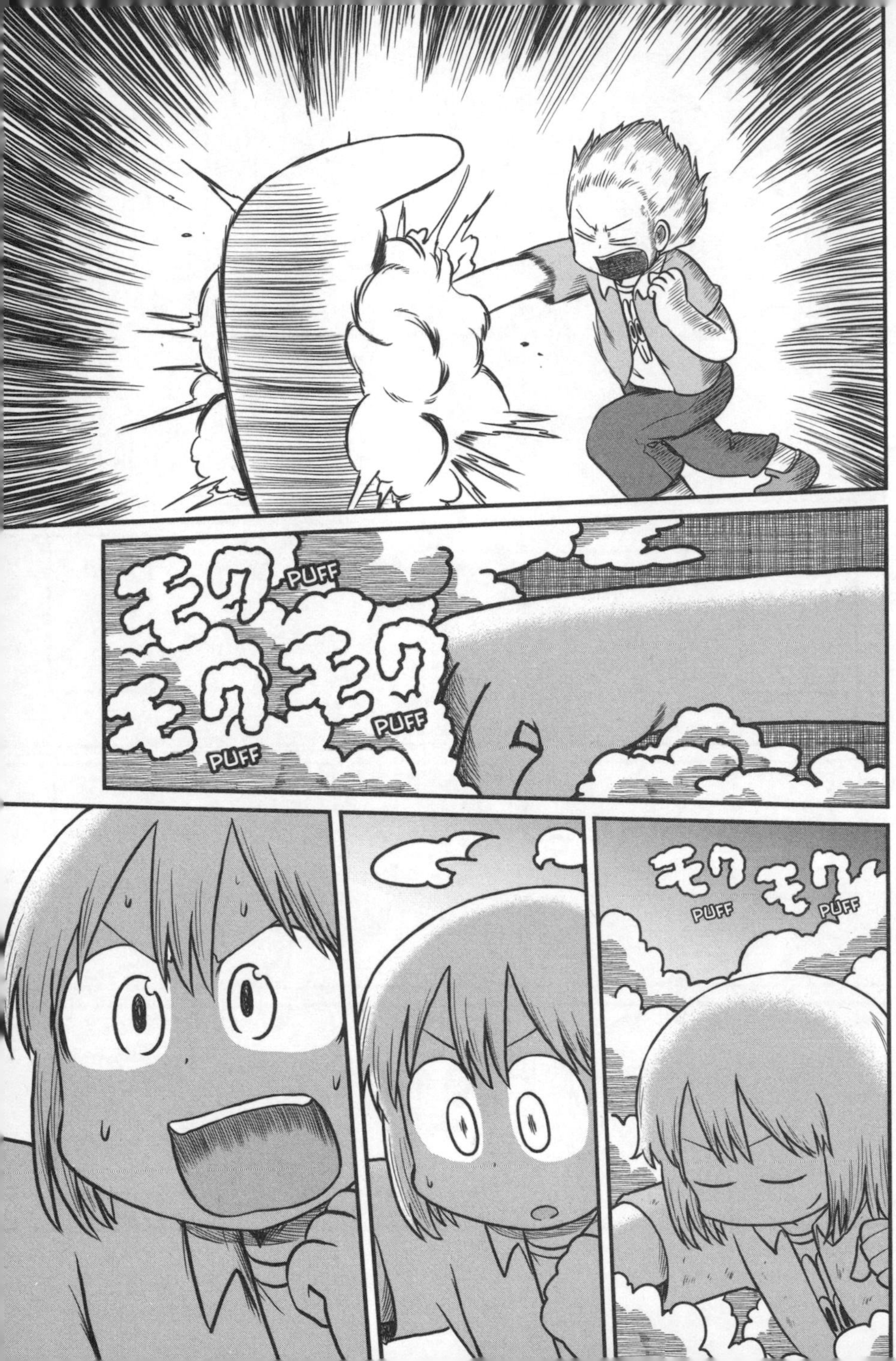
モク
PUFF
モク
PUFF
モク
PUFF
モク
PUFF
モク
PUFF

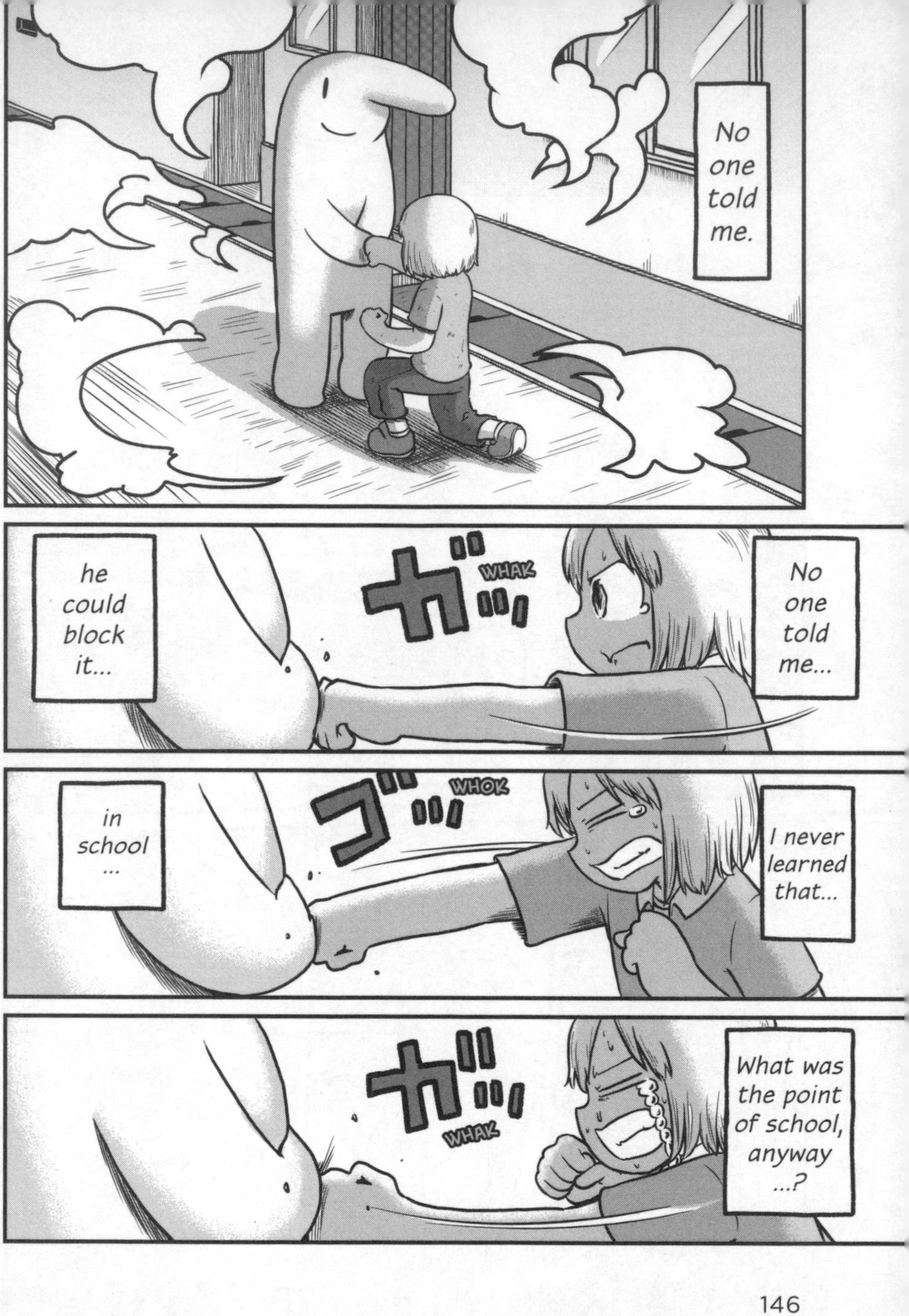
No one told me.
No one told me...
ガッ
WHAK
he could block it...
I never learned that...
ゴッ
WHOK
in school ...
What was the point of school, anyway ...?
ガッ
WHAK

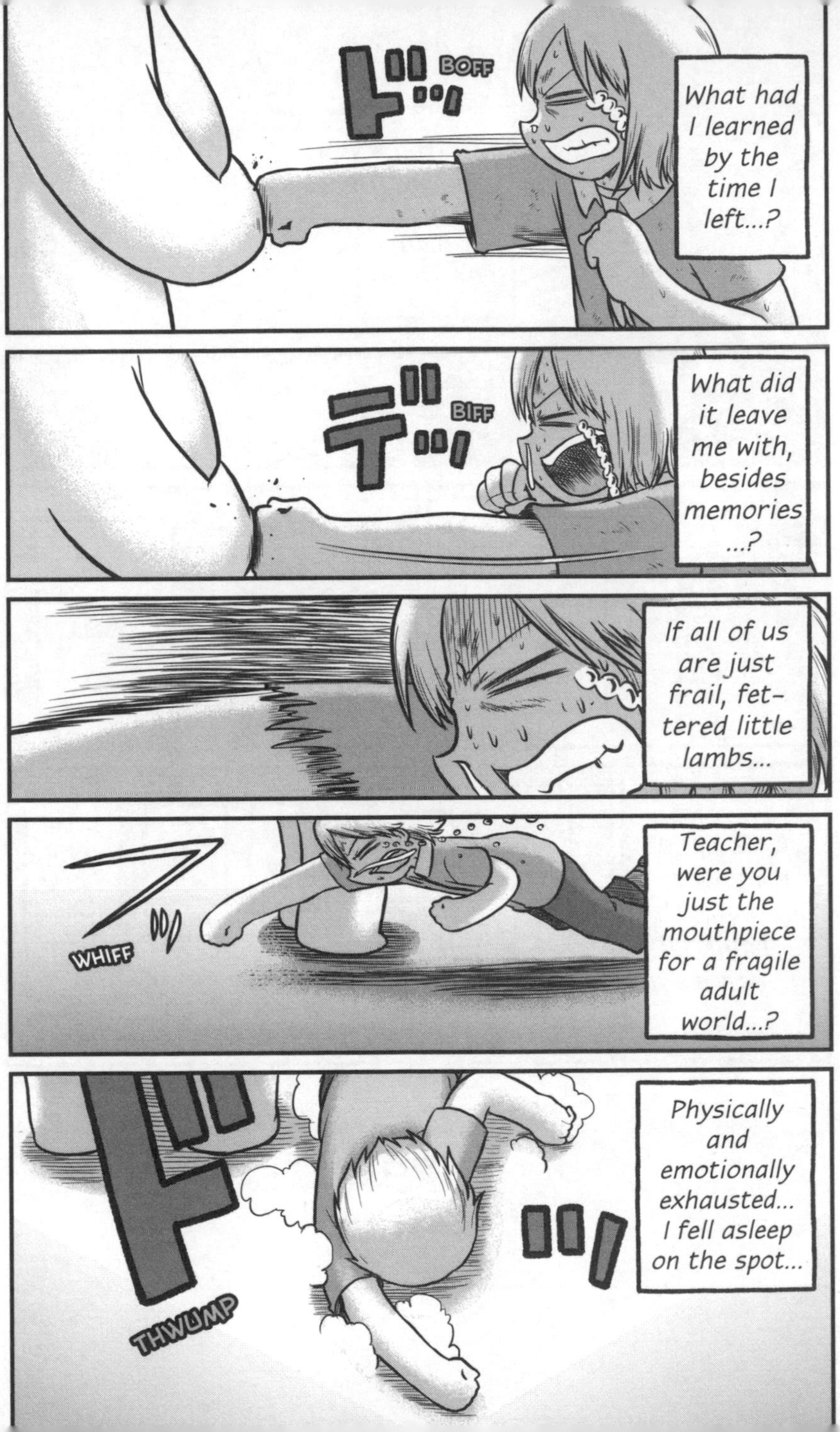
What had I learned by the time I left...?
BOFF
What did it leave me with, besides memories ...?
BIFF
If all of us are just frail, fet-tered little lambs...
Teacher, were you just the mouthpiece for a fragile adult world...?
WHIFF
Physically and emotionally exhausted... I fell asleep on the spot...
THWUMP

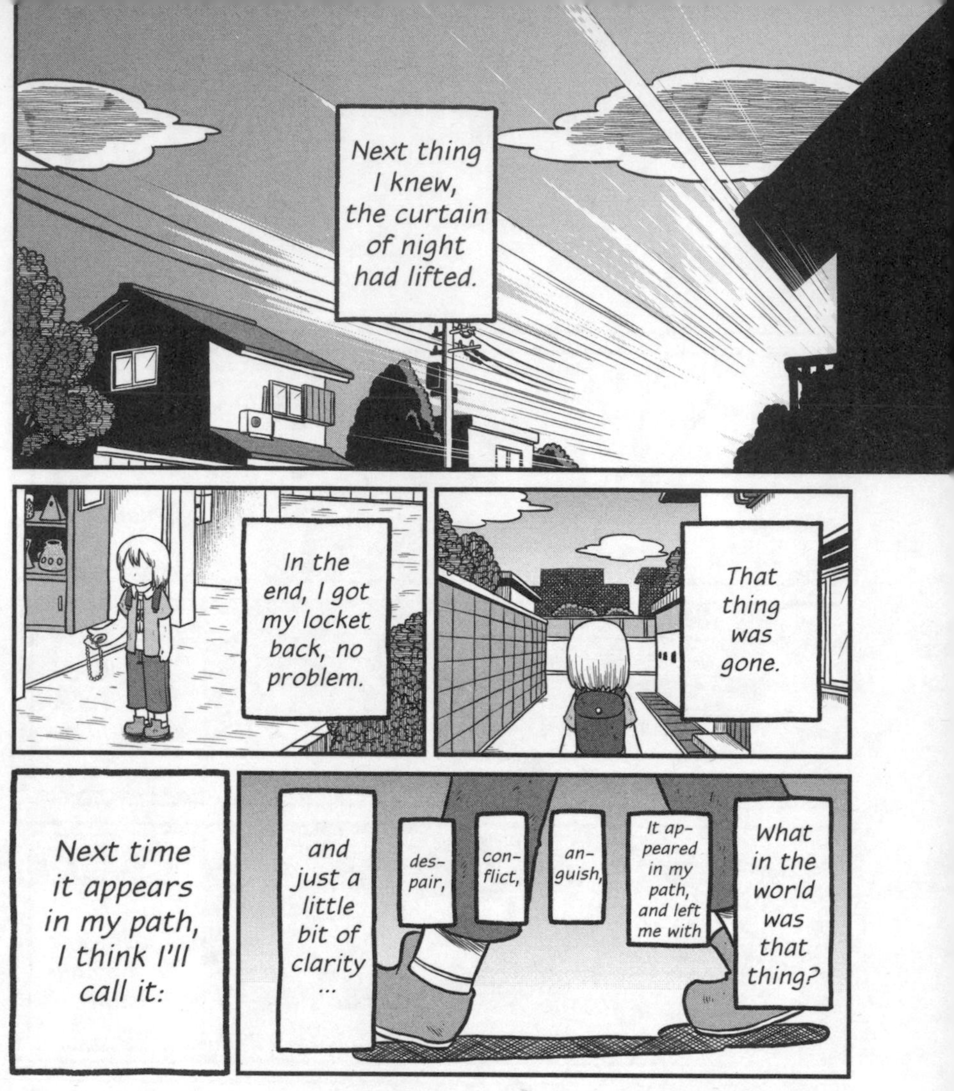
Next thing I knew, the curtain of night had lifted.
That thing was gone.
In the end, I got my locket back, no problem.
What in the world was that thing?
It appeared in my path, and left me with
anguish,
conflict,
despair,
and just a little bit of clarity…
Next time it appears in my path, I think I'll call it:

"life."

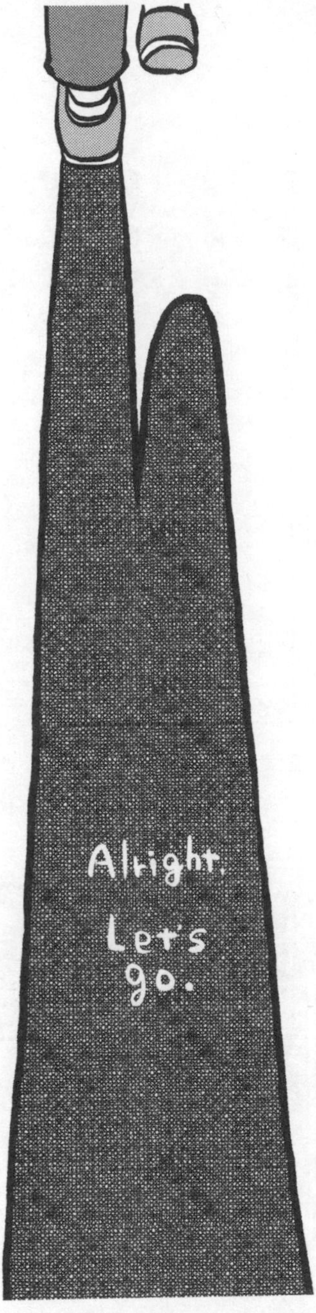
Alright.
Let's go.

CITY

CONTENTS

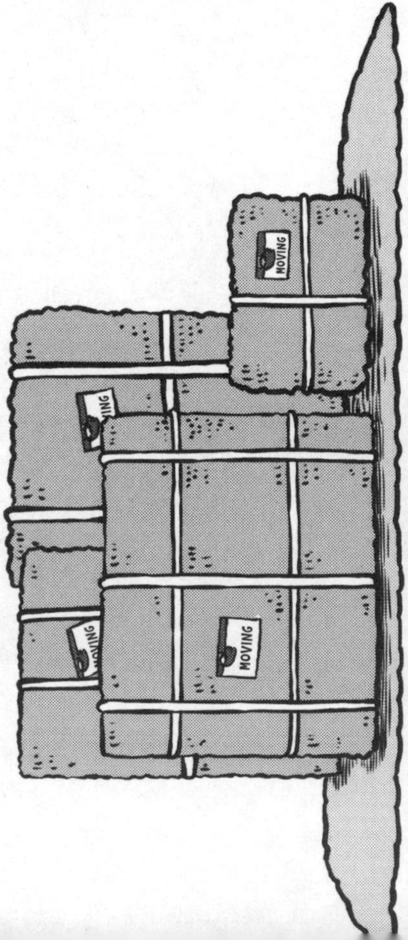

MOVING
MOVING

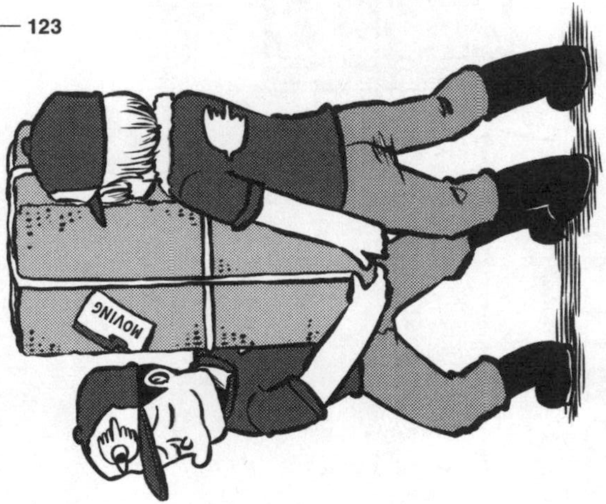
MOVING

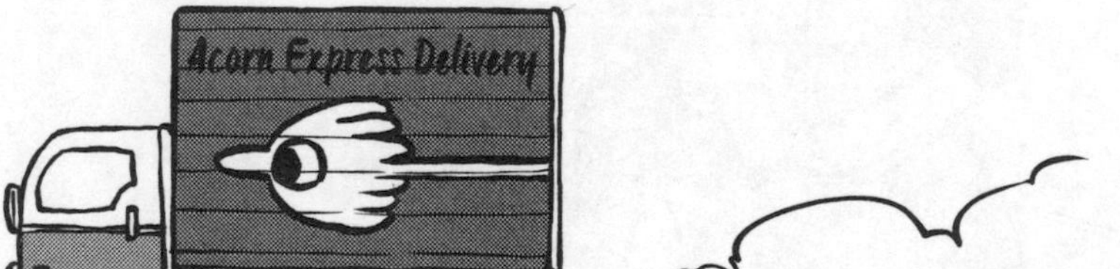
Acorn Express Delivery

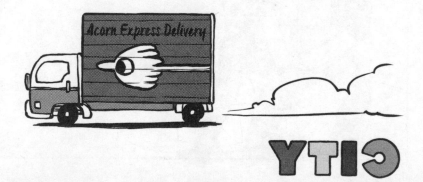

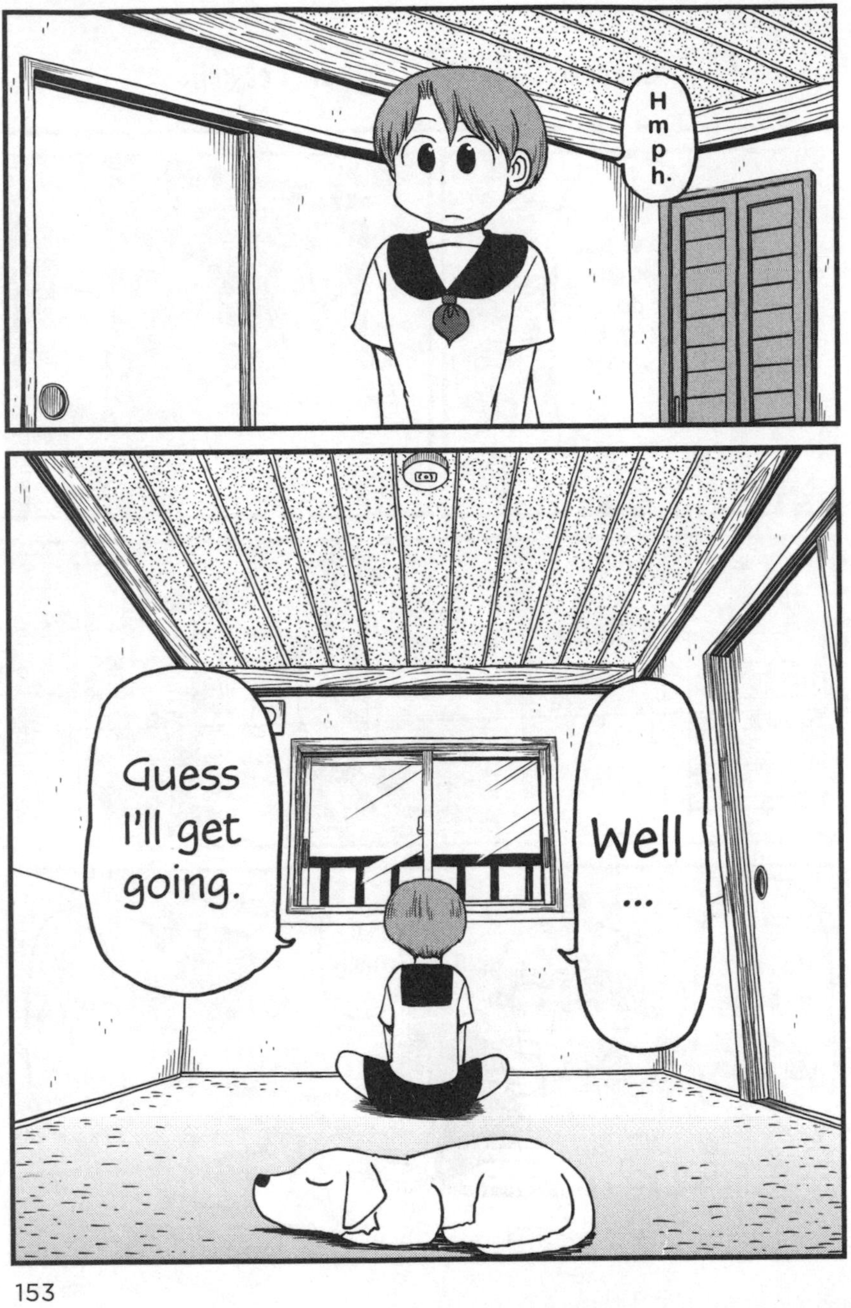
Hmph.
Well ...
Guess I'll get going.

Chapter 167 ◇ Final Farewells

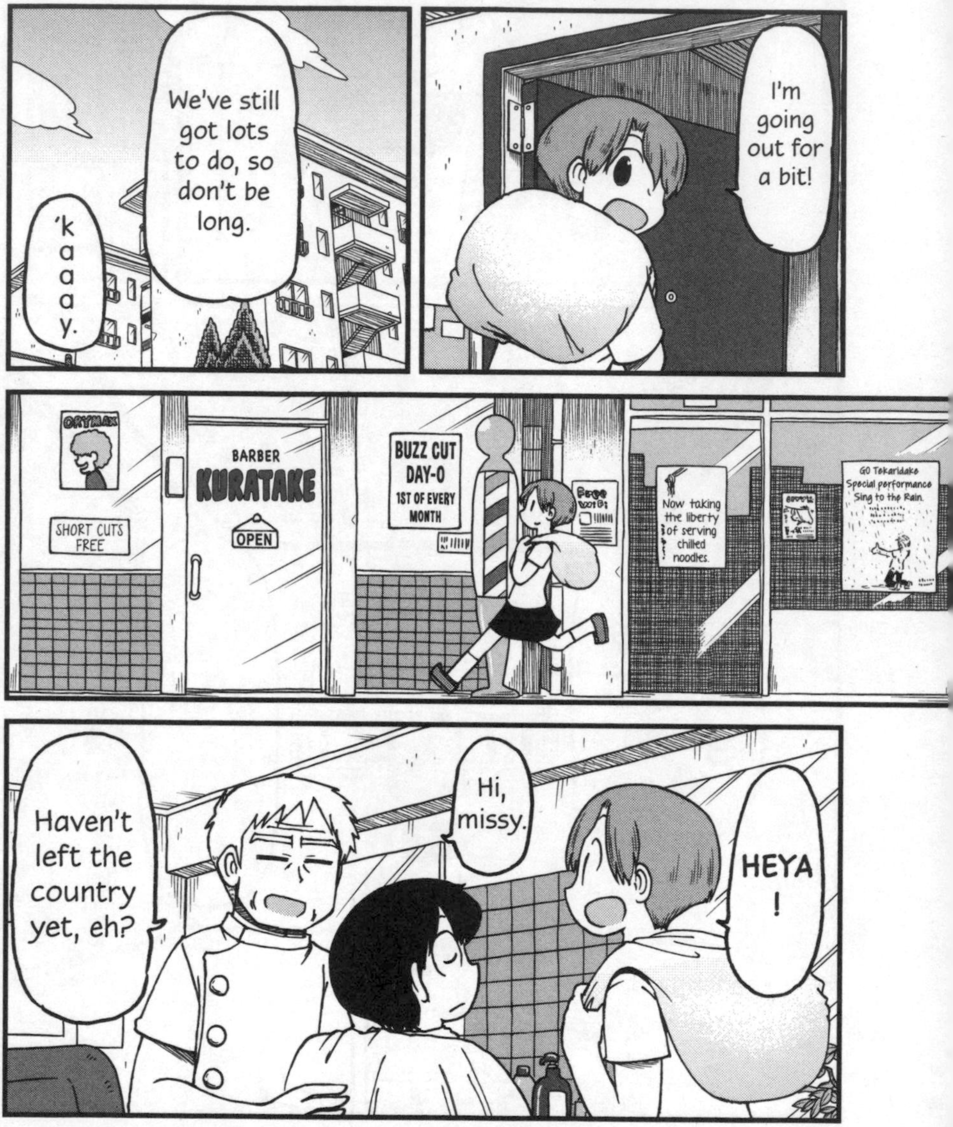
I'm going out for a bit!
We've still got lots to do, so don't be long.
'kaaay.
GO Tekaridake Special performance Sing to the Rain.
Now taking the liberty of serving chilled noodles.
BUZZ CUT DAY-O 1ST OF EVERY MONTH
BARBER KURATAKE
OPEN
SHORT CUTS FREE
HEYA!
Hi, missy.
Haven't left the country yet, eh?

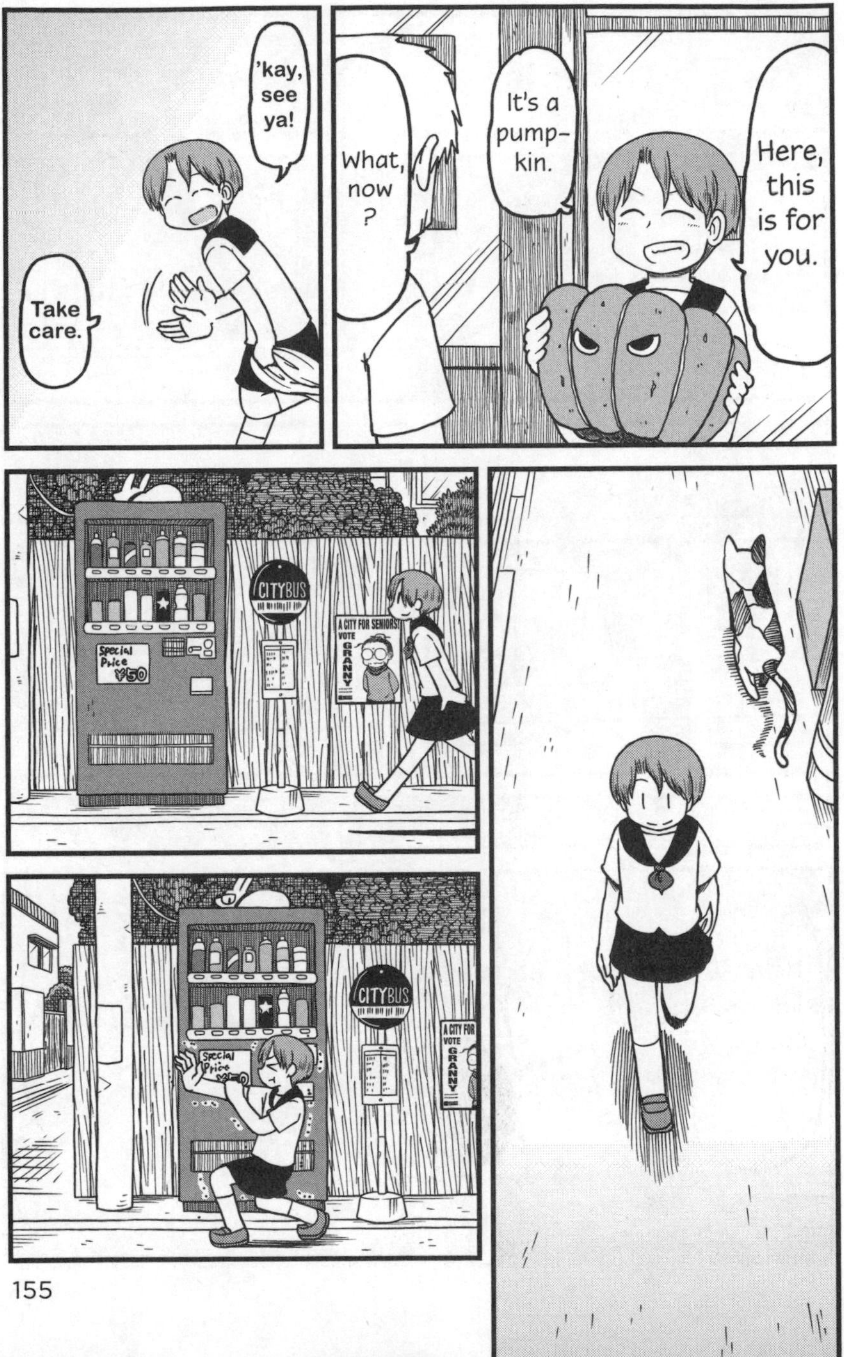
Here, this is for you.
It's a pumpkin.
What, now?
'kay, see ya!
Take care.
CITY BUS
A CITY FOR SENIORS!
VOTE
GRANNY
Special Price ¥50
CITY BUS
A CITY FOR
VOTE
GRANNY

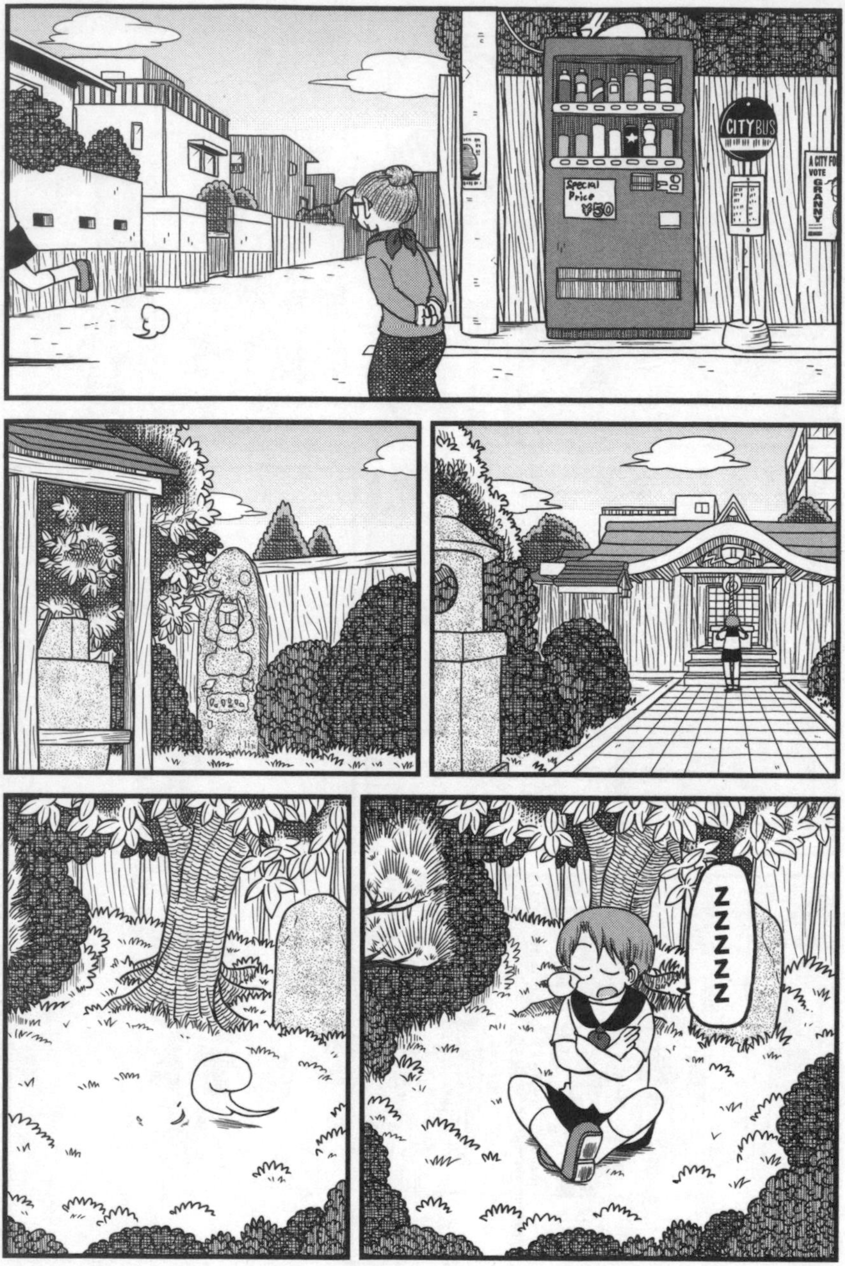
VOTE
GRANNY
CITY BUS
Special Price ¥50
ZZZZZ

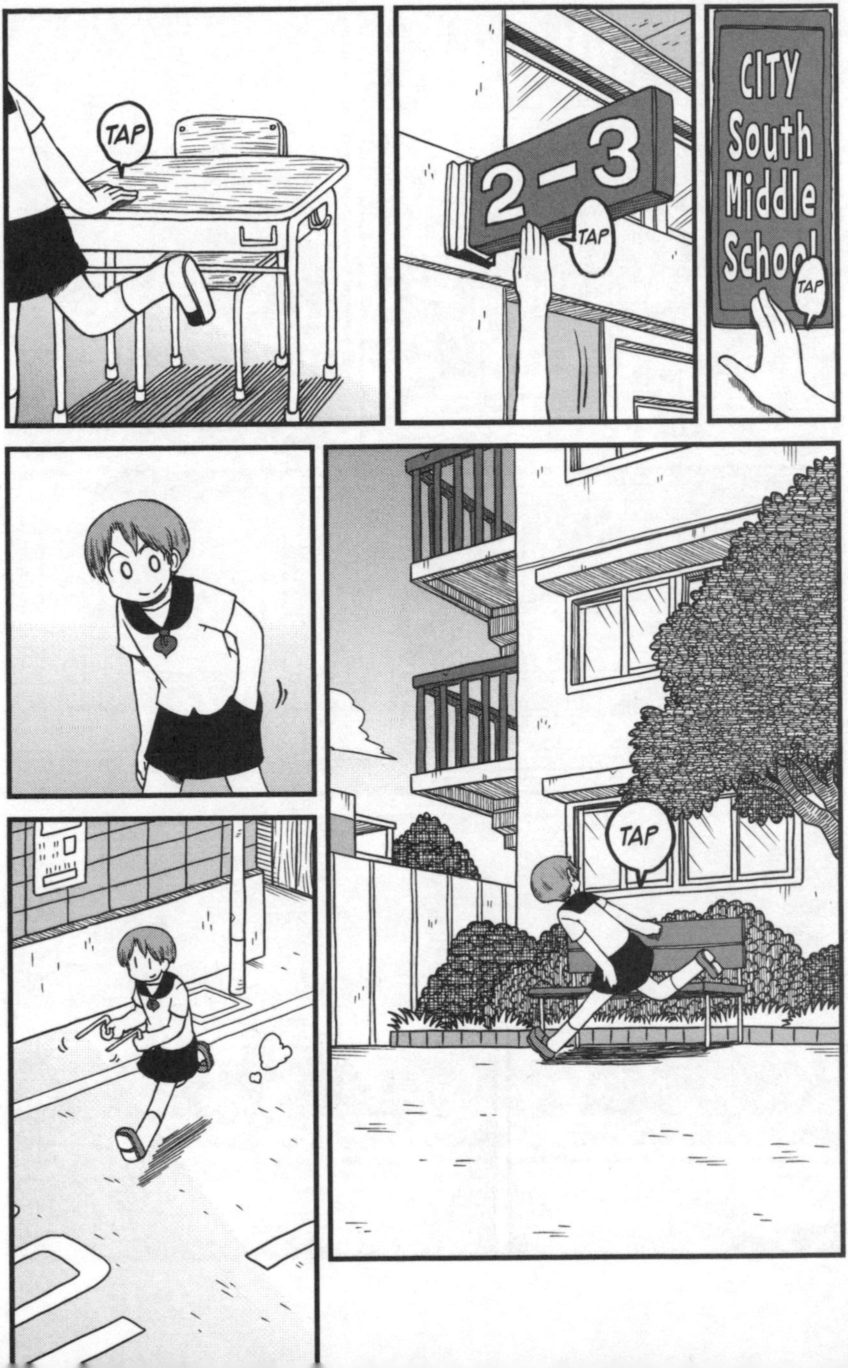
CITY
South
Middle
School
TAP
2-3
TAP
TAP
TAP

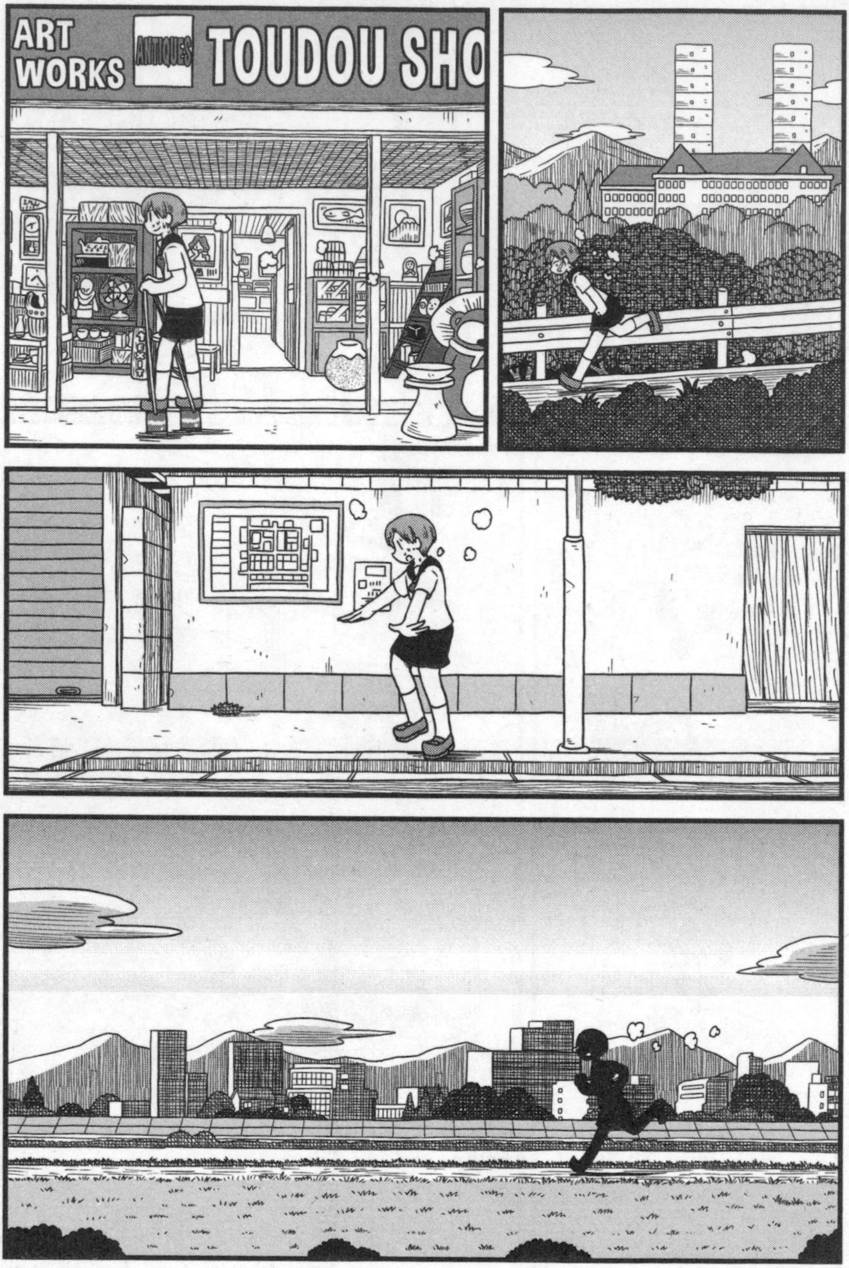
ART WORKS
ANTIQUES
TOUDOU SHO

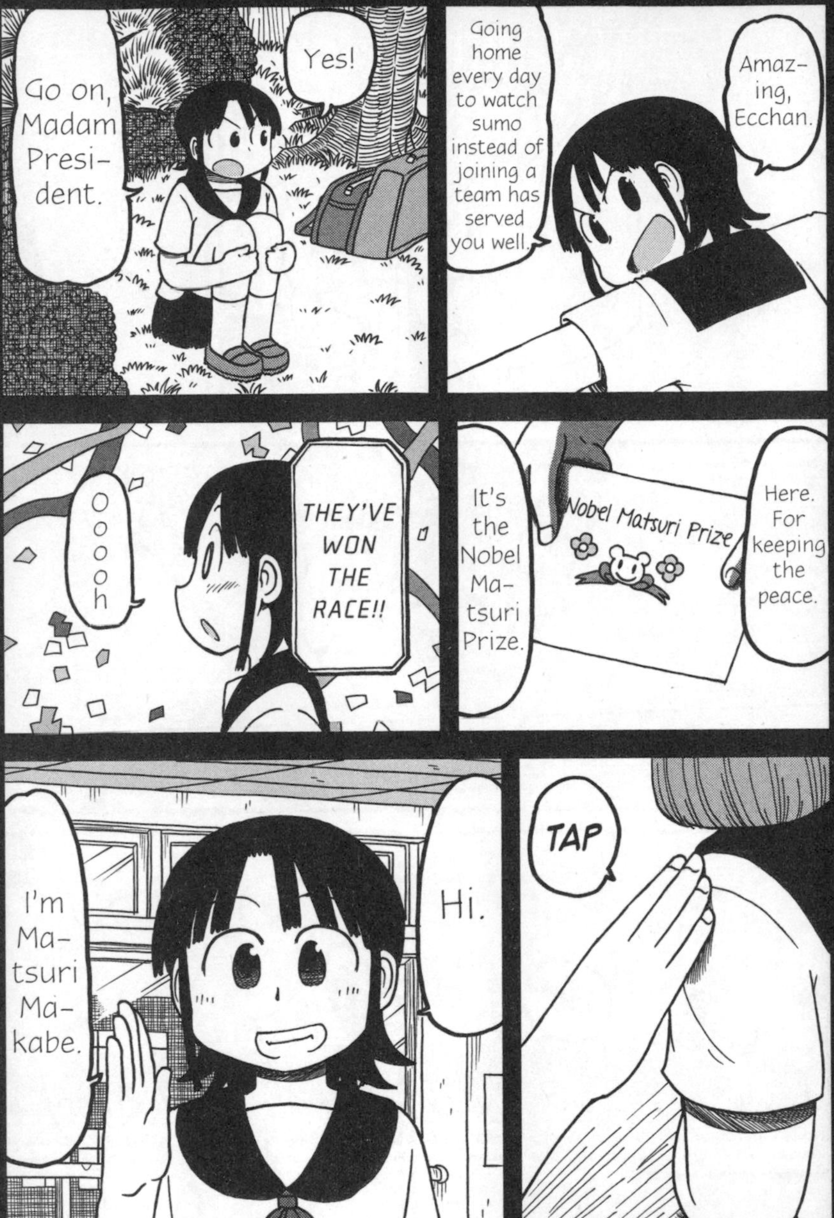
Amaz-ing, Ecchan.
Going home every day to watch sumo instead of joining a team has served you well.
Yes!
Go on, Madam Presi-dent.
Here. For keeping the peace.
Nobel Matsuri Prize
It's the Nobel Ma-tsuri Prize.
THEY'VE WON THE RACE!!
Ooooh
TAP
Hi.
I'm Ma-tsuri Ma-kabe.

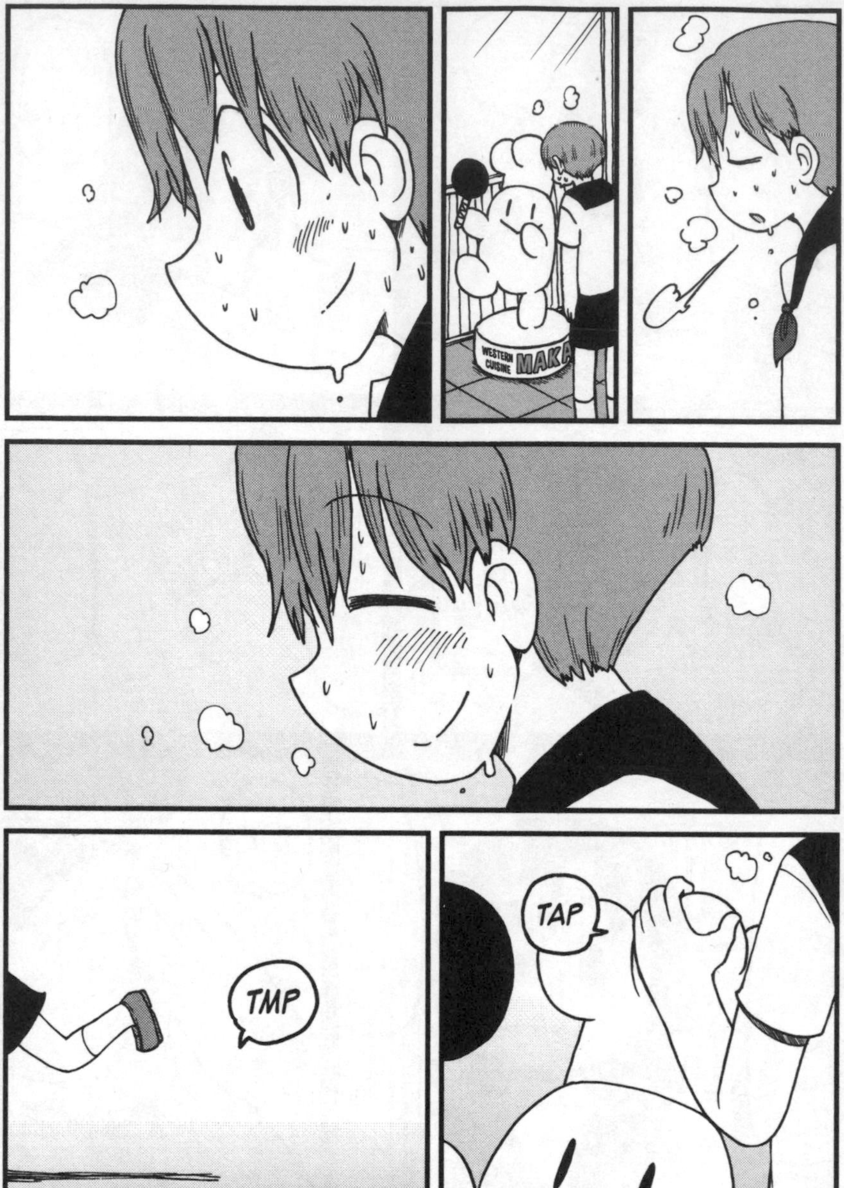
WESTERN CUISINE MAKA
TAP
TMP

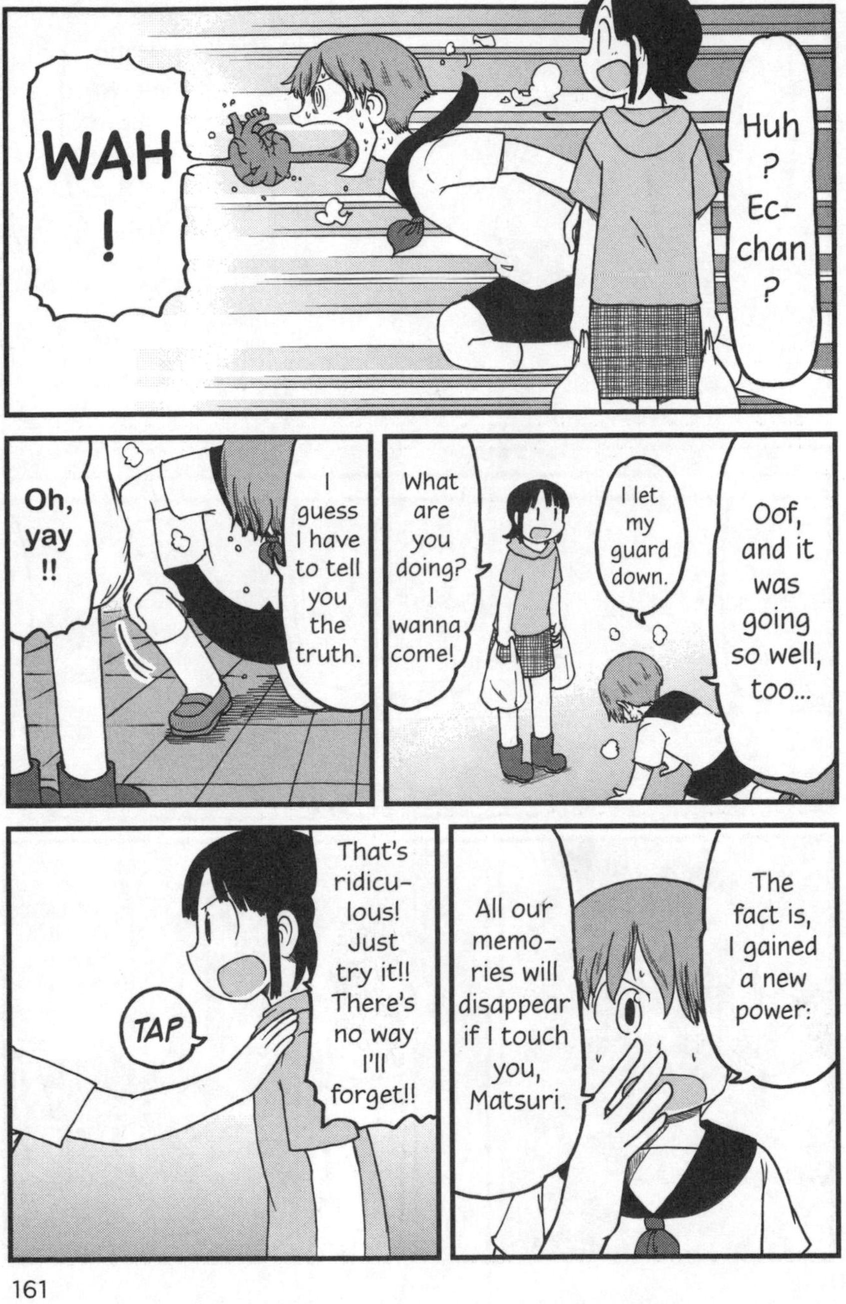
Huh? Ec-chan?
WAH!
Oof, and it was going so well, too...
I let my guard down.
What are you doing? I wanna come!
I guess I have to tell you the truth.
Oh, yay!!
The fact is, I gained a new power:
All our memories will disappear if I touch you, Matsuri.
That's ridiculous! Just try it!! There's no way I'll forget!!
TAP

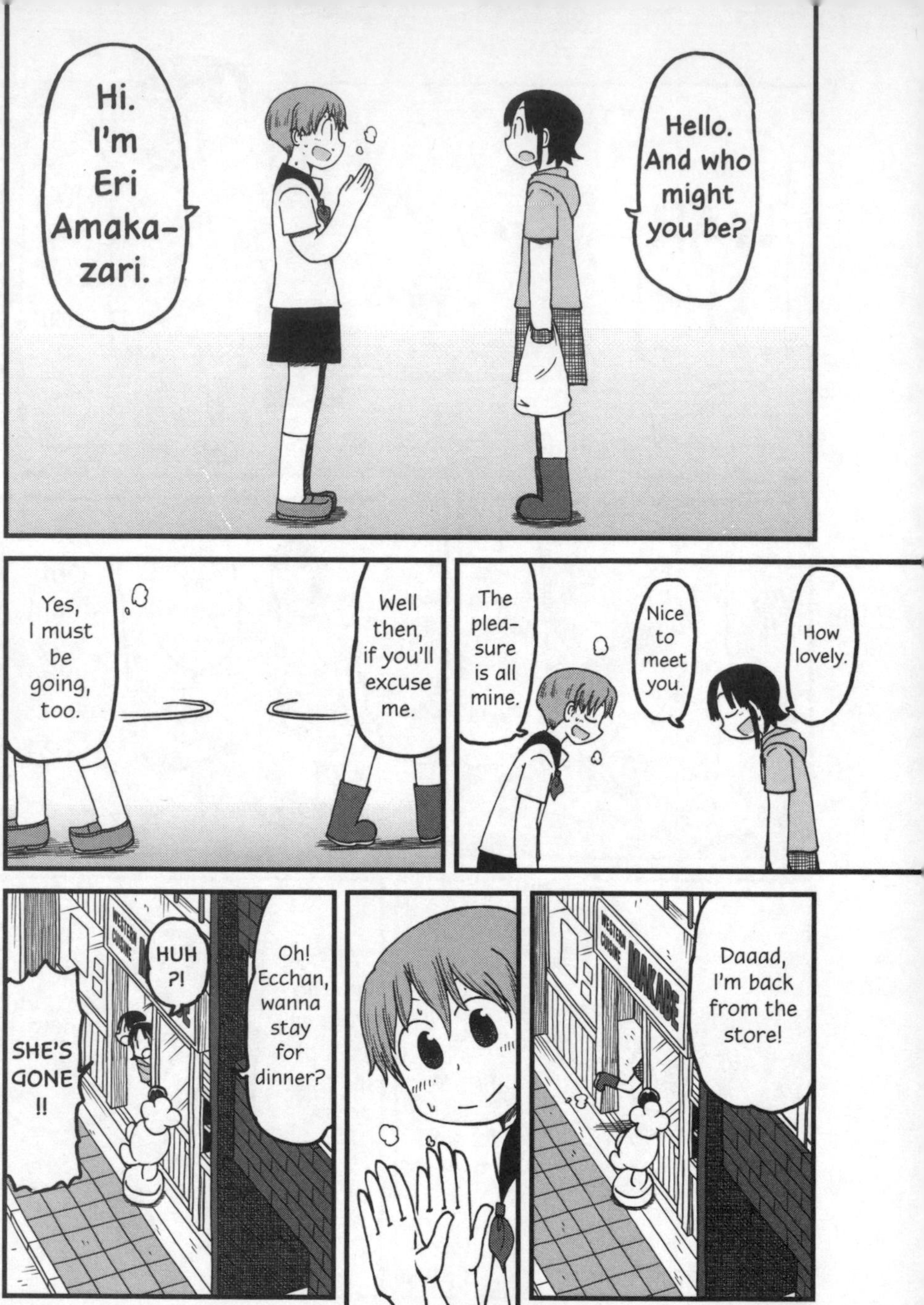
Hello. And who might you be?
Hi. I'm Eri Amakazari.
How lovely.
Nice to meet you.
The pleasure is all mine.
Well then, if you'll excuse me.
Yes, I must be going, too.
WESTERN CUISINE MAKABE
Daaad, I'm back from the store!
Oh! Ecchan, wanna stay for dinner?
WESTERN CUISINE
HUH ?!
SHE'S GONE !!

CITY

Recent Author Photo

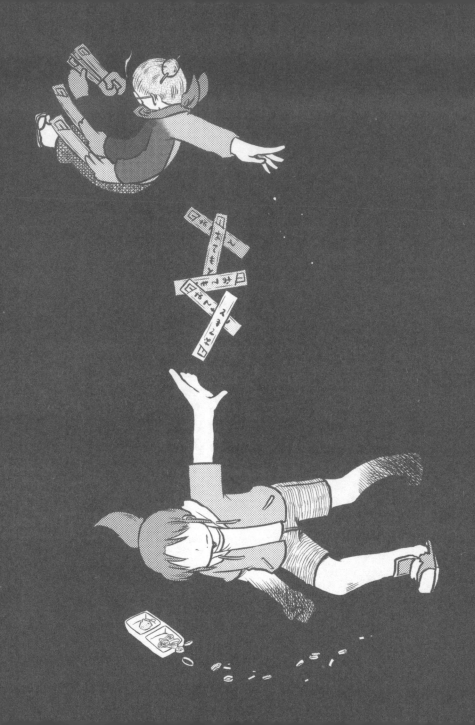

CITY
12

define "ordinary"

in this just-surreal-enough take on the "school genre" of manga, a group of friends (which includes a robot built by a child professor) grapples with all sorts of unexpected situations in their daily lives as high schoolers.

the gags, jokes, puns and random haiku keep this series off-kilter even as the characters grow and change. check out this new take on a storied genre and meet the new ordinary.

all volumes
available now!

nichijou

my ordinary life

keiichi
arawi

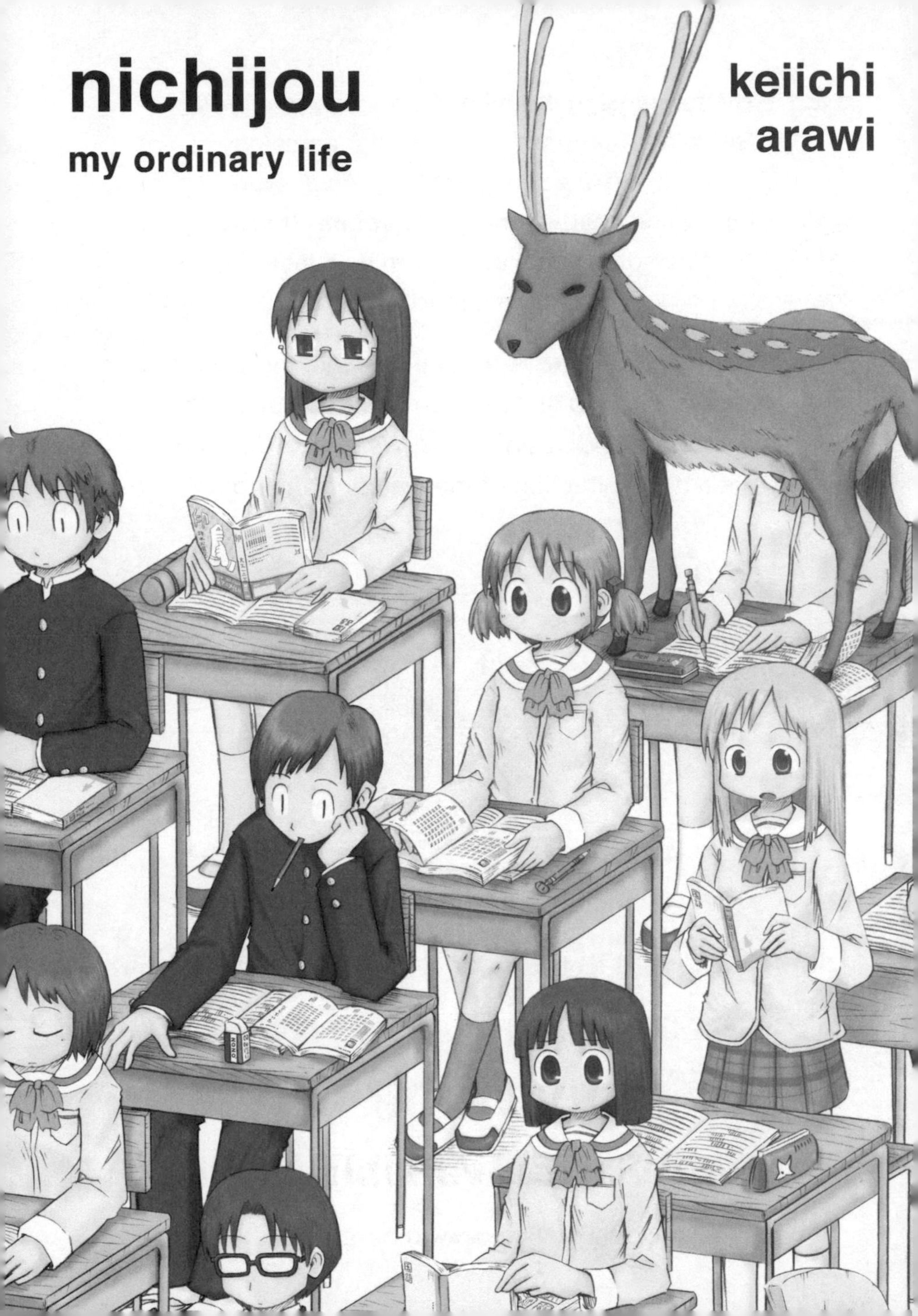

The follow-up to the hit manga series ***nichijou***, ***Helvetica Standard*** is a full-color anthology of Keiichi Arawi's comic art and design work. Funny and heartwarming, ***Helvetica Standard*** is a humorous look at modern day Japanese design in comic form.

Helvetica Standard is a deep dive into the artistic and creative world of Keiichi Arawi. Part comic, part diary, part art and design book, ***Helvetica Standard*** is a deconstruction of the world of ***nichijou***.

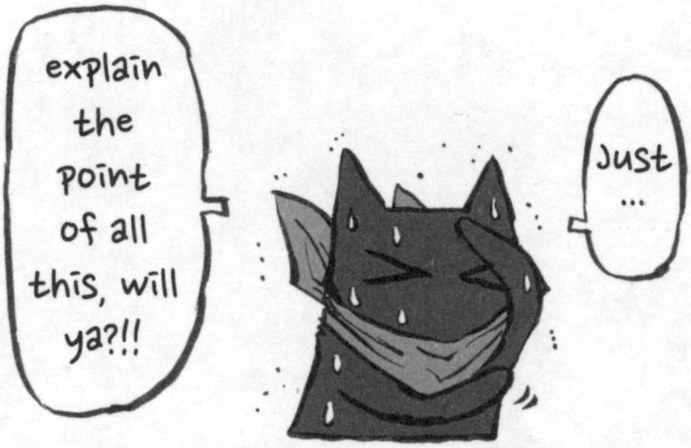
Just ...
explain the point of all this, will ya?!!

Helvetica Standard
Bold

Helvetica Standard
Italic

Both Parts Available Now!

Keiichi
Arawi

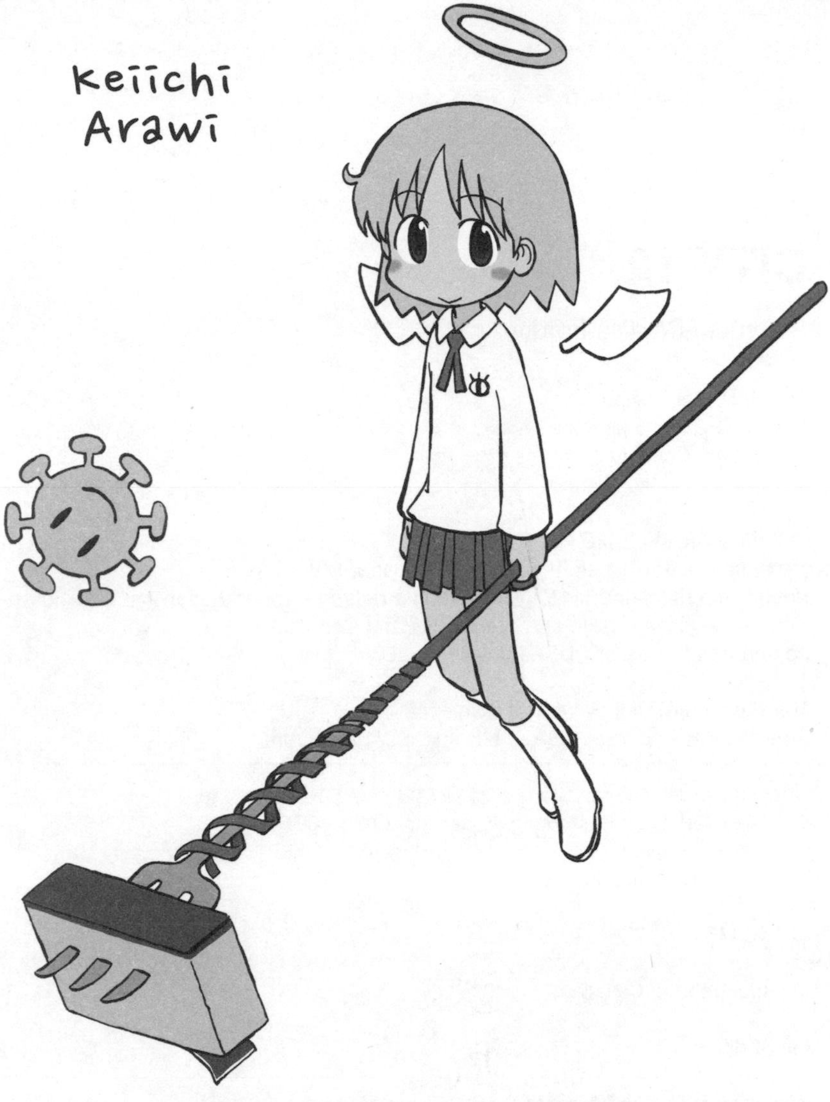

Helvetica
Standard

CITY 12

A Vertical Comics Edition

Editor: Daniel Joseph
Translation: Jenny McKeon
Production: Grace Lu
Hiroko Mizuno

First published in Japan in 2020 by Kodansha, Ltd., Tokyo
Publication rights for this English edition arranged through Kodansha, Ltd., Tokyo
English language version produced by Vertical Comics,
an imprint of Kodansha USA Publishing, LLC

Translation provided by Vertical Comics, 2021
Published by Kodansha USA Publishing, LLC, New York

Originally published in Japanese as *CITY 12* by Kodansha, Ltd.
CITY first serialized in *Morning,* Kodansha, Ltd., 2016-

This is a work of fiction.

ISBN: 978-1-647290-49-8

Manufactured in Canada

First Edition

Kodansha USA Publishing, LLC
451 Park Avenue South
7th Floor
New York, NY 10016
www.kodansha.us

Vertical books are distributed through Penguin-Random House Publisher Services.